NEW PROCLAMATION

Year B, 2000

Easter through Pentecost

EASTER

Linda M. Maloney

PENTECOST

Gordon W. Lathrop
Neil Elliott
Frank C. Senn

FORTRESS PRESS
Minneapolis

NEW PROCLAMATION
Year B, 2000
Easter through Pentecost

Cover and book design: Joseph Bonyata
Illustrations: Tanja Butler, *Graphics for Worship,* copyright © 1996 Augsburg Fortress.

ISBN 0-8006-4242-2

The paper used in this publication meets the minimum requirements of American National Standard for Information Sciences—Permanence of Paper for Printed Library Materials, ANSI Z329.48-1984. ™

Manufactured in the U.S.A. AF 1-4242

04 03 02 01 00 1 2 3 4 5 6 7 8 9 10

CONTENTS

The Season of Pentecost
Gordon W. Lathrop

The Season of Pentecost
Neil Elliott

The Season of Pentecost
Frank C. Senn

PUBLISHER'S FOREWORD

MORE THAN TWENTY-FIVE YEARS AGO Fortress Press embarked on an ambitious project to produce a lectionary preaching resource that would provide the best in biblical exegetical aids for a variety of lectionary traditions. This resource, *Proclamation,* became both a pioneer and a standard-bearer in its field, sparking a host of similar products from other publishers. Few, however, have become as widely used and well known as *Proclamation.*

Thoroughly ecumenical and built around the three-year lectionary cycle, *Proclamation*'s focus has always been on the biblical text first and foremost. Where other resources often have offered reprinted sermons or illustrations for the preacher to use or adapt, *Proclamation*'s authors have always asserted the best resource for the preacher is the biblical text itself. *Proclamation* has always been premised on the idea that those who are well equipped to understand a pericope in both its historical and liturgical context will also be well equipped to compose meaningful and engaging sermons. For that reason, *Proclamation* consistently has invited the cream of North American biblical scholars and homileticians to offer their comments because of their commitments to the text.

New Proclamation represents a significant change in Fortress Press's approach to the lectionary resource, but it still retains the best of the hallmarks that have made it so widely used and appreciated. Long-time users of the series will immediately notice the most major change, that is, the switch from eight to two volumes per year. The volume you are holding covers the lectionary texts for approximately the second half of the church year, from Easter through Pentecost. By going to this two-volume format, we are able to offer you a larger, workbook-style page size with a lay-flat binding and plenty of white space for taking notes.

Because the Evangelical Lutheran Church in America adopted the Revised Common Lectionary as its recommended lectionary source several years ago, the lectionary from the *Lutheran Book of Worship* no longer appears in *New Proclamation*. This allows our authors to write more expansively on each of the texts for each of the three lectionary traditions addressed here. When a text appears in fewer than all three of these lectionaries or is offered as an alternative text, these are clearly marked as follows: RC (Roman Catholic); RCL (Revised Common Lectionary); and BCP (Episcopal, for Book of Common Prayer).

Although psalms are not usually used as preaching texts, *New Proclamation* offers brief commentary on each assigned psalm (or, as they are usually listed, the Responsive Reading) for each preaching day so that the preacher can incorporate reflections on these readings as well in a sermon. Call-out quotes in the margins help signal significant themes in the texts for the day.

New Proclamation retains *Proclamation*'s emphasis on the biblical text but offers a new focus on how the preacher may apply those texts to contemporary situations. Exegetical work is more concise, and thoughts on how the text addresses today's world and our personal situations take a more prominent role.

Each section of this book is prefaced by a brief introduction that helps situate the liturgical season and its texts within the context of the church year. Unlike *Proclamation,* which was not dated according to its year of publication, this volume of *New Proclamation* is dated specifically for the year 2000 when the texts for Series B next appear. Although preachers may have to work a bit harder to reuse these books in three years' time, they will also find that the books should coordinate better with other dated lectionary materials that they may be using at the same time.

Other conveniences also appear in *New Proclamation.* Preachers who conduct services at different times on Easter will find Linda M. Maloney has commented on two different sets of texts that are appropriate for each of those times. Bibliographies and notes accompany most of the sections as well.

For all its changes, *New Proclamation* does not claim to reinvent the preaching lectionary resource. It is, in many ways, a work in progress, and readers will see even more helpful changes in future volumes. One thing that has not changed, however, is the commitment to offer preachers access to the ideas of the best biblical scholars and homileticians in North America. Linda M. Maloney, Gordon W. Lathrop, Neil Elliott, and Frank C. Senn have each risen to the occasion to address these texts in fresh ways and to make *New Proclamation* truly new. We are grateful to them for their contributions to this new effort.

THE SEASON OF EASTER

LINDA M. MALONEY

WHAT DOES IT MEAN TO LIVE in a post-Easter world?

Is the season of Easter the time of rejoicing the church projects, or is it for many Christians—if they think seriously about it—a let-down from the more focused devotion of Lent, a too-rapid demand for rejoicing when we have not fully wrestled with sorrow, or, paradoxically, a time that forces us to face the troubling facts of death and the unknown?[1]

Although we *say* that Easter is the great high feast of the Christian year, most of us would have to admit that we prefer Christmas. The birth of the Son of God as one of us is far more tangible and comforting—not quite graspable, but still somehow more familiar—than the resurrection of the man Jesus, his transcendence of mortality as our forerunner and redeemer. It is much easier to sing "who would not love thee, loving us so dearly" before the crib than beneath the cross.

The resurrection of Jesus, human like us and Son of God in glory, both reminds us of our own mortality and seems to call into question the value of our human lives. Not long ago the French Dominican Jacques Pohier underwent a shattering crisis because he dared to question the validity of a doctrine of resurrection; it seemed clear to him that to shift all our hopes somewhere beyond death and to insist that "our true home is in heaven" is to disvalue all that we know of human reality, our lives on earth. It can also be a convenient cop-out: in face of all the world's suffering, much of it inflicted by our own nation in our name, we can offer the certain hope that God will wipe away every tear in the (future) reign of God and think less painfully about our responsibility to comfort the sorrowful here and now.

Our usual way of dealing with the problem is, in fact, to reject the humanity of Jesus; our internal scenario projects him as God-come-to-earth, appearing to be human for the most part (the ancient heresy of Docetism) and undergoing some of the trials and sufferings of a human being, even to death, death on a cross—but then retiring to heaven, putting aside the human guise, and resuming his Godhead once for all. We sing: "Crown him . . . who once on earth, the incarnate Word, for ransomed sinners slain, now lives in realms of light, where saints with angels sing . . . . Crown him the Lord of heaven, enthroned in worlds above. . . ."[2] This effectively distances him from us, and we can cease to worry about how his story continues to be our own.

The shattering truth is quite different: the resurrection of Jesus means that he remains forever one of us, for he is raised not as a disembodied spirit, an ex-human being, but "in the flesh," in his clarified resurrection body—different to be sure, but ultimately recognizable to his friends and even to his former enemies like Paul. To put it another way, Jesus' descent into the world, and even the underworld, as the creed affirms, represents a plunge into creation, "farther up and farther in," as Aslan cries to the children in Narnia. The mission of his followers from that point forward is to ensure that the universe becomes more and more truly the enfleshment of the risen Christ.

I once asked an Australian priest how the churches in the southern hemisphere coped with the relentlessly northern-oriented liturgical seasons, the association of Easter with springtime and Christmas with the cold of winter. Her response was that the people of the southern hemisphere in fact have an advantage over the benighted north: their Easter happens when nature is declining rather than blossoming, so they are forcefully reminded that resurrection is far more than the natural renewal of life. It is an event beyond all time and space, eschatological, metahistorical, before which the springtime renewal of life pales to nothing. Our association of Easter with springtime (to say nothing of its trivialization by birds and bunnies) only distracts us from the *mysterium tremendum*.

JESUS' DESCENT INTO THE WORLD, AND EVEN THE UNDERWORLD, AS THE CREED AFFIRMS, REPRESENTS A PLUNGE INTO CREATION.

Robert J. Schreiter reads the Easter stories in a very serious context indeed: that of the terrible suffering inflicted by human beings on other human beings in many parts of the world. He shows how, by reading our own stories in the context of Jesus' story, we can begin to take steps toward reconciliation. The Easter season is, in fact, about reconciliation: God's reconciling the world to Godself in Jesus, our own coming to terms with being redeemed, and our moving into a new relationship with a Jesus crucified and risen. It is a hard and wrenching process, one often belied by the rejoicing mood of the season. As Schreiter points out, "an empty tomb confronts us with a yawning abyss of absence, . . . an absence that threatens to swallow us up in nothingness, to annihilate our own existence." That absence, like a black hole in the universe, evokes confusion and fear. Schreiter continues:

> The absence of the body from the tomb breaks again the relationship that burial tried to establish. Death is always a rupture of relationships, and grieving and mourning are a way of trying to reestablish relationships, albeit now in a different way. . . . Much of what Jesus does [in the Easter stories] is to shape new kinds of relationships with his disciples. The most important relationship of presence to combat absence will be in the Eucharist.[3]

The whole Easter season is a time for moving from mourning to rejoicing; it should and must not be mandated as a lightning transition: "Get over it!" Our Eucharistic celebrations will be the focus of encounter in this process.

How does the lectionary help us to cope with this painful transition, with the troubling of our lives that Easter must be, if taken seriously? Its primary strategy is to lead us through the farewell discourses in John's Gospel, which make up the bulk of the gospel readings for the Easter season. Of all the Gospels, the Fourth is most clearly written from a post-Easter perspective, and the farewell discourses are indeed words for a post-Easter people. In the pages that follow we will try to see how the Sundays of the Easter season are designed to help us establish a relationship with the Risen Lord and with each other that will empower us for living after Easter, toward Pentecost, and beyond.

THE RESURRECTION OF OUR LORD—EASTER DAY

APRIL 23, 2000

Revised Common	Episcopal (BCP)	Roman Catholic
Acts 10:34-43 or Isa. 25:6-9	Acts 10:34-43 or Isa. 25:6-9	Acts 10:34b, 37-47
Ps. 118:1-2, 14-24	Ps. 118:14-29 or 118:14-17, 22-24	Ps. 118:1-2, 16-17, 22-23
1 Cor. 15:1-11 or Acts 10:34-43	Col. 3:1-4 or Acts 10:34-43	Col. 3:1-4 or 1 Cor. 5:6b-8
John 20:1-18 or Mark 16:1-8	Mark 16:1-8	John 20:1-19

The lectionary for the principal service on Easter Day offers a variety of texts related to resurrection: all but three (Isa. 25:6-9; 1 Cor. 15:1-11; Mark 16:1-8) are likewise options for Years A and C. Here the Roman Catholic lectionary offers the fewest choices; the user of the RCL or BCP may wish to consider adopting the readings that are unique to Year B to avoid too much repetition from year to year. Alternatively, one may consider that using John 20:1-18 for Easter Day and John 20:19-31 (the sole option) for the Second Sunday of Easter will afford the preacher the rare privilege of completing a continuous reading of an entire chapter of a gospel within an eight-day cycle, a time frame that enables the listeners to hold the narrative units together in a more coherent way than is often the case.

The gospel lections present very different pictures. Mark's appears stark, blunt, and primitive, devoid of the transcendent. Its elements are the women, the spices, the stone, a "young man" not otherwise interpreted. Jesus is "not here" and is to be sought not in heavenly glory but "in Galilee." The women flee in panic: Daryl Schmidt's translation aptly captures the trailing but abrupt ending: "talk about terrified . . . ."[4] John's tomb scene, on the other hand, is complex and full of theologically tinted details. Mary Magdalene, the central figure, moves back and forth, as do the two male disciples; there is an extended dialogue between Mary and Jesus, again with great theological weight; and Mary fulfills her commission, proclaiming to the other disciples: "I have seen the Lord!"

From another perspective, however, we may say that both gospel endings effect the same circular movement by pointing us back to the beginnings. The reader of Mark is told that Jesus is to be sought "in Galilee," where the story began. If the women are silenced by awe and terror, the gospel itself nevertheless conveys the young man's message, and so we turn back and begin to read again: "Now after John was arrested, Jesus came to Galilee, proclaiming the good news of God, and saying, 'The time is fulfilled, and the kingdom of God has come near'" (Mark 1:9)—a message filled with a new content in light of the ending. John's tomb scene also turns us back to the beginning: there we read that Jesus was begotten of God, and Jesus has spoken of God throughout the gospel as his "Father." Now for the first time he speaks of "my Father and *your* Father . . . my God and *your* God" (John 20:17). Through the power of the resurrection we are drawn into the family circle; again we can begin to reread the gospel with new eyes.

We could say, then, that the readings for Easter Day combine to recommend a strategy for living after Easter: focusing on the life, death, and resurrection of Jesus, none of them in isolation from the others. At the same time, the preacher should be aware—for alert listeners surely will be—that the readings present sometimes conflicting interpretations of the meaning of life, death, and resurrection and their implications for us. Let us examine each of the day's readings in turn with an eye to the possible conflicts and synergies they provide.

First Reading
ACTS 10:34-43 (RCL/BCP); 10:34b, 37-47 (RC)

This passage is part of Peter's discourse in the house of the centurion Cornelius. It gives a summary of Jesus' life, death, and resurrection, as well as the witnesses' mission to preach this message and to testify that Jesus is "the one ordained by God as judge of the living and the dead." Attention should be paid to the context signaled by the framing of the text (the first part of which is unfortunately omitted in the RC lectionary). The author of Acts has composed this speech as the climax of Peter's "conversion" to acceptance of the gentile mission, which is the subject of the whole of Acts 10. Cornelius, the God-fearing centurion, has received a message in a vision to send for Peter; in the next scene Peter himself receives a vision of unclean creatures, which the visionary voice says are to be eaten because "what God has made clean, you must not call profane" (10:15). Immediately afterward, Cornelius's messengers appear, and Peter is told by the Spirit that he should go with them. Arriving at Cornelius's house in Caesarea, Peter announces that, on reflection, he has decided that his vision should be applied to human beings: "God has shown me that I should not call any*one* profane or unclean" (v. 28). Cornelius then tells of his vision and of the readiness of all present "to listen to all that the Lord has commanded you to say" (v. 33).

The passage chosen for reading on Easter Day, then, is Peter's elaboration of the statement in v. 15, beginning: "I truly understand that God shows no partiality, but in every nation anyone who fears him and does what is right is acceptable to him." The closing frame repeats this, casting the circle still wider by including the prophetic message: "All the prophets testify about him [Jesus] that everyone who believes in him receives forgiveness of sins through his name" (v. 43). The universal salvation of the God-fearing is, in light of Jesus' life, death, and resurrection, particularized in belief in him.

One important implication of this framing of the story of Jesus is that there is continuity between the before and after. Christians' life after Easter, the redeemed life that is appropriated through faith, is not different from the way of salvation proclaimed by the prophets. The prophets' prescription, "fear God and do what is right," is really no different from Augustine's aphorism: "Love God and do what you will."

CHRISTIANS' LIFE AFTER EASTER, THE REDEEMED LIFE THAT IS APPROPRIATED THROUGH FAITH, IS NOT DIFFERENT FROM THE WAY OF SALVATION PROCLAIMED BY THE PROPHETS.

ISAIAH 25:6-9 (RCL/BCP alt.)

This reading from Isaiah portrays the eschatological banquet of the redeemed. Its emphasis on the destruction of death makes it an especially appropriate selection for this day. The foods mentioned (fat/oil, marrow, strong wine) mark this banquet as a communion sacrifice *(šělamím),* but it is the eschatological communion, because God will share with the people the fat that is normally reserved for God. The vanquishing of death is accomplished through this communion in divine life that is symbolized by sharing in food that belongs to God.

RESPONSIVE READING
PSALM 118

The different lectionaries offer a variety of combinations of verses, but all are taken from Psalm 118. This is the last in the cycle of "Egyptian Hallel" psalms used in connection with great festivals. Parts of it may well have been intended as a speech for a king who comes to the Temple to offer thanks for a victory. Parts of this psalm, including vv. 22-23 (included in each of the three lectionaries) were favorites for quotation in the New Testament (for example,

Matt. 21:42; Acts 4:11; 1 Peter 2:7). The speaker, seeking entrance to the Temple, testifies that God has borne witness to his worthiness by delivering him from danger when others had abandoned him. The church sees this as prefiguring Jesus' fate: abandoned by every human companion, he has been rescued and exalted by God.

Second Reading
1 CORINTHIANS 15:1-11 (RCL); 5:6b-8 (RC alt.)

Paul's account of the resurrection witness from 1 Corinthians 15 is the suggested second reading in the RCL. The context in which this passage was written is important because it presents a very different interpretation from some of the other readings for the day and the season.

Paul's concern in 1 Corinthians 15 is to combat an extreme form of "realized eschatology" in Corinth, one that proclaimed that the resurrection of believers had already occurred. In the rest of the chapter, following the narrative account of "what I received," Paul argues forcefully that Christ has been raised and that Christians should look forward to the day of their own resurrection in the image of his. That whole argument could be very interesting for our theme of "life after Easter," but the lectionary does not include it.

What makes this passage clash with the gospel readings for Easter Day is that Paul has quite deliberately written the women's witness out of the story. His list of those who have handed on the tradition to him includes only males. (The NRSV has politely made the five hundred *adelphoi* in v. 6 "brothers and sisters," but it is not clear whether that was Paul's intention, and in any case we hear nothing of the *named* witnesses: Mary Magdalene, Mary of James, Salome, Joanna). Instead we are told of appearances to Cephas, to James, and—clearly outside the "received" tradition—to Paul himself. Scholars in turn have seized on this account, obviously written before the gospels were formulated, to assert that the stories of the women's witness were "later compositions." Such an interpretation ignores the possibility that Paul had an agenda of his own and certainly shaped his testimony accordingly. In the case of Corinth this was probably an aspect of Paul's controversy with women leaders; they have just been ordered to "keep silent" (14:34-36), and in chapter 15 Paul proceeds to "silence" their role models. There is sure to be some cognitive dissonance in listeners' minds between this passage and the gospel reading that follows, and the preacher should not gloss over it.[5]

COLOSSIANS 3:1-4 (BCP/RC alt.)

(Note: if Acts 10:34-43 is not used as the First Reading, it may be used as the second in the RCL and BCP.)

If Paul was really the author of Colossians (still a debated issue) there is a startling contrast between his views of resurrection as expressed in 1 Corinthians 15 and what he says in Colossians 3:1-4. In 1 Corinthians he insisted that *Christ* has been raised but *our* resurrection is yet to come. Here we find "Paul" writing "if *you have been raised* with Christ . . . *you have died.*" Again it is important to pay attention to the context in each case, but one could legitimately express doubt that these two passages came from the same hand.

What we can certainly say is that they provide us with two alternative strategies for living in a post-Easter world. The first, in light of 1 Corinthians 15, is to accept Christ's resurrection as a promise of our own, which will occur after death, and to focus on life here and now, being "steadfast, immovable, always excelling in the work of the Lord, because you know that in the Lord your labor is not in vain" until the day when death, the last enemy, shall be destroyed. The other strategy, suggested by Colossians, is rather to regard the fullness of salvation as accomplished in baptism and to see ourselves as living already in the first flush of resurrection life. (In context this passage introduces the paraenetic section of the letter. It does not constitute a rejection of the world, but certainly asserts that other than worldly values are to be preferred to those of this passing era.) Paradoxically, it may be the first strategy that calls us most intensively into our present lives, with the resurrection a hope for the future. The irony is that a hope of a future resurrection may be more compatible with careful attention to the needs of this world than an exalted "present eschatology" that focuses on the "spiritual realities" already within our grasp.

GOSPEL

MARK 16:1-8 (BCP/RCL alt.)

This is the reading proper to Year B. It is read (except for v. 8) at the Easter Vigil in Roman Catholic churches. (Episcopal churches always read Matt 28:1-10 at the Vigil.) It is the sole option for Easter Day in the BCP, and is one of two possible selections in the RCL.

What most fascinates, or troubles, readers of Mark's gospel is the abruptness of its ending. That abruptness was so disturbing even within a few years of the gospel's composition that several attempts were made to "complete" the narrative. Those attempts survive as the so-called "shorter ending" (an addition to v. 8) and "longer ending" (vv. 9-20), which are found in Scripture, usually in brackets, but are not included in the Easter pericope. There is practically no doubt that the gospel itself ended where it now ends, in v. 8, with *ephobounto gar:* "for they were afraid."

John Painter has defined Mark 16:1-8 as a "failed quest" narrative.[6] The women come seeking Jesus but do not find him, even though the obstacle they feared (the stone before the tomb) has been removed. They are then given a new direction for their quest: they will see Jesus in Galilee. This new direction is unexpected, but it should not be, because, as the heavenly messenger says, Jesus had told the disciples that he would go before them to Galilee after he was raised up (14:28). Nevertheless, it seems that the new quest fails also: the women do not tell the disciples, but "say nothing to anyone" because of their fear. Still, the very existence of the gospel belies this failure. And traditions of a reunion in Galilee survive in Matthew and John.

Two observations are in order: First, the ending of Mark apparently carries through the constant theme of the failure of disciples. It seemed, for a time, that the women disciples, who only emerge as an identified group in the last two chapters, would succeed where the men had consistently failed. They have remained faithful through the crucifixion; they alone have the courage to go to the tomb to pay the final honors to the crucified man—a dangerous thing to do. Here at last we think to find model disciples. But in the end the women, like the men, seem unable to trust the power of God. The irony that so strongly marks this gospel survives to the end: people commanded to keep silent have spoken (1:45; 7:36-37); now those who are commanded to speak are tongue-tied.

So our hope for model disciples is shattered; yet at the same time we are heartened. We, after all, are failed disciples too. It is not as though there had been a set of perfect apostles at the beginning, putting the rest of us to shame. From beginning to end, the progress of the gospel has been a story of failure and disappointment, of new beginnings and renewed failures, to which God never ceases to respond with forgiveness. The angelic message extends pardon to Peter (he, the denier, is singled out by name) and to all the failed disciples. For Mark, failure is part of continuing discipleship. As Joanna Dewey writes:

> The audience is reassured that they may fail, turn again, and continue following Jesus. Mark's message may even be that human failure is the beginning of true discipleship. So the listeners are called to be faithful followers, expecting healing, expecting persecution. And above all they are called to trust the power of God.[7]

But did the women fail, after all? The gospel ending tells us that they did not speak, but did they *never* speak? If the eyewitnesses never spoke, whence the gospel? It is worth considering whether to the first hearers of this message the women's silence conveyed something other than failure of faith or failure of nerve. Perhaps their silence represents, instead, the genuine experience of faith: numinous awe in the presence of the divine. Should the first response to the *mysterium tremendum* of Easter be to proclaim or to stand silent before God's miracle?

The first hearers of Mark's gospel, who, like us, were living in a post-Easter world, would have known that the mission of the first witnesses was at an end; if the gospel was to be proclaimed, the task fell now to them. But what if they themselves were fearful and silenced? In such a situation they could look at the first disciples, afraid and silent at the beginning of their lives of discipleship, and know that the fear had been overcome, the silence broken. This new generation, too, though fearful and silent at the beginning, could hope to find in the very cross itself the courage to speak.

We may also find in the ending of Mark a point of tension among the gospels, a tension between Galilee and Jerusalem as the focal points of the emerging church. In Luke 24:49 and Acts 1:4 we hear Jesus tell the disciples not to leave Jerusalem, but to await there "the promise of the Father." Matthew and John also record appearances of the Risen One in Jerusalem, yet end their stories in Galilee. John Painter surmises a background of conflict between the Jerusalem church and the mission-oriented Markan church in Galilee, a tension also reflected in Acts (see the remarks above on Acts 10, and see below on other passages from Acts read during this season). According to Mark the disciples should have known, from the words of Jesus himself, that they were to return to Galilee, and from that place, "Galilee of the gentiles," go on to proclaim the gospel to the whole world. To Mark, remaining in Jerusalem represents unfaithfulness to Jesus' command, refusal to leave the safety of "headquarters," and unwillingness to meet the Lord "on the way."

WHERE IS OUR GALILEE? ARE WE REMAINING IN JERUSALEM WHEN WE SHOULD BE ON THE ROAD?

The question for us, as twenty-first-century disciples, may well be: where is our Galilee? Are we remaining in Jerusalem when we should be on the road? Are we keeping silence about the gospel, even though the resurrection message calls on us to proclaim it? Or is our silence appropriate until we, as individuals and as church, have made the pilgrimage to Galilee?

JOHN 20:1-18 (RCL alt.); 20:1-19 (RC alt.)

This is the most elaborated of the resurrection narratives, with five fully-developed scenes: Mary Magdalene at the tomb, her meeting with Peter and the beloved disciple, their visit to the tomb, and finally her encounter with the angels and the risen Jesus. (The RC lectionary uses only 20:1-9, then resumes on the second Sunday of Easter with vv. 19-31, thereby eliminating the account of Mary's meeting with the Lord and her apostolic commission.)

In this account the beloved disciple and Mary Magdalene emerge as strong models for discipleship: he the loving follower who believes without having seen (v. 8; cf. v. 29), she the equally loving visionary who persists in seeking her Lord until she finds him, who as one of his true sheep recognizes his voice (cf. 10:4, 16), and who carries out the apostolic mission, declaring to the other disciples, "I have seen the Lord" (v. 18). The bond of love between Jesus and his followers is especially powerful in this gospel, nowhere more than in this chapter: there are strong echoes of the Song of Songs throughout the scenes with Mary Magdalene.[8]

A significant moment in this gospel for those of us living in a post-Easter world is Jesus' command to Mary: "Do not hold on to me" (v. 17). The relationship Jesus had with his disciples during his pre-Easter life cannot continue in the same way, nor can it be replicated. He must "ascend to the Father," that is, take his place at the heart of creation, not absent but rather omnipresent.

Response to the Readings of Easter Day and the Easter Season

The overall strategy for living in a post-Easter world may simply be, as suggested above, to focus on the life, death, and resurrection of Jesus as one inseparable set of events. But the several readings proposed for the day offer a variety of tactical approaches.

One approach is to focus on the "things that are above" as the ultimate goals and standards for life. These things constitute the fullness of human life, the true fulfillment into which Jesus, as our precursor, has entered. We are called to shape our world, to the extent possible, in light of those realities and in line with those values.

Another "angle of vision" finds the fulfillment not "above," but "within"—another kind of spatial metaphor. (All our language about resurrection and its consequences is necessarily metaphorical.) In affirming that the life of Jesus and of all those who are raised in him is changed, not taken away, we also affirm the goodness of human life and of all created existence. Jesus' resurrection does not take him away from human reality, but more deeply and fully into it so that the whole of creation is suffused with his risen life.

Finally, responses on our part to the Easter mystery may be unique to ourselves, perhaps proper to each of us at different times. The response of silent awe may be the first, or for some of us the only, way to respond: contemplation may be our calling. Others are summoned, like Mary Magdalene, to "go to the brethren" and proclaim the good news—news that the event realized in Jesus Christ affirms once for all that God shows no partiality, but prepares a messianic banquet for the whole world. If we are silent and baffled about how or whether to give witness to the gospel, we know that from the beginning this was the dilemma of disciples, so we are not alone.

The challenge for the preacher is to enable the audience to grasp these narratives as life-propositions, ways of being-in-the-world that we may appropriate, but *not* as retreats into the past, playing ancient Bible-land (as Krister Stendahl has said). What does it mean for us as twenty-first-century disciples to appropriate the world of Paul's or Mark's or Luke's or Isaiah's story as our own?

EASTER EVENING

APRIL 23, 2000

REVISED COMMON	EPISCOPAL (BCP)	ROMAN CATHOLIC
Isa. 25:6-9	Acts 5:29a, 30-32 or Dan. 12:1-3	Acts 10:34a, 37-43
Ps. 114	Ps. 114, or 136, or 118:14-17, 22-24	Ps. 118:1-2, 16-17, 22-23
1 Cor. 5:6b-8	1 Cor. 5:6b-8 or Acts 5:29a, 30-32	Col. 3:1-4 or 1 Cor. 5:6-8
Luke 24:13-49	Luke 24:13-35	Luke 24:13-35

THE NARRATIVE OF THE DISCIPLES ON THE ROAD TO EMMAUS seems ready-made for an Easter evening service. It is a unique episode, not untypical of Luke's writing, but with few echoes elsewhere. The other readings are connected to it in the loosest possible fashion, linked only by their references to the resurrection.

FIRST READING

ISAIAH 25:6-9 (RCL)

(See Easter Day, morning.)

ACTS 5:29a, 30-32 (BCP)

The scene is the apostles' second arrest and appearance before the Sanhedrin: having been warned not to teach in the name of Jesus (Acts 4:18), they have defied the order and continued to teach in the portico of the Temple. The high priest charges that by their teaching they are bringing Jesus' blood on the people of Israel, and Peter does not deny it; he refers to "Jesus, whom *you* had killed." Nevertheless, he asserts that God's purpose was to raise up Jesus as Leader and Savior "that he might give repentance to Israel and forgiveness of sins." God's purposes are not mocked even by the disobedience of God's people. Indeed, the most shameful thing that could happen to anyone in Israel, the thing that brought with it an everlasting curse, namely being "hanged on a tree" (cf. Deut. 21:23, to which Paul refers in Gal. 3:13), is the fate that befell Jesus. Nevertheless, he is exalted to the right hand of God. To this the disciples, together with the Holy Spirit (cf. 4:31; 15:28), are witnesses.

The scene underscores the remarkable transformation that has been wrought in Jesus' followers by his resurrection and the gift of the Holy Spirit. In defying the Sanhedrin they risk suffering the same fate as their Lord, yet they are not deterred. For the time being they are spared, but very soon martyrdom will be the fate of Stephen (chapter 7), then of James, son of Zebedee (chapter 12)—and, the listeners know, of a great many other disciples.

DANIEL 12:1-3 (BCP alt.)

This passage from Daniel is chosen because it contains the first certain reference to resurrection in the canonical Scriptures. A universal resurrection is not envisaged: only some are raised, but apparently not because they are good or evil, since some will receive everlasting life and others everlasting punishment. This idea that some will be raised while others will simply perish remained one of the significant strands of apocalyptic and eschatological thought in Judaism. It is difficult to know whether Paul subscribed to some form of this, or whether he envisioned a universal resurrection; in 1 Cor. 15:22 he says that "as all die in Adam, so all will be made alive in Christ," but in the very next verse speaks of "Christ the first fruits, then at his coming those who belong to Christ," and the rest of the passage speaks not of punishment, but of the destruction of all Christ's enemies.

Responsive Reading

PSALM 114 (RCL/BCP)

This psalm recalls the Exodus theme of the Passover and Easter feasts, as does Psalm 136.

Second Reading

1 CORINTHIANS 5:6b-8 (RCL/BCP)

Most of us are familiar with the Jewish practice, mandated by Exod. 12:15, of cleansing the house of all forms of yeast or leavening in preparation for Passover. What is not so well known is that the "leaven" the Bible speaks of is not the clean and pleasant-smelling yeast that makes bread baking a pleasure for all in the house. The "leaven" of ordinary people in the ancient world was a foul-smelling and moldy lump. It made the bread rise, but both the smell and taste were corrupted by it. Such bread was considered unworthy to be offered on the Lord's altars (cf. Lev. 2:11). Note the context of Paul's use of the metaphor: he is excoriating the Corinthian community for tolerating within itself a source of corruption, people who practice sexual immorality. They are the analogy for the leaven (misnamed "yeast" in the NRSV). Paul sees it as the task of the Christian community to keep itself free of corruption so that its self-offering to God may be pure of this kind of "leaven." Hopefully, of course, the purified community will not be as flat and tasteless as most communion bread!

Gospel
LUKE 24:13-49 (RCL); 24:13-35 (BCP/RC)

The richly detailed narrative of the disciples' encounter with Jesus on the road to Emmaus forms a kind of transition from the dramatic and shocking events at the tomb to Jesus' revelation of himself to all the disciples gathered in Jerusalem. The disciples move from absence—"he is not here"—through gradual understanding, to recognition, and ultimately to Jesus' tangible presence. Although the chapter concludes with Jesus' self-revelation in very physical terms, his commissioning of the disciples, and his final withdrawal, it is this central scene that most truly addresses the hearts of post-Easter disciples, for the mode in which the two believers encounter Jesus, "in the breaking of bread," is the way in which we latter-day followers meet him, and one another.

THE MODE IN WHICH THE TWO BELIEVERS ENCOUNTER JESUS, "IN THE BREAKING OF BREAD," IS THE WAY IN WHICH WE LATTER-DAY FOLLOWERS MEET HIM, AND ONE ANOTHER.

The story is told with all the skill of a novelist. The scene is described in detail: the place, the road, the evening meal. Even the movements and postures of the characters are shown, allowing us to picture the action: the disciples are talking with one another as they walk; the unknown person approaches and matches their pace; when he asks his question they stop still as they enter into the discussion with him. The expression, "As they came near the village" (v. 28), tells us that the preceding dialogue and the stranger's explanation of the Scriptures had been conducted as the three walked along. "He walked ahead as if he were going on" again shows us the action; having been persuaded, he goes "in" to stay with them. Finally, we see the three at table, Jesus' actions in taking, blessing, and breaking bread, and finally the disciples' hasty departure and return to Jerusalem.

In light of Luke's tendency to pair stories of men and women, the unnamed Emmaus disciple may well stand for all the unnamed women in the New Testament. There is no inherent reason to assume that both the disciples are male. Moreover, there is more than a little irony in the sequence in vv. 22-25: Cleopas speaks of the women's testimony, which the others did not believe (see v. 11) even though they "found it just as the women had said." To this Jesus replies: "Oh, how foolish you are, and how slow of heart to believe all that the prophets have declared!" Indeed, and these women prophets last of all!

In his commentary on Luke's gospel, scholar Luke Timothy Johnson has pointed to three literary and religious functions served by this story.[9] First, as we have noted, it provides a transition from the empty-tomb scene to the appearance of Jesus among his disciples. Second, it is a narrative tour de force that interweaves a number of people's "stories" into a single strand. Johnson points out how this same technique is used in the Cornelius narrative and subsequent events in Acts 10–15, where Cornelius's and Peter's "conversions" are bound together and ultimately become the basis for a "conversion" of the entire community with regard to the gentile mission. Here, in Luke 24, we have a story of disciples on the road telling of what happened in the city and what was told to them in turn by the women, who had still another experience of being reminded of Jesus' words; all of that is caught up and transformed by the stranger's telling of the words of the prophets "about himself," and finally the two disciples return to tell the whole story to the assembly in Jerusalem which, in turn, tells *them* of other such events. The smooth fabric of the story is woven of myriad fibers.

THE STORY OF JESUS IS TOLD AND INTERPRETED WITHIN—AT THE HEART OF—THE STORY OF A WHOLE PEOPLE IN ITS HISTORY WITH GOD.

Third, and probably most important, the narrative is developed theologically as a process of community interpretation. The story of Jesus is told and interpreted within—at the heart of—the story of a whole people in its history with God. It has meaning only in its embeddedness in that history. This narrative shows us how believers came to "make meaning," to understand what they had witnessed.

> The "opening of the eyes" to see the texts truly and the "opening of the eyes" to see Jesus truly are both part of the same complex process of seeking and finding meaning. Without "Moses and the prophets" they would not have had the symbols for appropriating their experience. Without their experience, "Moses and the prophets" would not have revealed those symbols. Luke shows us how the risen Lord taught the Church to read Torah as prophecy "about him."[10]

This interpretive process serves to build not only a community narrative, but a community. All those who were scattered, the individuals and groups who have been running to and fro through this chapter, are drawn together into one place and one shared story. They are ready for the full encounter with Jesus that begins at v. 36. But we may look at the story as extending beyond its own boundaries. This gospel began in the Temple, in the Holy of Holies, before God. It encompassed Jesus' life, death, and resurrection, and in this chapter the stories of people facing their new situation, revisiting the story, making meaning. That is our situation. We are engaged, as a community, in making meaning of the lives we live after Easter. The full encounter for which that process of community interpretation is preparing us we await at the parousia. Meanwhile we still hear the Lord speak to us in the assembly and interpret the Scriptures as telling about him; we encounter him in the breaking of bread and our eyes are opened to recognize him in those gathered with us at the table. We travel together through the post-Easter night toward the dawn encounter.

SECOND SUNDAY OF EASTER

APRIL 30, 2000

Revised Common	Episcopal (BCP)	Roman Catholic
Acts 4:32-35	Acts 3:12a, 13-15, 17-26 or Isa. 26:2-9, 19	Acts 4:32-35
Ps. 133	Ps. 111	Ps. 118:2-4, 13-15, 22-24 or 118:19-24
1 John 1:1—2:2	1 John 5:1-6	1 John 5:1-6 or Acts 3:12a, 13-15, 17-26
John 20:19-31	John 20:19-31	John 20:19-31

FIRST READING

ACTS 4:32-35 (RCL/RC)

This is the second of Luke's summary descriptions of life in the first Christian community (cf. 2:42-47). As the first description was preceded by the account of Pentecost, Peter's sermon, and the many conversions that ensued, so this summary concludes the account of the healing of the lame man (one of the "wonders and signs" mentioned in the previous summary at 2:43; cf. 4:30) and of the apostles' trial and testimony before the Sanhedrin, culminating in a community assembly (4:23-31) in which those events were interpreted as the work of God.

The fruit of these wonders and signs is the growth of the church as a community marked by unanimity ("one heart and soul," v. 32) and sharing of possessions in such a way that no one is in need. Property owners like Barnabas (vv. 36-37) sell their lands or houses when there is need for funds, and these are distributed by the apostles according to that need. This prepares the way both for the Ananias and Sapphira story in chapter 5 and for the difficulties over distribution in chapter 6, which lead in turn to the appointment of other church officers and ultimately to the dispersion of the church beyond Jerusalem, according to Luke's structuring of the story.

To better link this pericope with today's gospel reading, reference should be made back to v. 31, which tells how the whole community was "filled with the Holy Spirit and spoke the word of God with boldness," an echo of Jesus' commission in John 20:21-23.

ACTS 3:12a, 13-15, 17-26 (BCP)

The Episcopal lectionary assigns to this Sunday Peter's speech after the healing of the lame man. Its theme of the fulfillment of prophecy picks up the heart of the Emmaus pericope and carries Luke's emphasis on Jesus as prophet into the second book of his two-volume work. Unlike the similar discourse in chapter 2, which introduced a positive development (the conversion of many and the growth of the community), this one broaches a negative: the sharpening conflict evoked by the Jesus-preaching, signaled by the arrest of the apostles. Therefore in this speech Luke has Peter lay more stress on the wrong attitudes and actions of his audience in failing to recognize Jesus as the prophet sent by God and on the need for repentance (reinforced by a whole series of scriptural allusions and citations in vv. 22, 25-26).

JESUS' GLORIFICATION IS THE RESULT OF HIS HAVING OVERCOME THE POWER OF SIN, AND HIS DISCIPLES SHARE IN THAT GLORIOUS STRENGTH.

Crucial to the speech, however, is the opening statement that God has glorified Jesus—not merely through this work of healing, but through all the events of his life, death, and resurrection, culminating in his exaltation to God's right hand. Here is where the emphasis must lie during the Easter season—not on repentance, however necessary that is in the whole scheme of Christian life. Jesus' glorification is the result of his having overcome the power of sin, and his disciples share in that glorious strength, as the gospel pericope shows.

ISAIAH 26:2-9, 19 (BCP alt.)

This reading combines parts of a victory song and an apocalyptic psalm, ending with an affirmation that in its original context referred to the exiled people's status as "dead," a status that will yet be overcome by God when they are restored to their land (cf. v. 2). The faithful may take comfort in God's smoothing of their path; on the other hand, the post-Easter believers may find themselves yearning for a sense of God's presence as they strive to "learn righteousness."

Responsive Reading

PSALM 133 (RCL); 111 (BCP)

Psalm 133, a wisdom psalm about the joys of family harmony, goes well with the tale of harmony in the Christian community told in Acts 4. Psalm 111 fits better with the selection from Acts 3 prescribed by the Episcopal lectionary, praising God for mighty deeds and fidelity to the divine promises.

Second Reading

1 JOHN 1:1—2:2 (RCL)

The first "letter" of John (really a polemical treatise or exhortation, with no epistolary features) is often thought of as one of the great works on love: "God is love, and those who abide in love abide in God" (4:16) and "Beloved, let us love one another" (4:7). But in fact, the bulk of the exhortation consists of harsh polemic against a "them" who are opposed to "us," though there is no certainty about the exact character of the "them" because all we know comes from the author's clearly biased portrayal. Whoever "they" are, they have departed from the church represented by the author; they have approached another community, and it is the author's purpose to warn that community, and any others to whom the dissidents might turn, not to be "deceived" (2:26). He even accuses them of being "Antichrists" (2:18)! The phrases throughout the work that begin "If we say . . ." or the like are intended to contrast the writer's view (and that of his community) with that of the "others" (in the pericope for today we find "If we say that we have fellowship with him while we are walking in darkness" and "If we say that we have no sin" as well as "If we say that we have not sinned"). The author's opponents may well have said that they had fellowship with Christ; they would certainly have denied that they were walking in darkness. Whether they claimed to have no sin is dubious: they may, rather, have held a different view of atonement from what the author wanted to postulate.

Given this background, we can see the selection in today's set of readings as Janus-faced: on the one hand it extols many of the elements in the gospel pericope, but what a contrast it presents to the picture of the Christian community drawn in Acts 4! When that initial unanimity broke down (if indeed it ever existed), how quickly the Christians began to attack and tear one another!

There is much dispute about the relationship of 1 John to the Fourth Gospel, especially whether it predates or postdates the gospel. Certainly the two works are part of the same tradition. The beginning of 1 John even seems to echo the prologue to John: "In the beginning was the Word" and "We declare to you what was from the beginning." The elements of seeing and touching developed in John 20 are found here, as is the theme of testimony (cf. John 20:30-31). We also find here the theme of eternal life, the dualism of light and darkness, and the cleansing from sin through the blood of Jesus.

The preacher may choose to develop these themes in harmony with the gospel in positive terms, but it would probably be wrong to whitewash 1 John altogether and paint too rosy a picture of life in the early Christian communities. Such a portrayal can only cause our present congregations, few of which lack a "war department," to despair at their failure to attain this utopian ideal. It helps us to know that our predecessors, even those who were very close to the risen Jesus, also struggled to walk in the light.

1 JOHN 5:1-6 (BCP/RC)

The general remarks on 1 John given above apply here as well, though the rhetoric is generally positive. "Everyone who believes . . ." could indeed be *everyone* (if we had not read the rest of the letter!). The emphasis on obedience to God's commandments as the sign of love implies that there are those who claim to love and yet do not obey the commandments (which are left unspecified). The theme of water and blood again reflects the continuity between the tradition in 1 John and that of the Fourth Gospel, as does the reference to the witness of the Spirit. In fact, 1 John 5:1, 5 repeats the two confessions that originally concluded the Gospel and summarize Johannine Christology: that Jesus is the Messiah and Son of God (cf. John 20:31).[11] At the same time, the reference to "our faith" in v. 4 is at odds with the Gospel, which regularly uses the verb "believe," but never the noun "faith."[12] The reference to Jesus' coming "by water and blood" is cryptic. It may allude to his baptism and the cross (but cf. John 1:13). The association of the Spirit with truth accords with the farewell discourses that will provide the Gospel pericopes for most of the Easter season. (See also the commentary on this passage as the second reading for the sixth Sunday of Easter, pp. 44–45.)

GOSPEL

JOHN 20:19-31

In a genuine sense the successive scenes in John 20 depict the experience of all post-Easter disciples. We have heard the testimony of the eyewitness, Mary Magdalene, but the proclamation of the message of resurrection does not dispel doubt. The disciples are still huddled in the house behind locked doors, fearful of those who had pursued and executed Jesus.[13] Jesus himself appears. He proclaims "peace," fulfilling his promises in 14:27 and 16:33. When he shows proof that he is really himself, the disciples experience joy as well.

There is a chain of faith journeys in the Fourth Gospel; three of those journeys culminate in this chapter. Both Mary Magdalene and the beloved disciple accomplish the movement from deficient faith to full faith, and each completes the sequence by proclaiming the Good News: Mary Magdalene in her witness to the disciples, the beloved disciple through the witness of the Fourth Gospel itself (cf. 21:24). Thomas's progress from deficient faith to full faith to proclamation is described in the short space of five verses, thus summarizing and encapsulating the process that has been witnessed in other lives throughout the Gospel.

The disciples have experienced peace and joy in recognizing the Risen One; now they must complete their work by proclaiming him. They will be to the world what Jesus has been; therefore they need the same kind of support he had: Jesus' Father must now be Father to them (cf. John 20:17), and they must receive the Holy Spirit so that they can be holy as Jesus is holy.[14] As Jesus came to "take away the sin of the world" (1:29), so now the disciples will confront and take away the world's sin (20:23).[15] Though their experience has been and will be mixed (fear and joy), Jesus' love for them, even for those who, like Judas, fail most abjectly, is unfailing. Through that love they are empowered to bring his peace and joy to future generations of frightened disciples.[16]

HOW CAN WE PUT ASIDE OUR FEAR AND EXPERIENCE JOY WHEN FOR MANY OF US THE WORLD REMAINS SUCH A THREATENING PLACE?

Ultimately, the faith (or "believing") to which disciples are called is an eschatological reality because it is faith in the risen Jesus. The gospel places great stress on believing in the risen Lord (20:8, 18, 20, 25, 27-29). But resurrection is an eschatological event, a thing out of time. As John Painter writes:

> Believing is an eschatological phenomenon because it is a response to the eschatological event. It involves a *perception* that was possible only after the glorification of Jesus. It is a gift of the eschatological age, made *possible* by the coming of Jesus, but made *actual* by the coming of the Paraclete.[17]

Paradoxically, however, because Jesus has broken the bonds of death, of time, and of space, he is free from the ordinary limitations of the human condition (without ceasing to be one of us), and consequently he can be experienced in the places where we live our ordinary lives.[18] Thus the Fourth Gospel preserves the tension of "already" and "not yet" that is at the heart of both Jewish and New Testament eschatology. It is a tension that is difficult for most of us to sustain at every moment, and it is certainly a major part of our difficulty in coping with life in our post-Easter world. How can we put aside our fear and experience joy when for many of us the world remains such a threatening place? Would we not prefer, like Thomas, to have someone "with skin on" to show us the way, rather than the mysterious and numinous Paraclete? The gospel extended comfort to those in its own time who "had not seen and yet had believed." Can we really take possession of that comfort as yet another millennium rolls away?

The act of believing is an act of total dependence on God,[19] probably the least attractive act imaginable for our autonomy-worshiping century. And yet it is our only hope, our only way out of fear. The author of the Fourth Gospel held out that hope for us, writing "so that you may come to believe" (20:31). Remember: "Jesus did many other signs in the presence of his disciples, which are not written in this book" (v. 30). It does not say that he did all those signs before the book was written. We are his disciples if we love one another, says the author of 1 John, and surely he is still doing signs in our presence; if we cannot believe without seeing, still it may be that we can see, and so believe.

THIRD SUNDAY OF EASTER

MAY 7, 2000

REVISED COMMON	EPISCOPAL (BCP)	ROMAN CATHOLIC
Acts 3:12-19	Acts 4:5-12 or Micah 4:1-5	Acts 3:13-15, 17-19
Ps. 4	Ps. 98 or 98:1-5	Ps. 4:2, 4, 7-9
1 John 3:1-7	1 John 1:1—2:2, or Acts 4:5-12	1 John 2:1-5a
Luke 24:36b-48	Luke 24:36b-48	Luke 24:35-48

FIRST READING

ACTS 3:12-19 (RCL); 3:13-15, 17-19 (RC)

(See second Sunday of Easter, Alternate First Reading, p. 19.)

ACTS 4:5-12 (BCP)

The Episcopal lectionary offers for today's First Reading, as one alternative, Acts 4:5-12 (which will be the First Reading in the RCL and, in part, in the Roman Catholic lectionary, on the Fourth Sunday of Easter).

The scene is the trial of Peter and John before the Sanhedrin, described by Luke as "rulers, elders, and scribes." This trial is the sequel to the apostles' healing of the lame man at the Temple as described in the previous chapter. The key theme that links this reading to the gospel pericope is the emphasis on the "name" of Jesus as the source of healing and saving power (see vv. 7, 10, 12). The author of Luke and Acts is well known for "biblicisms," or imagery and theological reflections that imitate or connect with Old Testament or Semitic thought. In such a context the "name" stands for the identity of the person; knowing someone's name gives one access to the power of that person (cf. Exod. 3:13-14; Ezek. 20:8-9). In the Johannine literature, which dominates the rest of the Easter season, Jesus comes in the name of God and therefore exercises God's power. The name of Jesus is itself powerful, as shown again and again in Acts (cf. 2:38; 3:6; 4:7, 10, 12, 17-18, 29; 5:28, 40-41; 8:28; 10:43).

The whole pericope is a Lukan composition. The named opponents include all the leading groups in Israel ("rulers" = the previous high priest, Annas, who had been deposed by the Romans but retained great authority, plus his coterie; "elders" = the heads of the most influential lay groups; "scribes" = those with professional learning in Scripture) *but not* the Pharisees, who (apart from Paul, who is converted) do not appear in Acts as opponents of the Christians. The Pharisees are a part of greater Israel (as distinct from its rulers and authorities) that stands ready to hear the message of salvation. Although the apostles have been arrested for preaching about Jesus (see v. 2), and although in the sequel to this scene they will be warned no longer to preach in his name (a warning that will be utterly ignored), the accusation brought against them in v. 7 has to do with the healing. In the little missionary speech of Peter that makes up the heart of today's reading, Luke has skillfully played on the double meaning of "heal" and "save," the same word in Greek *(sōzein)*. Works of healing are but the outward manifestations of the universal salvation that has been wrought by God in Jesus.

MICAH 4:1-5 (BCP alt.)

This passage is a duplicate of Isa. 2:2-4. It is a vision of the eschatological, peaceful reign of God when all the people of the earth will be gathered into the reign of Israel's God. Again the reference to the "name" of God in v. 5 furnishes a point of connection to the gospel pericope.

Responsive Reading

PSALM 4

An evening song of confidence corresponding to the morning prayer of Psalm 3, the fourth psalm acknowledges divine rescue and expresses trust, all this as a frame to an instruction. The instruction also urges confident trust in God. The reference in v. 2 to "vain" words is a subtle allusion, in the context of the Psalter, to Psalm 2:1 (and therefore the whole psalm). Psalm 2, in turn, is key to the Christian community's interpretation of the events in Acts 4 (cf. Acts 4:5, 25-26). There is a good opportunity here, for once, to develop the interconnection of the psalm with the First Reading.

PSALM 98; 98:1-5 (BCP alt.)

Psalms 96–98 form a trilogy of hymns celebrating divine sovereignty. They are post-exilic compositions that emphasize the connection between God's action in history at the present time (98:1-3) and the eschatological future when God will "judge" or "govern" the world with righteousness and equity. Again there are significant opportunities for the preacher to develop the connection between the psalmist's view of history and the ideas expressed in the readings from Acts that pervade this season.

SECOND READING

1 JOHN 3:1-7 (RCL)

Although most commentators agree that a new section of 1 John begins at 2:28 and continues at least through 3:10, the lectionary lops off both the beginning and end of the frame, making it difficult to situate these verses in context and see them as anything other than a disjointed series of sayings. Verses 1-3 are a kind of aside or exclamation over the wonders of God's love, while vv. 4-7 begin a set of contrasts between the righteous and sinners, with the latter part missing, so that the material in these verses remains undeveloped.

The statements in vv. 1-3 about our status as God's "children" (*tekna,* a special word for believers in the Johannine literature, which for the most part reserves *huios,* "son," for Jesus) link with the theme of the "name." As the author of the letter says, being "called" children of God means that we really are God's children; moreover, this will be public knowledge. As Raymond Brown wrote, "Through God's love Christians are given a new (eternal) life and a new identity, and so they have a new name."[20] In Jesus, Christians share in the divine life and therefore rightfully bear the Name, exercising its power as well.

The remainder of today's selection reflects the hostility between the author and his group, on the one hand, and the secessionists or dissidents on the other. The author's opposition to them is, as throughout the letter, couched in dualistic terminology reflecting that of the Gospel of John, especially the opposition of sin and righteousness, light and darkness, truth and lie.

1 JOHN 2:1-5a (RC)

Commentators have struggled, generally in vain, to reconcile (1) the author's condemnation of those who say "we have no sin" (cf. 1:8); (2) his saying that Christians cannot claim to be sinless and that if they do sin they have

Jesus Christ as their advocate (2:1-2); and (3) his assertion elsewhere that true Christians cannot and do not sin (cf. 3:6, 9). It appears that both the author and his opponents subscribed to some sort of perfectionism, according to which Christians, if they are truly in Christ, are preserved from sin. However, Raymond Brown suggested that the key to their difference may lie in the pericope discussed above, namely in the assertion that Christians are God's children, "born of [God]" (2:29).[21] The child is not perfected in its begetting or birth, though the elements of its perfection, its *telos,* are present in it, waiting to be developed. Mistakes will be made along the way, yet as long as the child is true to its "genetic heritage" it must progress toward the full development of what it truly is. This seems to be the best explanation of Johannine perfectionism, though it remains somewhat contradictory from our twenty-first-century perspective.

In the remainder of this pericope, vv. 3-5a, emphasis is placed on obedience to God's commandments as the means to perfection or, from another point of view, the sign of that perfection. Those who are born of God will quite naturally act according to the divine "genetic information," the plan laid down by God for the perfection of humanity, manifested in God's commandments. It is not a matter of extraneous performance, but of acting according to one's true nature.

ARE WE LIVING THE RESURRECTION LIFE ALREADY, OR IS THE PERFECTION THAT IS APPARENTLY DEMANDED OF US SOMETHING UNATTAINABLE IN THIS LIFE?

This issue of perfectionism is important for post-Easter Christians. Are we living the resurrection life already, or is the perfection that is apparently demanded of us something unattainable in this life? It may help if we understand, with the author of 1 John, that the life implanted in us at baptism will inevitably flourish and flower unless we place obstacles to it—for example, by depriving it of light (knowledge of the truth) or the nourishing soil of a community of support.

1 JOHN 1:1—2:2 (BCP)

(See second Sunday of Easter, pp. 20–21.)

GOSPEL

LUKE 24:36b-48

This penultimate scene from Luke's Gospel depicts Jesus' final appearance to his disciples. The gospel pericope stops short of the last verses, containing the promise of the Holy Spirit and a short version of the story of Jesus' ascension. The lectionary's surgery on the Lukan text not only smacks of "play-acting" a reenactment of the forty days, but it obscures for the congregation the programmatic ending of the gospel and the way it anticipates the action in Acts, as well as Luke's vision of the whole of Christian history.

In this scene Jesus attempts twice to overcome the disciples' distress: first with his greeting of peace (the very peace that his appearance on earth has effected: see Luke 1:79; 2:14, 29), and then by showing his hands and feet and eating in their presence. Luke struggles to express, with the narrative means at his disposal, the fact that Jesus is *present* to his disciples even though, as the angels had said to the women (v. 5), "he is not here." He remains himself, a son of humanity, forever one of us, and yet his physical presence is withdrawn from us by his bursting the bonds of space-time through his death and resurrection. We still struggle and stumble after words to describe this indescribable truth; Luke has done better than most.

Despite Jesus' best efforts, the disciples' fear is not fully overcome. Again Luke grapples with a set of emotions hard to depict in words and produces a Greek construction difficult to render in English. Luke Timothy Johnson translates it "disbelieving and marvelling because of their joy."[22] The phenomenon the gospel author is struggling to put into words may furnish an important key to our own difficulty in coming to terms with living after Easter. There is that element of "too good to be true" in the Easter message. It is more than that: it is too good for us even to hope that it might be true, if we really take it seriously. On the surface, and if we do not think about it too hard, we may feel that forgiveness of sins and eternal life are, after all, just what we deserve for living a good life. But when we "put aside childish things" we are face-to-face with the fact that we could never hope to deserve any such thing; we could never hope even to receive such a free gift, were it not that our God is incomprehensibly good and loving toward us.

At the Passover Seder, part of the *haggadah* is the *"dayyenu"* litany: "it would have been enough for us." As God's mighty deeds for Israel are recited, the company responds, each time, that if God had done that, and only that, *"dayyenu,"* ("it would have been enough for us"). And indeed, each of God's deeds, even the smallest, would have been enough for us, and more than enough for us, but all of them together were *not enough for God.* God had to go the whole way, become one of us *(one of us!)* in Jesus, the Anointed One, suffer our rejection, die, and be raised from the dead, restored to the fullness of human life (and our human life is restored in him) rather than leave one possible action undone that might finally convince us that God loves us beyond all measure, beyond all limits, beyond death itself. Is there any possible response to such a manifestation of love but a combination of fear, joy, awe, and disbelief? If we ever stood face-to-face with the truth, I suspect we would be completely rapt; and after all, life—life after Easter—has to go on. So we are like the disciples: glancing, glimpsing, touching lightly, trying to take it in without being taken over by it.

Ultimately, of course, we do have to be taken over by it, even if we do not fully grasp it. Jesus goes on to "open the minds" of the assembled disciples as he had opened the minds of the two on the road to Emmaus. Just as the words of Scripture had furnished the hermeneutic key for the travelers to understand the meaning of Jesus' life, death, and resurrection, so now these words are the key to understanding the whole testimony of Scripture about what has happened and what is to come. Because the disciples now recognize that Jesus is the Messiah about whom Scripture had spoken, they are to be witnesses (v. 48), and through them "repentance and forgiveness of sins is to be proclaimed in his name to all nations, beginning from Jerusalem" (v. 47). These are the fruits of the messianic age, the message that is to go forth from Jerusalem and be proclaimed to all peoples, as the disciples come to understand in the course of the narrative that follows in Acts.

FOURTH SUNDAY OF EASTER

MAY 14, 2000

REVISED COMMON	EPISCOPAL (BCP)	ROMAN CATHOLIC
Acts 4:5-12	Acts 4:(23-31) 32-37 or Ezek. 34:1-10	Acts 4:8-12
Ps. 23	Ps. 23 or 100	Ps. 118:1, 8-9, 21-23, 26, 28-29
1 John 3:16-24	1 John 3:1-8 or Acts 4:(23-31) 32-37	1 John 3:1-2
John 10:11-18	John 10:11-16	John 10:11-18

THE FOURTH SUNDAY OF EASTER is one of several "Good Shepherd" Sundays scattered through the liturgical year. The psalm most commonly used is Psalm 23; the reading from 1 John 3:16-24 begins with "he laid down his life for us" and the gospel pericope echoes: "the good shepherd lays down his life for the sheep." We usually expect the First Reading and gospel to coordinate, but in this case only the BCP makes that possible by suggesting Ezekiel 34:1-10 as an alternate First Reading. The passages from Acts chosen for this season, though not quite a *lectio continua,* are only loosely coordinated to the gospels, if at all.

FIRST READING

ACTS 4:5-12 (RCL); 4:8-12 (RC)

(See third Sunday of Easter, pp. 24–25)

ACTS 4:(23-31) 32-37 (BCP)

In the chapter on the second Sunday of Easter (pp. 18–19) we already discussed the summary in Acts 4:32-35, so let us concentrate on 4:23-31 (which it would be a real pity to omit, since it is one of the liveliest and yet most solemn scenes in Acts). Here for the first time, and in the most careful detail, Luke presents a theological (ecclesiological) paradigm that he will repeat at intervals throughout Acts. It shows how a Christian community can and should (according to Luke's thinking) recognize, acknowledge, and appropriate God's action in the world and in history.

In the scene here presented, the apostles, after being released for the second time by the Sanhedrin, return to "their own," that is, their fellow Christians, and give an account of what has happened. On hearing it, the assembly bursts into interpretive prayer. (This is portrayed by Luke as a mass phenomenon analogous to the collective speaking in tongues at Pentecost: "they raised their voices together." Luke has composed a dramatic episode to depict in a single scene what would have been a long process of theological interpretation and appropriation.) The events that have transpired in Jesus' life, death, and resurrection, and in the present time of the church, are first placed in a scriptural context (Psalm 2), then (and thereby) interpreted as the working out of the divine plan. The kings and rulers have gathered together "against your holy servant Jesus" *in order* to carry out the divine plan, willy-nilly. Their evil intentions were for naught, for they only led to good.

The prayer then shifts to petition: the Christians ask first that they may "speak [God's] word with all boldness" and second that God will continue to heal and to perform signs and wonders (a stock biblical phrase) through the name of Jesus. The prayer is immediately answered both with a sign (earthquake) and with the fulfillment of the request to "speak the word of God with boldness" (v. 31). This shows that their interpretation of events is correct; all that has happened (and, by implication, all that will happen) is according to the divine will, which cannot be thwarted.

The unanimity of believers described in the rest of the chapter is one of the greatest "wonders" bestowed on the church (and how seldom in evidence lately!). One may well suspect Luke of some hyperbole, as his picture of the harmony in the early church is for the most part a good bit rosier than what the writings of Paul or the Johannine corpus would suggest. Still, if Christians really could be brought to focus on God's will and to seek it without supposing that they already know it, what signs and wonders might yet come to pass?

IF CHRISTIANS REALLY COULD BE BROUGHT TO FOCUS ON GOD'S WILL AND TO SEEK IT WITHOUT SUPPOSING THAT THEY ALREADY KNOW IT, WHAT SIGNS AND WONDERS MIGHT YET COME TO PASS?

EZEKIEL 34:1-10 (BCP alt.)

The image of the king or other leader as shepherd is quite common in the Old Testament—usually positive (cf. Isa. 44:28, of Cyrus; elsewhere of David in his ascent of the throne: cf. 2 Sam. 5:2; 7:7-8; also of God: Pss. 23, 28, 78, 80;

Gen. 49:24). In Ezekiel 34 it becomes an accusation: the leaders of Israel have been bad shepherds, feeding *on* the sheep rather than feeding them. There is very similar language in Jer. 23:1-2, but Ezekiel develops the metaphor more fully than any other Old Testament writer.

There are strong echoes of Ezekiel's language in John 10, especially the parallels between the bad shepherds of Israel and the hirelings who have no particular care for the sheep, as well as the notion of "scattering." In the verses that follow (Ezek. 34:11-16) the connection is even stronger, for there Yahweh dismisses the wicked shepherds and promises to shepherd Israel: "I myself will be the shepherd of my sheep, and I will make them lie down, says the Lord God. I will seek the lost, and I will bring back the strayed" (vv. 15-16). This makes Jesus' saying, "I am the good shepherd," one of the most powerful "I am" sayings in the Fourth Gospel, for his hearers would have understood very clearly that he was identifying his own mission with that of God.

Responsive Reading

PSALM 23

In the Psalter this song of confidence is the sequel to Psalm 22, which is almost as familiar because Jesus recites its opening verse from the cross. In context in the Psalter, then, Psalm 23 carries forward some of the themes of its predecessor: for example, the banquet of the poor (22:26) and the royal reign of Yahweh (in biblical discourse the king is a shepherd to the people). The plea for rescue and for God's nearness, so urgent in Psalm 22, is answered: the shepherd restores life (23:3a); God abides with the petitioner (23:4). The telling of the name of Yahweh promised in 22:22 is fulfilled in Psalm 23, which begins and ends with the Lord's name. This psalm portrays God in two mutually supportive metaphors: as shepherd and as host. As such, God extends care to individuals, to the community of those who fear God, and even to the nations who turn to Yahweh.

PSALM 100

Augustine wrote: "Let praise become your food. By praising you will acquire new strength, and the one you praise will become sweeter to you."[23] No one can go wrong by using Psalm 100 as his or her song of praise. It is entitled "a psalm for the *tōdāh*," that is, for thanksgiving to God for good things received. One way to interpret the scene Luke describes in Acts 4:23-31 is to say that the author was influenced by the Hebrew custom of *tōdāh*, in which the one giving thanks recited the divine favors that were received and for which the thank-offering was being brought. Psalm 100 is thus appropriate in the context of that reading, while Psalm 23 carries through the shepherd metaphor found in the gospel.

Second Reading

1 JOHN 3:16-24 (RCL)

As we continue the more or less sequential reading of 1 John that began with the second Sunday of Easter in the RCL, we find that the unit in 3:18-24 is preceded in the lectionary passage by two verses belonging to the previous unit. Probably they are there because v. 16, "we know love by this, that he laid down his life for us—and we ought to lay down our lives for one another" echoes the Good Shepherd passage in today's gospel. (There would also be a good fit between v. 27, on the sharing of goods, and Acts 4:32-37, but that is in a different lectionary!).

For the author of 1 John it is a matter of course that Jesus' example in laying down his life for us demands an equal response on our part: we should be prepared to lay down our lives for one another. And if this is true, how much the more should we be willing to sacrifice what is less valuable than life itself, namely this world's goods. The author may well imply a criticism of the "secessionists" from the Johannine community (as Raymond Brown called them) if they had more of this world's goods than his poor community and yet refused to share with their ex-brethren. On the other hand, that same author demanded that his community members refuse even to exchange greetings with or offer hospitality to the secessionists (2 John 10)![24]

The next part of the passage is complicated in thought and structure. The author appears to be offering encouragement in two situations: either an individual is conscious of sin, in which case she or he has assurance of forgiveness through the atonement of Christ (cf. 1:8—2:2), or if an individual is living a life as one of God's children so fully that she or he is not conscious of sin, that person can be confident before God even now. The idea that anyone could feel confident of being sinless seems foreign to us, but the author may be combating an opposing position, according to which all Christians should be confident of their salvation and not have to pay attention to their deeds.

Another difficulty with this passage lies in v. 23, where God's commandment is said to be "that we should believe in the name of his Son Jesus Christ and love one another." How can belief be commanded? And if it is, does that make faith a "work"? Certainly the Johannine author's notion of God's commandment is different from what we find in the Synoptic Gospels. For the author of 1 John—and for the author(s) of the Fourth Gospel as well—belief in Jesus is an interpretation of God's love (see 1 John 4:9-10). We are commanded to believe because that is our only access to understanding and appropriating God's love for us. Thus faith is not a "work," but a way of seeing, and hence of being, in relation to the love of God. The history of persecution reflected in the Gospel and in 1 John made that community concentrate on love of the "brothers and sisters" rather than of the more generalized "neighbor" of the Synoptics.

The last verse of this passage marks a transition in 1 John, presaging the next section, on discernment of spirits. It also marks a turning point for the lectionary of the Easter Season, which from this point onward begins to look forward to the sending of the Holy Spirit at Pentecost.

1 JOHN 3:1-8 (BCP); 3:1-2 (RC)

(See third Sunday of Easter, p. 26.)

GOSPEL

JOHN 10:11-18 (RCL/RC); 10:11-16 (BCP)

All three lectionaries prescribe the Johannine passage on the Good Shepherd for this Sunday. Like all such passages in the Fourth Gospel, this is an allegory, not a parable. Every element has an equivalent outside-the-story world, in reality: shepherd, sheep, hired hand. In light of the Old Testament traditions (see the discussion of Ezek. 34:1-10 above, pp. 31–32) Jesus' hearers would have been in no doubt about who the various characters in the allegory were. There is an indirect accusation (by way of the Old Testament allusions) that Israel's current leaders were participating in the slaughter and scattering of the people, in contrast to Jesus, who will "lay down his life" for them. In saying this, Jesus goes beyond any of the previous "shepherd" sayings: nowhere is it said that the ruler, the leader, or God will sacrifice his/her own life for the people. Jesus is uniquely the Good Shepherd because he knows his people with the same intimacy with which he knows the Father and the Father knows him.

The relationship between Jesus and those who believe in him is parallel to the relationship between the Father and Jesus. Moreover, just as Jesus belongs by nature to the Father because he is the Son, so believers belong by nature to Jesus, the one who reveals the Father.[25] Jesus, who will give up his life for the believers, has a legitimate claim to them; the claim of their other leaders, who will sacrifice their followers rather than bring harm on themselves, is illegitimate.

In vv. 17-18 Jesus adds something that is very important in the scheme of the Fourth Gospel: not only will he lay down his life for his sheep, but he will do so freely, by his own choice. This summarizes the Johannine view of the meaning of the cross; readers will remember this statement when the actual Passion is described later.

Perhaps the most important point for post-Easter Christians to note is that through his death and resurrection, freely chosen in response to the Father's command (v. 18), Jesus has laid claim on them. Because he has claimed them through his self-donation, they are irrevocably his. Hireling shepherds may flee and abandon the sheep (which are not theirs), but Jesus will never abandon those who are his own. "Having loved his own who were in the world, he loved them to the end" (13:1). But the "end" is a new beginning, the gift of a new life to Jesus' own: namely, all who are in the world, for there can be only one flock, claimed and owned by the one Shepherd.

WHAT ARE THE IMPLICATIONS OF BEING "OWNED" BY JESUS CHRIST? DOES THAT RUB AGAINST THE INDEPENDENT, INDIVIDUALIST GRAIN OF TWENTY-FIRST-CENTURY WESTERNERS?

What are the implications of being "owned" by Jesus Christ? Does that rub against the independent, individualist grain of twenty-first-century westerners? And yet when Jesus says that "no one can serve two masters," the implication is that none of us will be masterless: we will inevitably serve someone or something. The task of the season of Easter may be one of taking stock, admitting who our ruler and guide really is, and deciding whether to accept the proffered gift of the Holy Spirit. Accepting that gift will bind us irrevocably to the one master who has laid down his life to claim us.

FIFTH SUNDAY OF EASTER

MAY 21, 2000

REVISED COMMON	EPISCOPAL (BCP)	ROMAN CATHOLIC
Acts 8:26-40	Acts 8:26-40 or Deut. 4:32-40	Acts 9:26-31
Ps. 22:24-30	Ps. 66:1-11 or 66:1-8	Ps. 22:26-28, 30-32
1 John 4:7-21	1 John 3:(14-17), 18-24 or Acts 8:26-40	1 John 3:18-24
John 15:1-8	John 14:15-21	John 15:1-18

FIRST READING
ACTS 8:26-40 (RCL/BCP)

There is a marked contrast between the scenes in the gospel pericopes assigned for today and the scene from Acts chosen by two of the three lectionaries. In place of the sheltered supper room we are carried away, with Philip, to the windswept plains of Gaza; from temporary security to open and perilous mission; from talking *intra nous,* just "Jesus and us," to talking to utter strangers. The stranger in this story is very strange indeed, exotic even to Philip, but especially so to us: a man of a different race, a higher social status, and a different sexuality. As Clarice Martin has forcefully pointed out, critics have tried to downplay this differentness. Nevertheless, "the Ethiopian eunuch's ethnographic identity qualifies him to symbolize the universal scope and outreach of the Christian gospel as inclusive of ethnically diverse persons from all nations."[26] As an Ethiopian he fulfills the prophecy of Psalm 68:31 that Ethiopia would "stretch out her hands to God," and as a eunuch he reveals the fulfillment of Isaiah's prophetic demand that eunuchs and foreigners should be equal members of the people of God (56:3-7).

The obvious reference to Isaiah raises the question whether the author of Acts regards the eunuch as a gentile or a Jew. If he is a gentile, then it is wrong to view the story of Cornelius in Acts 11 as the account of the first gentile conversion. If, on the other hand, he is a Jew or a Jewish proselyte, what of the prohibition in Deuteronomy 23:1 against men who are sexually mutilated being part of the Lord's assembly? Some argue that Isaiah's prophecy is about the eschatological future. But clearly the author of Acts believed that the time of fulfillment had arrived in Jesus: whether his Israel was real or idealized, he portrays this man as a Jew or Jewish proselyte; that is why he shows him in the act of returning from Jerusalem where "he had come . . . *to worship.*" He and Philip engage in a Jewish exegetical discussion that leads to Philip's explaining the text of Isaiah in eschatological terms, that is, in terms of his own experience of Jesus' life, death, and resurrection. The Holy Spirit, having brought Philip here for this very purpose, moves the heart of the Ethiopian to faith in Jesus, and he is baptized.

And then? The eunuch "went on his way rejoicing." He passes out of the story for good—but where does he go, and what happens after? Obviously he goes home to Ethiopia and returns to the service of Candace, the powerful queen mother of that noble African civilization. Does he then remain alone, a lonely Jewish Christian to the end of his days? Surely not! He is in fact the first to accomplish what Jesus had foretold in Acts 1:8: "you will receive power when the Holy Spirit has come upon you; and you will be my witnesses . . . to the ends of the earth." Luke sets up a pattern in which the Christian message is carried symbolically to the "ends of the earth," first to the south, regarded since Homer's time as the utmost reach of the known world in that direction, and then in the other direction, to Rome.

THIS FIRST CHRISTIAN MISSIONARY TO THE "ENDS OF THE EARTH" IS A MAN OF A DIFFERENT RACE, A HIGHER SOCIAL STATUS, AND A DIFFERENT SEXUALITY.

But especially notable is that this first Christian missionary to the "ends of the earth" is, as I have said above, a man of a different race, a higher social status, and a different sexuality. Luke frequently pictures persons of high social standing as adherents to Christianity. But if this is one of his typical "paired" stories, in this case matching the story of the conversion of Cornelius and his household, then we have a marked contrast between the man of Ethiopia, black and a eunuch, and the man of Rome, white and head of a household. In the current crisis of the church over the membership and ministry of persons of non-majority sexual orientation, we would do well to reflect on the story of the man of Ethiopia. If the Holy Spirit chose a black man with a "different" sexuality to be the first recorded missionary to all of Africa, what are we about when we question the Spirit's choice of persons not like ourselves in our own time? Should we not say, with Peter, as he defended his baptism of Cornelius to the elders of the church in Jerusalem, "who was I that I could hinder God?" (Acts 11:17).

ACTS 9:26-31 (RC)

The Roman Catholic lectionary offers the conclusion to the story of Paul's conversion, ending with one of Luke's summary accounts of the growth of the church. The "Hellenists" in conflict with Paul here are Jews, not diaspora Jewish Christians like those in Acts 6:1. In the Acts account, Paul's conflicts will be mainly with these "Hellenists," both in Jerusalem and later in Asia Minor and Greece. Luke portrays Paul as fundamentally in harmony with the Jerusalem leadership of the church (see v. 28), though historically this seems not to have been the case. At this point in Acts, the church is flourishing in Judea, Galilee, and Samaria; the stage is set for the next outward leap, beyond the Jewish homeland and into the lands of the gentiles.

DEUTERONOMY 4:32-40 (BCP alt.)

This alternate reading in the Episcopal lectionary coordinates with the gospel reading (John 14:15-21) through the admonition to keep God's commandments. The passage contains a recitation of God's mighty deeds from Egypt to Sinai, with the added element of God's choice of Israel because of God's love for them. The motive for obedience, here as in the gospel pericope, is a loving response to love already shown.

Responsive Reading

PSALM 22:24-30 (RCL); 22:26-28, 30-32 (RC)

Parts of the thanksgiving portion (vv. 22-26) and hymn (vv. 27-31) of Psalm 22 are chosen for this Sunday very probably because it says that "all the ends of the earth shall remember and turn to the Lord; and all the families of the nations shall worship before him" (v. 27). The individual lament and thanksgiving expand in vv. 23-26 to a song of the community of those who fear God. In the final section the group of those giving praise again expands in space and time. Universal adoration is to be practiced by all nations and also by all generations. The fact that the dead also adore God (v. 29) marks this portion of the psalm as a late composition.

PSALM 66:1-11 (or 1-8) (BCP)

This praise of God's mighty deeds would coordinate well with the Deuteronomy reading, but it also accords with the reading from Acts 8, for in it "all the earth" worships God and is called to "come and see" what God has done for Israel. The testimony in this part of the psalm comes from the whole community; the latter part is an individual thanksgiving.

Second Reading

1 JOHN 4:7-21 (RCL)

This rather long reading from 1 John centers on the most famous verse in the letter: "God is love, and those who abide in love abide in God, and God abides in them" (v. 16b). So famous is the verse, and its immediate context, that 1 John is, as noted earlier (pp. 20–21), primarily thought of as a paean to love. Seldom do we reflect on how restricted that love is: "those who love God must love their brothers and sisters also"—but evidently not the dissidents or secessionists who are seen to have failed in love.

It is important to guard against a misuse of this pericope to stress the "Christian God of love" in contrast to the "Old Testament God of justice."[27] The God who is revealed as love in the New Testament is none other than the God who is revealed as loving in the Old Testament (see the earlier remarks on Deut. 4:32-40, p. 38).

The emphasis on abiding in God and keeping God's commandment links this passage to the gospel pericope on the vine and branches (see especially John 15:10).

1 JOHN 3:18-24 (RC); 3:(14-17) 18-24 (BCP)

(See fourth Sunday of Easter, pp. 33–34.)

Gospel

JOHN 15:1-8 (RCL); 15:1-18 (RC)

To say anything new or fresh about this highly popular metaphor—the vine and the branches—seems a hopeless task. What Christian has not had her or his consciousness saturated with the image: evoked in stained glass windows, carved on altars and altar rails and pulpits, embroidered on vestments. The author of the Fourth Gospel has made minute allegorical application of each of the elements (vine, branches, vinedresser, fruit) and it would be just as well not to attempt a similar contemporary application, which would quickly become tedious.

The central point, of course, is the intimate and ongoing relationship of vine (trunk) and branches. Without the former, the latter quickly wither and die; for this evangelist the signs of being cut off from the source of life are quickly evident. For the author and the Johannine community, what sustained them individually and kept them together was an ongoing bond with and experience of the living Jesus. That experience became normative for group members: if they did not have it, they were obviously cut off from the vine.

Clearly this is a crucial question for post-Easter Christians, now as then: Do we have a sense of our continued bond with the living Christ? Are the difficulties we experience merely pruning, or are we cut off from the source of vitality, without which we cannot hope to bear fruit? And what is the fruit we hope to produce? Is it a matter of our own moral perfection, or that of our community (as was probably true for the Johannine community), or is it a question of mission? It seems that we (as a community) must take care neither to lose our rootedness in the vine nor to cease growing: either event would be fatal to our ongoing life as Christians.

ARE THE DIFFICULTIES WE EXPERIENCE MERELY PRUNING, OR ARE WE CUT OFF FROM THE SOURCE OF VITALITY, WITHOUT WHICH WE CANNOT HOPE TO BEAR FRUIT?

(See also the commentary on John 14:15-21 below.)

JOHN 14:15-21 (BCP)

Instead of the vine and branches, the Episcopal lectionary prescribes a passage from the end of the preceding discourse. One fruitful way of approaching these very familiar gospel pericopes is to bring them into dialogue with other readings assigned to the same day. This approximates one of the popular techniques of Jewish and early Christian exegesis: answering the question of one text by applying another, often very different text. What if we relate Acts 8:26-40 and John 14:15-21 as question and answer?

Each of these passages contains an "if": the gospel pericope begins "If you love me . . ." and in Acts 8:37 (a verse that is probably not original and so is omitted in the lectionary) Philip says to the Ethiopian, "If you believe . . ." What is the follow-up to each of these "ifs"? In the gospel we read: "If you love me, you will keep my commandments." In the dialogue between Philip and the Ethiopian, the latter asks, "What is to prevent me from being baptized?" and Philip answers: "If you believe with all your heart, you may." The Ethiopian replies: "I believe that Jesus Christ is the Son of God."

If these are the answers, what are the questions? One is: how can the Ethiopian know enough to believe "with all his heart" after such a short catechesis? Surely because, as Jesus promises in the gospel, he has received the Spirit of truth who now abides in him. He can go on his way rejoicing, confident that he is not orphaned even when he returns alone to his own country. He "believes with all his heart," which means that he also loves. So the question turns back to the gospel text: "If you love me, you will keep my commandments." What are these commandments? Certainly for the Ethiopian the ones he has already known as a Jew, but the gospel gives another answer just before this: "I give you a new commandment, that you love one another. Just as I have loved you, you also should love one another. By this everyone will know that you are my disciples, if you have love for one another" (John 13:34-35; cf. 1 John 4:21). The Ethiopian has the same charge as all disciples: to live by the commandments he already knows and to go beyond them by applying them all in love. But another question arises: How can he love other disciples when he is all alone? Where is his community of support? Who will sustain his faith?

At this point the story becomes very modern. Some of us are fortunate enough to grow up and remain in our communities of faith, like branches on a well-planted vine, but in America at the dawn of the twenty-first century that is an increasingly rare kind of life. Most of us move from place to place: the national average is now something like ten moves in a lifetime. Many of us move from church to church, not just parish to parish, but denomination to denomination. How, in all this restless movement, do we find a place to hold on to, a community to sustain us, a word that is certain in good times and bad?

There are two parts to the promise offered today: First, the Spirit of truth abides with us, and will be in us forever. We are not orphans, but are incorporated into the risen life of Jesus, grafted into the true vine and imbued with life in God and in the Spirit of God. Second, the Spirit of truth is to be shared, is sharing itself: like the Ethiopian, we are called to go on our way rejoicing, to make disciples "even to the ends of the earth" by sharing the good news that is ours, even with the most unexpected of people. The Spirit took a chance on that Ethiopian, going with him to evangelize Africa—going forth without a catechism or a creed, only the good news of Jesus and his Jewish faith and the Spirit within him. What kind of community did he form? It was a community with a different culture, certainly, people of a different race, formed within a different social structure—perhaps even with a different set of ethical standards in matters sexual and otherwise. But it was a community sustained by the Spirit and built on the faith we all share: "I believe that Jesus Christ is the Son of God."

SIXTH SUNDAY OF EASTER

May 28, 2000

Revised Common	Episcopal (BCP)	Roman Catholic
Acts 10:44-48	Acts 11:19-30 or Isa. 45:11-13, 18-19	Acts 10:25-26, 34-35, 44-48
Ps. 98	Ps. 33 or 33:1-8, 18-22	Ps. 98:1-4
1 John 5:1-6	1 John 4:7-21 or Acts 11:19-30	1 John 4:7-10
John 15:9-17	John 15:9-17	John 15:9-17

First Reading

ACTS 10:44-48 (RCL); 10:25-26, 34-35, 44-48 (RC)

This little scene concludes the story of the conversion of Cornelius (or perhaps we should call it the conversion of Peter and his companions). Having begun with the story of Peter and Cornelius on Easter Sunday, we have now come full circle and read the end of the story before entering the brief Ascension season. (The Roman Catholic lectionary precedes vv. 44-48 with a few snippets from earlier in the chapter to set the scene.) At the conclusion of Peter's testimony, the Holy Spirit "falls" on all the listeners—the whole of Cornelius's extended household, we must suppose. The event is an echo of the Pentecost scene, for the outward manifestation of the reception of the Spirit is "speaking in tongues" (the same words used for the disciples' initial experience in Acts 2:4, though the translation of the two verses in the NRSV obscures this). Peter's fellow Jewish Christians are astonished that this gift is being given to the gentiles, in the same manner as it had been given to them.

Much is sometimes made of the fact that these new believers receive the Holy Spirit *before* being baptized, but that only underscores the similarity to the Pentecost event, where nothing is ever said about the initial disciples being baptized. Later, baptism became the normative channel through which the Holy Spirit came to the faithful. Luke apparently knows of or posits a kind of development of baptismal practice from this initial phase, through one in which various kinds of pre-Christian or extra-Christian baptismal rituals were accepted as preparation, to a final stage at which only Christian baptism ("in the name of the Lord Jesus") was the vehicle of the Spirit (see Acts 18:24-25; 19:1-7).

Philip bestowed baptism at the Ethiopian's request. Peter seems to be a harder case: it takes the manifestation of the Holy Spirit to convince him, at last, that baptism cannot be withheld from these new gentile converts. He makes the same argument to his fellow Jerusalem Christians in 11:17: "If then God gave them the same gift that he gave us when we believed in the Lord Jesus Christ, who was I that I could hinder God?" Could it be that this verse would make a better pastoral guide than some others more commonly in use?

ACTS 11:19-30 (BCP)

The Episcopal lectionary recommends, instead of the scene in the house of Cornelius, the summary account of the beginnings of the gentile mission that concludes Acts 11. Clearly it is still God who is at work, even in seeming adversity. The expulsion of Jewish Christians from Jerusalem (Acts 8:1, 4) leads to conversions in Judea, Galilee, and Samaria (not to mention Africa), in the coastal cities, and (we now learn) beyond the borders of Israel, in Phoenicia, Cyprus, and Syrian Antioch. At first the expelled disciples, though Greek-speaking, confine their proselytizing to their fellow Jews (v. 19). But those who are in any case from the diaspora quickly begin to spread the word among the Greeks (gentiles) as well. (The better text witnesses have "Hellenists," but the sense of the passage is clearly that these are gentiles, not Greek-cultured Jews.) This passage, in which Luke has certainly incorporated a number of independent traditions, really follows logically after 8:1-4. The bare historical narrative has been interrupted by the elaborate Lukan composition detailing the divine origins of the gentile mission, first with the Ethiopian, then with Saul/Paul, who will be the prime missionary, and finally with the Peter/Cornelius episode.

At this point it becomes possible to bring Paul back into the story through the agency of Barnabas, with whom he will work for several more chapters. They make their base in Antioch, the "third city of the world" in the Roman era, home to a large Jewish colony, and soon to be the staging point for the entire gentile mission. There, as the text notes, the disciples were first called "Christians," a name we are proud to wear today, but one that at the beginning was probably a jeer. We know from Tacitus that Romans evidently confused what they heard of "Christus" with "Chrestus," a common slave name. Since *christos* means "anointed," the epithet "Christians" may once have meant, to outsiders, something like "greasers" or at most "Jesus freaks." (Try "bikers" as a similar moniker for an outsider group in our own time.) The Jesus people, however, seized the word meant to ridicule them and made it the proudest title in the world (but that took a long time). Unfortunately its *mis*use in political and colonial contexts has made it suspect again: nowadays if people call you a Christian, do you want to claim what they are attributing to you?

ISAIAH 45:11-13, 18-19 (BCP alt.)

This part of Isaiah tells of God's mysterious working through the foreign monarch, Cyrus, to restore God's people to their land. The affirmation "I am the Lord, and there is no other" recurs five times in chapter 45. Cyrus, who does not even know Israel's God, becomes God's "anointed" *(christos)* to carry out God's plan. What a paradoxical sort of savior! But indeed it is God, the incomparable, who saves; Cyrus is only a "shepherd" who will obey God's orders. God is the ruler of all things and all peoples; again the theme of salvation "to the ends of the earth" echoes in the background.

Responsive Reading

PSALM 98

(See third Sunday of Easter, p. 26.)

PSALM 33

This extended hymn is part of a sequence (Pss. 31–33) in which the "steadfast love" *(ḥesed)* of Yahweh manifests itself in ever wider dimensions: for the individual (Ps. 31), for all who trust in God (Ps. 32), and here for all creation: the whole earth is full of the *ḥesed* of Yahweh. The psalm's message complements the theme of the spread of Christianity to all nations.

Second Reading

1 JOHN 5:1-6 (RCL)

This reading contains the end of one section of 1 John and the beginning of another; hence there is a shift of focus in the middle—in fact, in the middle of v. 4. (Commentaries generally divide this part of the letter into sections 4:7—5:4a and 5:4b—12.) One thing is constant, however: the author's polemic against his opponents. In the first part of the reading the argument is that those who love God will necessarily love God's children, and Christians are God's children, "begotten" (or born) of God. The fact that the secessionists or opponents do not (according to the author) love the brothers and sisters is prima facie evidence that they do not love God. Moreover, those who love God keep God's commandments, and since the opponents place no value on keeping commandments, it is doubly evident that they do not love God.

There is a modern equivalent to this situation, and an ironic paradox (latent in the first-century circumstances as well). Some members of our churches are concerned that others appear not to be keeping God's commandments. (Now, as then, there is obviously disagreement between the two sides about the actual content of those commandments.) But in their insistence that these other Christians should "shape up or ship out," these devout and sincere people are contributing to the kind of fission within Christianity that the author of 1 John denounces—and blames on his opponents! Does love of the brothers and sisters require something more than pointing out their faults?

ALTHOUGH WE ARE COMFORTED BY OUR POSSESSION OF THE MEMORIES OF THE EYEWITNESSES RECORDED IN SCRIPTURE, WE HAVE THE CONTINUAL WITNESS OF THE SPIRIT TO LEAD US INTO ALL TRUTH.

In the second part of the reading there seems to be an attempt to combat a teaching that would downplay the meaning of Jesus' sacrifice, although as Raymond Brown wrote, the passage (1 John 5:6-8) is

> an excellent example of the strengths and weaknesses of I John. The burning conviction of the author, the oratorical power of his short phrases, the vividness of the imagery of water, blood, and Spirit, and the probative force of three witnesses: These illustrate the flare and genius of the writer. The weakness, from our point of view at least, is the utter obscurity of what he is talking about.[28]

What may be most important to note in our context is that the selection ends with reference to the witness of the Spirit. As Georg Strecker has written, "the Christian community is not dependent solely on eye- and ear-witnesses who bring the past event of Christ near to them (cf. 1:1-4), because the truth of Christian faith is also guaranteed for it by the Spirit."[29] That is our situation: although we are comforted by our possession of the memories of the eyewitnesses recorded in Scripture, we have the continual witness of the Spirit to lead us into all truth.

1 JOHN 4:7-21 (BCP); 1 JOHN 4:7-10 (RC)

(See fifth Sunday of Easter, p. 39.)

Gospel

JOHN 15:9-17

The first part of this selection contains a chiastic progression (vv. 9-10, 12-17):[30] Jesus' commandment is love, and the maximum of love is to lay down one's life for one's friends. But Jesus' friends, those for whom he will lay down his life, are those who keep his commandment. At the beginning of the progression, "love" refers to the relationship between the Father and Jesus, and between Jesus and his disciples ("As the Father has loved me, so I have loved you; abide in my love," v. 9). By the time the "bottom" of the chiasm is reached, the primary reference of "love" is to the relationship among the disciples ("This is my commandment, that you love one another as I have loved you," v. 12). What makes the disciples friends of Jesus, then, is their love for one another. Their ability to love one another is certainly the fruit of the love of Jesus poured out for them; but the ultimate test (cf. Matt. 25:40) is their love for one another.

At the heart of the chiasm, between the instructions on love, stands v. 11: "I have said these things to you so that my joy may be in you, and that your joy may be complete." This introduces the theme of joy that will dominate the next two chapters. Remarkably, strangely, unbelievably, as Jesus goes toward his death his dominant emotion is joy, and it is this joy that he bestows on his followers as his most precious gift. We ourselves take great pleasure in causing joy in those we love, but we can never give them the joy that is particularly our own. Jesus, however, can do just that, because his joy is the Holy Spirit. Although Paul lists joy as the second of the "fruits" of the Spirit (Gal. 5:22), the Johannine author recognizes the very joy of Jesus himself as that same Spirit, who will be breathed on the disciples at Jesus' death (which, for John, coincides with his resurrection and glorification).

When I was in college (quite a long time ago now) we used to pray the Pentecost collect at the beginning of class, and in Latin class, of course, we prayed it in Latin. I am glad that I learned it in Latin (and in that older English version that stuck closer to the original sense). The modern translation—even in the "traditional" form in the BCP, which in this case is virtually identical to the "contemporary" collect—asks: "Grant us by the same Spirit to have a right judgment in all things, and evermore to rejoice in his holy comfort." Not, if you will pardon me for saying so, words to live by, unless maybe you make your living on the judicial bench. The original Latin asked: "*Da nobis in eodem Spiritu recta sapere, et eius semper consolationem gaudere.*" The literal English translation of "*recta sapere*" is "to relish what is right." Not just to "have a right judgment," if you please, but to *relish,* to munch on and savor and lick your lips and fingers over, the things that are right—indeed, the right itself. "*Sapere*" is for dark chocolate and fine wines and juicy peaches at high summer. No wonder the Pentecost disciples appeared to be intoxicated! They were relishing the right and rejoicing in the Spirit poured out on them. That is what the joy of the Holy Spirit, the joy with which Jesus went even to the cross, is all about, and that is the joy for which the Sundays before Pentecost are preparing us. If we didn't have a foretaste, we might be bowled over.

Not long ago I read an essay about Alice Waters, the founder of Chez Panisse and prophet of good food. As a young student she went to France for the first time, and encountered oysters and the cider of Normandy. She kept keeling over with—she supposed—the sheer joy of it. Only later, when, after returning to the United States, she tried to import some of that cider did she learn that it contained alcohol. Then she understood why—apart from the sheer joy of it all—she kept passing out. Many Christians are like Alice Waters. Lacking a genuine experience of encounter with the Holy Spirit, they are unprepared for it when it happens, and they are likely to be oblivious to what is happening to them, or else attribute the effects to something else. It was the concern of the authors of the Johannine literature—and should be the concern of today's pastors—to help these Christians open their eyes to what is really happening, to "relish what is right," and not to be led astray by false interpretations or lulled into simple lethargy.

All Christians, as the rest of the gospel pericope assures us, are chosen by Jesus to receive his joy, his Spirit, and because of this to bear fruit—delicious, lasting fruit that other generations of believers can relish. It is for their sake that we bear fruit, as the last verse reminds us, circling back again to the love commandment: "I am giving you these commands so that you may love one another" (v. 17). As Jesus has reminded us that the extreme of love is the surrender of oneself for others, we know when he commands us to love that we can only fulfill his commandment by imitating his self-surrender. That is the very "right," that is, genuine and Spirit-filled action, that we can truly relish, the source of our joy.

THE ASCENSION OF OUR LORD

JUNE 1, 2000

REVISED COMMON	EPISCOPAL (BCP)	ROMAN CATHOLIC
Acts 1:1-11	Acts 1:1-11 or Ezek. 1:3-5a, 15-22, 26-28	Acts 1:1-11
Ps. 47 or 93	Ps. 47 or 110:1-5	Ps. 47:2-3, 6-9
Eph. 1:15-23	Eph. 1:15-23 or Acts 1:1-11	Eph. 1:17-23 or 4:1-13 or 4:1-7, 11-13
Luke 24:44-53	Luke 24:49-53 or Mark 16:9-15, 19-20	Mark 16:15-20

BECAUSE THE LUKAN ACCOUNTS OF THE ASCENSION at the end of the gospel and the beginning of Acts are overlapping (and represent two slightly different perspectives by the same author) we should discuss them together, especially if they are to be proclaimed and preached at the same service. We will therefore alter our format in this chapter, looking first at the Luke/Acts readings and then at the others.

FIRST READING / GOSPEL
ACTS 1:1-11 / LUKE 24:44-53 (RCL); LUKE 24:49-53 (BCP)

The overlap of the Ascension accounts at the end of the Gospel and the beginning of Acts is a deliberate literary technique: the reader's attention is linked back to the events in the Gospel, then forward to the events in Acts that are anticipated by the language of the accounts. In addition, the shaping of the accounts rounds off and fulfills an important purpose of Luke's story of Jesus: placing him in the line of the great prophets of Israel, as the last and greatest of all.

As two men in dazzling garments (identified as Moses and Elijah) appeared with Jesus at the Transfiguration, and as two men in white garments appeared at the tomb to give instructions to the women, so now two men in white stand before the apostles, instructing them (Acts 1:10-11). As Moses was taken by God (and ascended into heaven in the accounts by Philo and Josephus, Luke's older contemporaries), and as Elijah went up to heaven in the whirlwind, so now Jesus "goes up" and is hidden from the witnesses' sight by a cloud (v. 9), a standard device in these scenes. (But note also the cloud in Luke's Transfiguration scene (Luke 9:34-35); there, unlike in Matthew and Mark, the disciples enter into the cloud, rather than merely being overshadowed.) As Elijah told Elisha he would receive "a double share of his spirit" if he saw his master going up to heaven (2 Kings 2:9-10), so now the apostles watch Jesus ascend, having already had his promise that his Spirit will descend on them very soon. The pointing of the account toward the gift of the Spirit is very strong: there is reference to the Spirit in vv. 2, 5, and 8.

Both the Gospel ending and the beginning of Acts are clearly Lukan compositions. Luke stresses that his gospel contains *all* that Jesus did and taught, and that Jesus gave full instructions to his disciples (for Luke the stress lies on the "apostles," that is, the Twelve). It is important to him to emphasize that the risen Jesus instructed the disciples for a full forty days, but also that he entrusted them with the same message conveyed by his earthly deeds and words; in this way Luke combats Gnostic notions of "secret teachings." The apostles have been chosen and instructed through the same Holy Spirit who will build up and empower the church.

Although the NRSV translates v. 4 "while staying with them," the alternate and more literal translation is "while eating with them." The meal context is typical for instruction in Luke's gospel (cf. chs. 5, 7, 10, 11, 14, 19, 22, 24). It establishes a continuity between the earthly Jesus, the risen Jesus, and the later church that will, like the Emmaus disciples, know the Lord "in the breaking of the bread" (Luke 24:35; cf. Acts 2:46; 10:41). The "promise" *(epangelia)* is the Holy Spirit; by alluding to the gift to be given "not many days from now," Luke prepares for the Pentecost scene in the next chapter.

The apostles' question follows naturally from the promise in v. 5. Jewish expectation was that the outpouring of the divine Spirit would inaugurate the end-time (cf. Joel 2:28—3:1) and with it the restoration of Israel (cf. Sir. 48:10). Luke shared that expectation, but he stresses that the timing and development of those events are not matters that humans can know. However, the inbreaking epoch will be a time of witnessing, the era of the church gathered from among Jews and gentiles. Jesus' promise reflects Isaiah 49:6, where God says to the servant: "It is too light a thing that you should be my servant to raise up the tribes of Jacob and to restore the survivors of Israel; I will give you as a light to the nations, that my salvation may reach *to the end of the earth*." The second half of that verse, in its Greek version, is quoted verbatim in Acts 13:47 to demonstrate that the mission to the gentiles is of divine origin. For Luke, the "restoration" of Israel requires the incorporation of the gentiles.

Although the Ascension scene is clearly a vision (see the remarks below on Ezekiel 1), Luke emphasizes the apostles' *seeing,* not because he wants this to pose as a historical account, but so that we will not forget that all the events described in the gospel and Acts derive from the testimony of *eyewitnesses.* There is nothing secret or hidden about them. The cloud, besides being a stock ingredient in such scenes, is also a sign of the divine presence; it recalls the Transfiguration scene, but also the cloud that accompanied Israel through the desert and that rested on Sinai. Jesus, entering into the cloud, is taken into the divine presence.

BECAUSE JESUS HAS BEEN TAKEN OUT OF OUR SIGHT, OUT OF OUR SPACE AND TIME, THIS MEANS THAT HIS POWER, HIS SPIRIT, HAS BEEN SET LOOSE IN THE WORLD . . .

A small boy, returning from church on Ascension day, anxiously asked his mother: "Where is God?" "You know," said his mother reassuringly. "God is everywhere." "No," he cried urgently. "I mean *where* is God?" "I don't understand," said his mother. "Why are you asking me this?" "Because," cried the boy, "the preacher said that Jesus is sitting on God's right hand, and I want to go and tell him to get off it!" If we feel similar confusion on being told today that Jesus is "seated at the right hand of God," that is only normal. Our reassurance comes from our faith that God is indeed everywhere, and Jesus with God; moreover, because Jesus has been taken out of our sight, out of our space and time, this means that his power, his Spirit, has been set loose in the world to be everywhere and at all times present with those who love him. Finally, Acts 1:11 assures us that just as Jesus has departed—certainly, visibly, really—so he will return, just as tangible, visible, and real, when the parousia arrives. Though the "when" and "how" may be unknown to us, the *that* is assured.

EZEKIEL 1:3-5a, 15-22, 26-28 (BCP alt.)

Parts of Ezekiel's inaugural vision, the first part of his call story, are offered for today's reading by the Episcopal lectionary and may be a fruitful choice for those who do not want to repeat the Ascension narrative in both the first and Gospel readings or who prefer to adhere to the scheme of Old Testament reading, New Testament reading, and Gospel. (The Acts pericope may still be chosen as the second reading.)

The important thing to stress with regard to Ezekiel's vision is that it is very deliberately couched in "visionary" language; that is, the extreme frequency of terms such as "like," "as," "resembling," "appearance," "something that looked like" signifies that this is no literal description of physical or physical-seeming phenomena. It is a stuttering attempt to describe the indescribable. "This was the appearance of the likeness of the glory of the Lord" (v. 28). Ezekiel's account thus gives a key to interpreting Luke's seemingly simple, plastic, everyday description of Jesus' Ascension. That, too, is a vision, and by no means to be read in literal fashion.

Responsive Reading

PSALM 47

The psalm extols God's universal sovereignty, calling on "all peoples" to praise God, who reigns supreme over all nations (v. 8). Only vv. 3-4 break the tone of universalism, with their emphasis on God's special love for Israel. The psalm concludes with a vision of God enthroned (compare the throne vision in Isa. 6:1). This correlates, in the context of the Gospel reading, with Daniel's vision of the Ancient One "taking his throne" (Dan. 7:9) and the "one like a human being, coming with the clouds of heaven" who "came to the Ancient One and was presented before him" (Dan. 9:13). So, in the evangelist's view, Jesus has entered the presence of God, veiled by "the clouds of heaven," and has been clothed with dominion over "all peoples, nations, and languages." To this his disciples will bear witness, being entrusted with a share in that power (cf. the miracle of tongues in Acts 2:5-11).

PSALM 93

Similar to Psalm 47, this is a hymn to God as sovereign. Again we find the reference to God's throne. Here, however, there is a broadening beyond the human reference of sovereignty over peoples and nations, for the non-human elements also testify to God's dominion; even as they seek to rebel, their failure to surpass God's power testifies to the divine omnipotence.

PSALM 110:1-5

This is one of the psalms most frequently cited (in its Septuagint version) in the New Testament. Although the Hebrew text is severely corrupted, the Greek version was reread from very early in the Christian era as messianic and christological. Verses 1 and 4 are most frequently cited: v. 1 in Mark 12:36 par.; Acts 2:34-35; 1 Cor. 15:22-23; Eph. 1:20-23; Heb. 1:13; 10:12-13 (among others); v. 4 is central to the conception of the letter to the Hebrews. The first part of the psalm describes a royal enthronement of the king as God's anointed and alludes also to the combined roles of priest and king customary for the earliest rulers of Israel; Christian rereading sees this as a historical prefiguring of Christ's role.

Second Reading

EPHESIANS 1:15-23 (RCL/BCP); 1:17-23 (RC)

As Bonnie Thurston has written in her commentary on Ephesians, this section "focuses on how God has used Jesus Christ to effect divine purposes."[31] Clearly the pericope is included among the readings for Ascension because of its reference to Christ's being "seated . . . at [God's] right hand in the heavenly places" (v. 20). The emphasis is on the exaltation of Jesus as Christ and Lord. However, the expression "the heavenly places" is found nowhere in the New Testament outside Ephesians (cf. 2:6; 3:10; 6:12). Here it represents an invisible, spiritual world removed from the material reality we know. An emphasis on this kind of interpretation of the Ascension would run directly contrary to the intention of Luke and of the gospel traditions generally (and indeed, the genuine Pauline traditions as well)—namely, their insistence that, through his Spirit, Jesus remains actively at work in *this* world. In fact, that is not the intention of the writer of Ephesians either, since he goes on to speak of Christ's being "the head over all things for the church, which is his body, the fullness of him who fills all in all" (vv. 22-23). The message of the Ascension is certainly that Jesus' life and power are no longer restricted by space and time, but indeed "fill all" the universe. It is not about his retirement to some timeless ethereal realm.

EPHESIANS 4:1-13 (or 4:1-7, 11-13) (RC alt.)

The Roman Catholic lectionary offers as an alternative reading the first thirteen verses of Ephesians 4. Here again we find an "ascension" reference in vv. 8-10 (although the lectionary allows for the omission precisely of these verses!). The quotation in v. 8, "when he ascended on high he made captivity itself a captive; he gave gifts to his people," is a quotation from Psalm 68:18 (though it differs significantly from the Hebrew version). This psalm is one of those suggested for reading in the Episcopal lectionary for the following Sunday, probably again because of its reference to ascension.

Verses 8-10 are in fact a digression within this first part of the paraenetic section of Ephesians. Otherwise the passage is characterized by a listing of the qualities of a Christian life, the gifts bestowed by Christ that sustain the unity of the church, characterized in this letter as the body of which Christ is the head. (This head/body image is typical only of Ephesians; in the authentic Pauline letters Christ is not differentiated from his body.) Again there is reference to the Spirit, though here the chief work of the Spirit is to bind the members together in peace. The Ephesians (and all Christians) are urged to live a life worthy of their high calling. We may see this as the natural sequel to the instructions given to the women at the tomb and to the apostles in the Ascension scene: Christ has been definitively called to his high destiny, and Christians to theirs.

CHRIST HAS BEEN DEFINITIVELY CALLED TO HIS HIGH DESTINY, AND CHRISTIANS TO THEIRS.

GOSPEL

MARK 16:9-15, 19-20 (BCP alt.); 16:15-20 (RC)

As noted earlier, (pp. 8–9) the canonical "longer ending" of Mark was added to the gospel at a later time. We cannot be sure how much later, but not much more than fifty years, since it was known to Tatian (ca. 140 C.E.) and Irenaeus (180 C.E.). It is a pastiche of information found in Matthew (v. 15), John (vv. 9ab, 10, 14) and Luke (vv. 9c, 11-15, 19-20); the language is clearly non-Markan, nor does the author display Mark's dramatic skill.[32] The only "new" element is v. 18, with its reference to snake-handling (but cf. Acts 28:3-6) and immunity to poison; this last is an occasional element in Christian literature beginning in the second century. This verse pushes us close to the talking beasts and improbable miracles of second-century apocryphal Acts of apostles and other early Christians. Probably for that reason, but more significantly because of their assurance that these verses are a later addition and shed no light on the interpretation of Mark, most commentators have nothing at all to say about Mark 16:9-20.

This situation is awkward for the person compelled to use Mark as the Gospel for the day. The best recourse is probably to focus on one of the other readings, or to develop one of the themes in the post-Markan pastiche, using the primary gospel source material (in Matthew, Luke, or John) as one's primary preaching source.

SEVENTH SUNDAY OF EASTER

JUNE 4, 2000

REVISED COMMON	EPISCOPAL (BCP)	ROMAN CATHOLIC
Acts 1:15-17, 21-26	Acts 1:15-26 or Exod. 28:1-4, 9-10, 29-30	Acts 1:15-17, 20a, 20c-26
Ps. 1	Ps. 68:1-20 or 47	Ps. 103:1-2, 11-12, 19-20
1 John 5:9-13	1 John 5:9-15 or Acts 1:15-26	1 John 4:11-16
John 17:6-19	John 17:11b-19	John 17:11b-19

THIS FINAL SUNDAY AFTER EASTER GIVES AN OPPORTUNITY, in the midst of the "novena" of waiting for Pentecost, to review and bring to a conclusion the process of reconciliation that has been taking place during the Easter season. The disciples in the story have gone from frightened silence before the empty tomb to having their hearts burn as Jesus explains the Scriptures to them, to receiving forgiveness and the power to forgive others, and finally to a commission to witness to what they have experienced "to the ends of the earth." Resurrection is no longer an abstract concept, but something experienced through the healing, forgiveness, and reconciliation bestowed by God as a result. The disciples have moved from despair and confusion to boldness and forthright witness.[33] Can the same be said for our congregations?

FIRST READING
ACTS 1:15-26 (BCP); 1:15-17, 21-26 (RCL); 1:15-17, 20a, 20c-26 (RC)

The lectionary "fills in" the time between Ascension and Pentecost with the intervening episode in Acts, the account of the choosing of Matthias to replace Judas and make up the full number of the Twelve, corresponding to the twelve tribes of Israel. Luke has here combined two pieces of tradition, one regarding Judas's death and the other concerning the selection of Matthias. Probably the quotation from Psalm 69:25 in v. 20a was part of the Judas story; Luke has coupled it with a quotation from Psalm 109:8 (ironically, in the psalm itself these are the words of the wicked who curse the innocent person praying the psalm) to form a link between the two stories.

The lectionary omits the little transitional section in vv. 12–14 that lists the core group of those present, including, besides the Eleven, "certain women, including Mary the mother of Jesus, as well as his brothers." It will therefore be important to clarify for hearers of the reading that the 120 persons include both women and men, so that the inclusive translation, "friends," for the opening *adelphoi* of Peter's address reflects the author's intention.

Luke has shaped the scene to emphasize that the choice of Matthias, like every event to be recounted in Acts, is God's work, part of the divine plan. Hence the solemn opening, "in those days," the reference to the fulfillment of Scripture (expressly said to be the word of the Holy Spirit), the citation of scriptural proof, and the statement that one of those who had accompanied Jesus and the Twelve throughout Jesus' ministry "must" become an official witness in place of the defector, Judas. The fate of Judas is itself portrayed as the precondition for the choice of a replacement, and therefore part of the fulfillment of God's design. The church's tradition—beginning with Mark's simple description of Judas's actions and extending, by way of the other evangelists' increasing revulsion, to some wildly developed legends in the second century and later—nevertheless does not contradict the firm assertion of faith that Christ's death brought healing for all, and that none of us can know the extent of God's mercy. Luke would not say differently.

The words attributed to Peter in vv. 21–22 have been called a Magna Carta for the Twelve. They summarize Luke's notion of apostolicity: the apostles are those who were with Jesus from the time of his baptism until his ascension and who are now to serve as witnesses of his deeds and words, but especially of his resurrection. The elements of apostolicity, for Luke, are thus (1) belonging to the Twelve, (2) exercising a "ministry," that is, an office of service, (3) giving witness, and (4) being chosen, gifted with the Spirit, and sent. This is the image of apostles that has fastened itself on most minds; it should be noted, however, that it does not apply to Paul, who most decidedly claimed for himself the title of apostle! He would have agreed with everything but the first element (belonging to the Twelve), as would, no doubt, Mary Magdalene, who met all the other criteria as well as did any of Jesus' male disciples, and more than some. (Luke himself, by delaying the account of the choice of the Twelve until chapter 6 of his gospel, casts doubt on their having been in fact present at Jesus' baptism!) In any event, the Lukan account insists on the choice of a twelfth *man* to make up the circle. Choosing the replacement by casting lots reflects Old Testament prescriptions (cf. Lev. 16) and shows that the choice really belongs to God.

In Luke's conception (and probably that of the early church) apostles had a function only in the earliest phases of the church's life—hence the placement of this event at the very beginning. As eyewitnesses, they guaranteed the truth of the tradition to be handed on, and they thus formed a bridge between Jesus' life and the future church. Twelve they were, for their lifetimes, but no successor apostles were ever chosen.

EXODUS 28:1-4, 9-10, 29-30 (BCP alt.)

Use of this reading (with Acts 1:15-26 as the second reading) will reinforce the traditional context of the Acts scene: it prescribes the engraving of the names of the twelve tribal ancestors of Israel on Aaron's vestments and the placement of the Urim and Thummim, used for casting lots to obtain divine guidance (see 1 Sam. 14:36-37; 28:6), in his breastplate. The reading should not be used, therefore, unless Acts 1:15-26 is the second reading.

Responsive Reading

PSALM 1

The initial psalm, contrasting the fate of the righteous and the wicked, correlates well with the two-part story in the First Reading. Objection has been raised to the NRSV translation, which pluralizes the psalm's statements for the sake of inclusivity. It is said that this obscures the messianic note of the psalm—in Christian context its special application to Jesus as the "one righteous man." Surely it may be said, however, that Jesus' life was not solitary, but solidary; he is first within the "congregation of the righteous" (v. 5), without whom no human life, including that of Jesus, has any genuine reality.

PSALM 68:1-20

A number of themes from the week are found in this psalm: the contrast of righteous and wicked, the triumphant ascent (of God), the ubiquitous cloud (v. 4; cf. v. 7). The psalm itself is a medley of nine shorter songs or parts of songs about divine rulership. Three themes are found in the verses included in the lectionary: God's scattering of enemies (1-3, 11-14), God's care for the people (4-6, 19), and the liturgical celebration of God's triumph (15-18).

PSALM 103:1-2, 11-12, 19-20

Gianfranco Ravasi has written of this psalm that it is "regarded as one of the gems of the Psalter and, by Christian readers, as an ideal prelude to the 'God is love' of 1 John 4:8."[34] The lectionary provides only a few fragments extolling God's benefits, God's steadfast love *(ḥesed),* and God's greatness, concluding with a doxology.

(For Psalm 47, an alternative in the Episcopal lectionary, see *Ascension Day, p. 51.)*

SECOND READING

1 JOHN 5:9-13 (RCL); 5:9-15 (BCP)

This final selection in the semi-continuous reading of 1 John touches on two themes that link to the first and third readings of the day: witnessing and prayer. Commentators are troubled by the apparent "pastness" of the divine witness as depicted here: "for this is the testimony of God that he has testified to his Son" (v. 9). Certainly the references to God's testimony throughout the Johannine writings are quite vague. But as we read the letter in the context of the Easter season we can surely say at a minimum that the Easter event itself is the mightiest testimony of God to Jesus as God's Anointed, "Son" of God in the terminology most favored by John. From the perspective of the letter itself this may be seen as something past, since within the lifetime of the writer or at least of eyewitnesses with whom the writer was familiar there was a "before" and "after" in their own lives. But that is not the case for today's believers. For them (though they may not reflect consciously on the fact) Christ's resurrection is an always-present event. Baptized into Christ's death and resurrection, they live their lives in the ongoing context of God's testimony to Jesus and, through him, to the believers themselves: that because of Jesus' life, death, and resurrection *nothing* (not time, not space, not even our own sins) can separate us from the love of God (Rom. 8:38-39). Moreover, God's testimony to Jesus continues in the church's sacraments, by which his saving death and everlasting life are daily made present in our midst.

God's testimony continues as well in the testimony of believers; the Johannine writer is no less sure of this than is the author of Acts. Those who believe share in the eternal life of the risen Jesus (note: "eternal" life is an ongoing *present* reality, not something reserved for those who have died!). They cannot fail to testify to the truth that is in them, for only in this way can God's testimony to Jesus (viewed as past) and the testimony of the eyewitnesses to God's action in Jesus be conveyed to future generations of believers.

The witnesses of future generations will be sustained by confident prayer, knowing that whatever they ask according to God's design will be granted (v. 14). They have the example of Jesus' confident prayer in John 17 (see today's gospel); following that model, they may live confidently in the present, and toward the future.

1 JOHN 4:11-16 (RC)

(See the fifth Sunday of Easter, p. 39.)

GOSPEL

JOHN 17:6-19 (RCL); 17:11b-19 (BCP/RC)

The final prayer of Jesus in John 17 contains three sections, with vv. 6-19 forming the second. In vv. 6-8 Jesus *describes* the disciples, telling the Father he has accomplished the work given him to do among them; then in vv. 9-19 he *prays* for them.[35] He parallels his mission with their mission: the post-Easter disciples must learn *that* they are to carry on Jesus' mission in the world and *how* to do it; the post-Pentecost disciples must be about their task (v. 18). The mood of Jesus' prayer, even though it is a farewell, is one of joy, and so the disciples should go into the world in joy (v. 13), for they are manifestations of the Father's glory (cf. vv. 1-5).

THE POST-EASTER DISCIPLES MUST LEARN *THAT* THEY ARE TO CARRY ON JESUS' MISSION IN THE WORLD AND *HOW* TO DO IT; THE POST-PENTECOST DISCIPLES MUST BE ABOUT THEIR TASK.

The dark side is by no means absent. Just as in the reading from Acts, so here there is reference in v. 12 to the "son of destruction" (NRSV "the one destined to be lost"), namely Satan,[36] who according to this gospel entered into Judas and made him the instrument of betrayal (cf. 13:2). So also Jesus says that "the world has hated them because they do not belong to the world" (v. 14). "Not belonging to the world" is a kind of litmus test throughout the Fourth Gospel (cf. 1:10-13), and yet Jesus was in the world, and his disciples must continue in the world, for how else shall the Word be made known? In v. 17 Jesus asks that the disciples may be made holy, as he is holy. "Holiness" is in itself a kind of set-apartness; to be holy is to be different from "the world" (in the pejorative sense frequent in the Johannine writings), though not separate from it. The disciples are not separate from the world God loves (cf. 3:16): their mission is to that world, for without their witness, how can it come to believe? But they are not "of" the unbelieving world, a world that refuses to believe. In the final section of the prayer (vv. 21-26) Jesus will pray for that other "world," namely those who will come to believe through the disciples' witness.

Because Jesus is about to depart, it is important that his disciples hear his prayer for them, for they know that his prayer is always heard (see 11:41). Knowing that Jesus' prayer for them will be answered, they need have no anxiety, but may be filled with joy even when "he is not here" in the way they have always known him.

Despite that absence in the conventional human sense, it remains true—for the Fourth Gospel as for the rest of the New Testament—that Jesus is profoundly present precisely in and through his departure. As L. William Countryman has pointed out, the unity of believers with one another for which Jesus prays "is nothing less than the unity of father and son before the creation of the world."[37] With that unity the gospel began; with Jesus' petition that the Father incorporate his disciples in that divine unity his words on earth come to an end. Through Jesus' ministry, and now through that of the disciples, the unity that is identical with the divine glory will be realized in a new way: it will develop in the world over time as more and more people come to know Jesus as the Sent One. This is not simply a "me and God" kind of unity; it is also believers' unity with one another. Through *that* unity the world will know that Jesus is the one sent by God (v. 23). It is not merely institutional unity that is at stake here, but something much greater:

> The unity for which Jesus prays is the divine unity, not any unity characteristic of human communities. Still there is a powerful issue of witness involved in this plea for unity: just as it is Jesus' own oneness with the father that makes of him the road by which others may come to God, so the believers' loving unity with one another represents our journey back along that road to our divine origin.[38]

We thus have spelled out for us, as we turn toward Pentecost, the way by which we, too, will return to God, the father of our Lord Jesus Christ. It is the way of loving unity with the One who is never absent from our lives as long as we are caught up in that divine love in company with and service to one another, our faces turned always toward the glory that is ours as the beloved children of God.

NOTES

1. For a somewhat similar reflection see Wes Howard-Brook, *John's Gospel & the Renewal of the Church* (Maryknoll, N.Y.: Orbis, 1997), 152, 158.

2. Words by Matthew Bridges, "Crown Him with Many Crowns," *The Hymnal 1982.* According to the Use of the Episcopal Church (New York: The Church Pension Fund, 1985), number 494.

3. Robert J. Schreiter, *The Ministry of Reconciliation: Spirituality and Strategies* (Maryknoll, N.Y.: Orbis, 1998), 35.

4. Daryl D. Schmidt, *The Gospel of Mark.* The Scholar's Bible 1 (Sonoma, Calif.: Polebridge Press, 1990), 151.

5. For a succinct summary of this problem see Antoinette C. Wire, "1 Corinthians," in Elisabeth Schüssler Fiorenza, ed., *Searching the Scriptures* 2: *A Feminist Commentary* (New York: Crossroad, 1994), 153–95, especially 189–90.

6. John Painter, *Mark's Gospel: Worlds in Conflict.* New Testament Readings (London and New York: Routledge, 1997), 210.

7. Joanna Dewey, "The Gospel of Mark," in Schüssler Fiorenza, ed., *Searching the Scriptures* 2, 470–509, at 507.

8. See Ann Roberts Winsor, *A King Is Bound in the Tresses: Allusions to the Song of Songs in the Fourth Gospel* (New York: Peter Lang, 1999).

9. Luke Timothy Johnson, *The Gospel of Luke.* Sacra Pagina 3 (Collegeville, Minn.: The Liturgical Press, 1991), 398–99.

10. Ibid., 399.

11. See Margaret D. Hutaff, "The Johannine Epistles," in Schüssler Fiorenza, ed., *Searching the Scriptures* 2, 406–27, at 421.

12. See L. William Countryman, *The Mystical Way in the Fourth Gospel: Crossing Over into God*, rev. ed. (Valley Forge, Pa.: Trinity Press International, 1994), 139.

13. See Francis J. Moloney, *The Gospel of John.* Sacra Pagina 4 (Collegeville, Minn.: The Liturgical Press, 1998), 530.

14. Ibid., 531.

15. See David Rensberger, *Johannine Faith and Liberating Community* (Philadelphia: Westminster, 1988), 144.

16. Moloney, *Gospel of John,* 533.

17. John Painter, *The Quest for the Messiah,* 2nd ed. (Nashville: Abingdon, 1993), 415.

18. See Howard-Brook, *John's Gospel and the Renewal of the Church*, 152.

19. Countryman, *Mystical Way,* 139.

20. Raymond E. Brown, *The Epistles of John.* Anchor Bible 30 (Garden City, N.Y.: Doubleday, 1982), 388.

21. Ibid.

22. Johnson, *Gospel of Luke,* 400.

23. *MPL* 37:1281.

24. See Brown, *Epistles of John,* 475.

25. See Robert Kysar, *John's Story of Jesus* (Philadelphia: Fortress, 1984) 52–53.

26. Clarice J. Martin, "The Acts of the Apostles," in Schüssler Fiorenza, ed., *Searching the Scriptures* 2, 792.

27. See Brown, *Epistles of John,* 552.

28. Ibid., 595.

29. Georg Strecker, *The Johannine Letters,* trans. Linda M. Maloney. Hermeneia (Minneapolis: Fortress, 1996), 185.

30. Raymond E. Brown, *The Gospel according to John XIII–XXI.* Anchor Bible 29A (Garden City: N.Y.: Doubleday, 1970) 667.

31. Bonnie Thurston, *Reading Colossians, Ephesians and 2 Thessalonians: A Literary and Theological Commentary* (New York: Crossroad, 1995), 98.

32. See Painter, *Mark's Gospel,* 215–17.

33. Cf. Schreiter, *Ministry of Reconciliation,* 97.

34. Gianfranco Ravasi, "Psalms 90–150," in William R. Farmer, et al., eds., *The International Bible Commentary* (Collegeville, Minn.: The Liturgical Press, 1998) 845.

35. See Moloney, *Gospel of John,* 459.

36. Ibid., 468, 470.

37. Countryman, *Mystical Way,* 116.

38. Ibid., 117.

THE SEASON OF PENTECOST

GORDON W. LATHROP

NEIL ELLIOTT

FRANK C. SENN

Pentecost and Its Echoes

Introduction

Gordon W. Lathrop

Pentecost is the fiftieth day of Easter. The day thus comes to the Christian congregation as the last and summary day of the great festival of the resurrection. Contrary to this book's layout, Pentecost ought not be seen as a new feast, the beginning of a new season. Rather, the festival celebrates the outpouring into our midst and into our hearts, by the power of the Holy Spirit, of all the reality of the cross and resurrection of Jesus, all the truth with which the observance of Holy Week and Eastertide have been full. Pentecost thus takes what belongs to Christ and declares it to us (John 16:14). Pentecost is the existential presence of the content of the Triduum and the Fifty Days of Easter as this content continues to be the ground of the church's faith, the center of the church's assembly, and the source of the church's witness in the world.

The texts for the Day of Pentecost continue lectionary patterns characteristic of most of the fifty days of Easter, bringing those patterns to a climax. A passage from John is read yet again as the Gospel, only now with the clear sense that the "going away" or death of Jesus, with which the farewell discourses of the Fourth Gospel are so concerned, is the indispensable basis for the coming of the Paraclete. Acts is read for a final time, only now with the strong story—the pivotal story at the junction of the Third Gospel with its second volume—of that outpoured Spirit which empowers the church's witness to all the nations. The only textual pattern that turns toward the coming Sundays—rather than expressing a culmination of the preceding Sundays in Easter—is the possibility, available in the RCL and the BCP, of reading a First Reading from the Hebrew Scriptures: from this Sunday on, the churches will once again hear the witness of the Old Testament in their assemblies. Otherwise, the point of the readings of the day, like the point of the festival itself, is the proclamation that the Spirit of those assemblies must always be poured out from the great mysteries of the death and resurrection of Jesus that we have just so centrally celebrated. That this festival is celebrated, in the northern hemisphere, in the now strong light of late spring or early summer, only adds natural intensity to what is essentially a theological point. The proclamation of the death and resurrection of Christ by the life-giving Spirit—this is our burning light, our warmth, our sun, our fire, our springtime of the world.

But Pentecost is so great a culmination of so great a festival that it is no surprise that this final day of the feast itself came to have echoes. On the "octave" of the Fiftieth Day, the eighth day of its celebration, the western churches began to keep a festival in honor of the Holy Trinity. In a sense, of course, this meant prolonging the Easter Days by yet another week. Such a week could be seen as unnecessary: with the Fifty Days over, we ought to get back to the more ancient festival—the greatest of all the Christian festivals—the celebration of the weekly and ordinary *Sunday*. Furthermore, the resultant festival seems odd. It is the only feast we keep in honor of a doctrine rather than a saving event. But if we take Trinity Sunday as the octave of Pentecost—the same as New Year's Day is the octave of Christmas—then we might understand the day more dynamically. It is the echo of Pentecost. It is a thing we have to say and sing once we have kept Good Friday and Easter and Easter's final day. God is three, a community, yet one. Our assemblies, empowered by the Spirit poured out from God and proclaiming the death of Christ, have been gathered into the very life of the triune God. "Trinity" is yet another way to sum up God's saving acts in Easter. It is not the name for a puzzle in the sky. The Holy Trinity, rather, speaks of *God with us*, active in judgment and mercy, enduring and conquering our death, raising us up to life, intending such life for all the world, creating a community in the Spirit to bear witness to that intention.

THE POINT OF THE READINGS OF PENTECOST SUNDAY, LIKE THE POINT OF THE FESTIVAL ITSELF, IS THE PROCLAMATION THAT THE SPIRIT OF THOSE ASSEMBLIES MUST ALWAYS BE POURED OUT FROM THE GREAT MYSTERIES OF THE DEATH AND RESURRECTION OF JESUS THAT WE HAVE JUST SO CENTRALLY CELEBRATED.

In the Roman Catholic Church, the old western echo of Pentecost has had a further trajectory. If Easter with its Fiftieth Day implied the feast of the Holy Trinity, then a further doctrine also needed to be celebrated. The assembly is gathered by the Spirit into the life of the triune God, said the Roman Church, above all by its participation in the Holy Eucharist. In the thirteenth century, the doctrine of Christ's presence in the Eucharist thus came to be celebrated in a post-Easter observance, with Thomas Aquinas himself composing texts for the liturgy. In the present time in North American Roman Catholic churches, the feast of the Body and Blood of Christ, which used to be observed as *Corpus Christi* on the first Thursday after Trinity Sunday, can be transferred to the Second Sunday after Pentecost and made into a second doctrinal Sunday, a second echo of Easter and its Fiftieth Day.

Both of these observances—Trinity Sunday in all the churches and the Body and Blood of Christ in the Roman Catholic Church—run the danger of reinforcing a kind of didacticism. By this conception, liturgies are held simply to teach us something, to see to it that we get it right. But the Spirit poured out in our assemblies, the presence of Jesus Christ in our midst, and thereby the presence of God's astonishing will to save the universe itself—these are far more than concepts or doctrines. If we celebrate these festivals as echoes of Pentecost, they are also brilliantly capable of singing and proclaiming the dynamic central meaning of our assemblies. In the power of the Spirit, we are gathered around Jesus Christ—in his word and in the holy meal of his body and blood—and so we are gathered into the very life of God and made witnesses of that life.

Pentecost is the fiftieth day of Easter. But it may best be seen as the ongoing event which constantly founds the meetings of the church every Sunday, every ordinary Sunday. Indeed, the Day of Pentecost itself, with both of its echo-feasts, is an articulated echo of Sunday, an important way of seeing what all Sundays mean. The church's assembly in the Spirit around the word of God and the Body-and-Blood meal of Jesus, Sunday in and Sunday out, proclaims the mystery of Easter and gathers the community into the triune God.

In what follows, the texts of these feast days are interpreted, beginning with the Gospel and then proceeding through the other readings and their alternates in the various lectionaries. Priority is given to the Gospel in a way that accords with the clear intention of the lectionaries themselves: although the Gospel is in last place when read in the church, it is in first place when we begin our study, as a hermeneutical key to our Christian undertaking with these texts. But all of the texts, from the various Western Christian and North American sources, are considered, in the hope that preachers will be enriched in their work by knowing the full range of possibilities alive in the churches on these ecumenically shared feast days. In dealing with these texts, current exegesis and relevant critical, literary, and historical possibilities are first briefly discussed, with an accent on the interplay of symbolic images in each text. Then the writing here usually turns to the concern preachers will have to articulate the meaning of these feasts through the terms of each of the texts. The whole complex of readings is then summarized, together, according to one vision of how the texts sound together *in the assembly*, on this feast day, next to singing and preaching and praying and the eucharistic meal and the sending to service in the world. If you are a preacher, may this little preparatory work be one small contribution to your imagination and to your courage to arise in the assembly with the judgment and mercy of God on your lips.

THE DAY OF PENTECOST

JUNE 11, 2000

REVISED COMMON	EPISCOPAL (BCP)	ROMAN CATHOLIC
Acts 2:1-21 or Ezek. 37:1-14	Acts 2:1-11 or Isa. 44:1-8	Acts 2:1-11
Ps. 104:25-35, 37	Ps. 104:25-37 or 104:25-32 or 33:12-15, 18-22	Ps. 104:1, 24, 29-31, 34
Rom. 8:22-27 or Acts 2:1-21	1 Cor. 12:4-13 or Acts 2:1-11	Gal. 5:16-25
John 15:26-27 or John 16:4b-15	John 20:19-23 or John 14:8-17	John 15:26-27 or John 16:12-15

There are many kinds of spirits in the world and lots of spiritualities. Many sorts of meetings may be "spirited." If we can sense the "spirit of a meeting" we may be in, the spirit in the room, that spirit may be something which oppresses or delights us. After all, Nazi rallies and American lynch mobs had very powerful spirits. So, sometimes, do concert audiences and fans at sporting events, and even crowds in shopping malls, though in these latter cases the spirit is usually sweeter. But the texts for the Day of Pentecost make clear that if our meeting—our assembly for worship—is really a meeting in the presence of the biblical God, then the Spirit that enlivens that assembly will be the Spirit of God.

And what is the Spirit of God? How do we know it? According to the Fourth Gospel, source for the Gospel reading on this day in all of our lectionaries, the Spirit is God present, seeing to it that the words and actions of Jesus Christ are alive in our midst as powerful words and actions, judging and forgiving, sending, giving life. The Spirit is all that belongs to Christ, all that pertains to him—and thus all that truly pertains to the ancient God—alive here and declared to us.

The reading from Acts makes a similar point. As the Lukan Gospel concludes and the second volume of the Lukan work begins, the church is charged to proclaim to the nations all that has transpired in Jesus, all that the first book has narrated. The outpouring of the Spirit enables the church to do just that, giving power that the words about Jesus Christ might be heard universally, the particular story of a Judean execution might be everywhere life-giving. The Holy Spirit is God as the force and presence of this story.

The other readings of the day, alternate first or second readings, celebrate what this Spirit does. Poured out from God, bearing life-giving witness to Christ, gathering us into the very life of the Trinity, this Spirit is still making exiled, "dead," and despairing people alive (Ezekiel), creating them as people of hope and witnesses to God in the world (Isaiah). This very Spirit groans with creation's longings and gives a downpayment on all of God's promises (Romans). This Spirit pours out gifts for living (Galatians).

There are many kinds of spirits and spiritualities in our world. By God's mercy may the Spirit of all of our Sunday meetings be that life-giving Paraclete proclaimed in these texts.

GOSPEL

JOHN 15:26-27; 16:4b-15 (RCL/RC)

The most widely used Gospel for this festival is an important passage in the "farewell discourses" of the Fourth Gospel. One way to view these discourses is to see that, after the dramatic introduction of chapter 13 (the footwashing and its following dialogue), the discourse of chapter 14 is then reduplicated and echoed in the discourse of chapters 15 and 16, and the whole is then summed up with the great prayer of chapter 17. Thus, it is no surprise that the first mentionings of the "other Advocate" and its work, found in 14:16-17 and 14:26 and identified there as "the Spirit of truth" and "the Holy Spirit," should be paralleled and intensified in our 15:27-28 and 16:7-11,13-15. But in our passage, the presence ("to be with you forever," 14:16) and the christological teaching work ("and remind you of all that I have said to you," 14:26) of this Advocate are described in even stronger imagery. The Advocate bears decisive witness in a *trial.*

A whole literature has developed about this Advocate. How shall we translate the word *parakletos*? "Helper," "Counselor," "Comforter," "Advocate"? Or shall we simply leave the word untranslated as "Paraclete"? And what religious and linguistic background may stand behind the Johannine use of the term, four of the five New Testament cases of which we have listed above? The fifth use, in 1 John 2:1, helps us to see why the Spirit is called "another" *parakletos* in the farewell discourses (14:16): Jesus himself is the first one. Without having to decide the translation and background questions, however, our passage makes clear that at least here *Advocate* is an appropriate translation. The Spirit here comes into court, bears testimony, pleads the cause of another, even acts as attorney, like one called to the side—*para-kletos, ad-vocatus*—of someone engaged in a forensic situation of judgment. According to the Fourth Gospel, it is Jesus himself—and, with him, the church—who is engaged in this legal battle with the world.

Of course, John's Gospel will go on, in the Passion narrative, to tell the story of the actual trial and execution of Jesus. Those who hear this story in faith, however, will know that hidden underneath the political, legal, and religious condemnation of Jesus is the condemnation of the world itself—the present order of power in the earth. No wonder that, in the Fourth Gospel, Jesus carries himself in the midst of his trial and torture as if he were the judge, though he himself judges no one (cf. 12:47)! Indeed, in paradoxical ways, Jesus has already acted as Advocate and Judge for the sake of believers in the course of the narratives of the Book of Signs (chap. 2–12). For example, in his vindication of the man born blind (cf. 16:2: "they will put you out of the synagogues") and his pronouncement upon those who say "We see," he is standing as if in court (9:39-41). The First Letter of John rightly summarizes the understanding of the Johannine community: "If anyone does sin, we have an advocate with the Father, Jesus Christ the righteous" (1 John 2:1).

THE ASSEMBLY IS TO BE THE PLACE WHERE THE REAL OUTCOME OF JESUS' TRIAL IS ANNOUNCED SO THAT PEOPLE MAY COME TO FAITH AND THE WORLD MAY LIVE.

But in the farewell discourses, it is the Holy Spirit who comes into court as advocate. And it is the Holy Spirit who proves "the world wrong about sin and righteousness and judgment" (16:8). The Spirit does this precisely by being "another Advocate," by standing in for Jesus who has now been killed, who now shares the lot of all the wretched dead, murdered by unjust courts and unjust powers. Indeed, the Spirit's enabling of faith in Jesus and the Spirit's proclamation of the resurrection of Jesus and of the condemnation of the "ruler of this world"—as the meaning of the death of Jesus—these are exactly the matters which prove the world wrong. For the Fourth Gospel, sin is not transgression of a religious law but the absence of faith in the Crucified-risen One (16:9). True righteousness is not any religious observance at all, but God's justification of Jesus (his death is seen by faith as "going to the Father," 16:10). And judgment is the *reversal* of all that the world counts as power (16:11; cf. 12:31). Far from being an assembly of mourners for the dead Jesus—"sorrow has filled your hearts," 16:6—the Johannine church is urged to understand itself as the place where the Spirit of God, God present and active and enlivening the truth, is proclaiming the real truth about the world as it may be known through the death and resurrection of Jesus. The assembly is to be the place where the real outcome of Jesus' trial is announced so that people may come to faith and the world may live.

Of course, these things are narrated in the farewell discourses as if they were spoken by Jesus before his death. It is important to remember the general structure of John's Gospel, however. Throughout the Book of Signs, repeated "signs" that reveal the truth about Jesus have been paired with discourses that say the same things as the signs, doing so in intense, repetitious, symbolic prose. The Sign of the Feeding of the Multitude (6:1-14), for example, is paired with the Bread of Life discourse (6:25-71). But in the Book of Glory, as the final section of the book (chap. 13-20) may be called, the discourse comes *first*, in the form of the farewell discourses. These provide the words for the Great Sign, Jesus' death and resurrection. The farewell discourses, thus, say in intense prose what the Johannine community understands the "going away" of Jesus, his death, to mean. Thus, in the *sign* of the Passion account, the Spirit is given over by the dying Jesus (19:30), poured out of his wounded side (19:34; cf. 7:38-39), and breathed out by his risen presence (20:22). Jesus literally, physically sends the Spirit from his death and resurrection, from his condemnation and, says faith, his vindication. In the *discourse* of John 15-16, the Spirit "will take what is mine and declare it to you" (16:14). These witnesses point to the same reality.

The farewell discourses proclaim the death and resurrection of Jesus into the life of the assembly. Indeed, they may be taken as expressing in intense prose the very meaning of the Sunday assembly—the "eighth day" assembly—which is expressed as *sign* in 20:19-29. The community gathers around the death and resurrection of Christ as life-giving for all the world. It is that very Sunday assembly itself which is repeatedly indicated by the plural "you" of the discourses.

The coming of the Spirit is then exactly the same as the community's experience of the resurrection of Jesus, the encounter with his wounds, the knowledge in faith that this murdered one has been vindicated and is with God as "Jesus Christ the righteous" (1 John 2:1). The Spirit enlivens the assembly with the words of Jesus and things of Jesus, and thereby with the very words and things of God (16:13-15). In so doing, the assembly itself is seen to be already participating in the last day—"the things that are to come" (16:13)—wherein the very words of Jesus have become the final judge (cf. 12:48) and the "ruler of the world" has been cast out. The space of the assembly is to be a space of life and of the victory of the resurrection; the assembly itself is to join in witness—legal "testimony," even—to the world (15:27).

Because the very content of this testimony will always need to be the acts, words, and things of Jesus, the Spirit can sometimes be said to be sent by the Father "in my name" (14:26) and sometimes sent by Jesus "from the Father" (15:26) or simply sent by Jesus (16:7). This varying speech, one of the sources of the disagreement between the Eastern and the Western churches about the Western addition of the *filioque* clause to the Nicene Creed, ought to be regarded simply as characteristic Johannine poetic and pleonastic speech. The *filioque* should not be allowed to divide East and West, and the west should probably willingly surrender it as a later addition to the classic text. After all, for the community of the Fourth Gospel, Jesus says that "all that the Father has is mine" (16:15). In any case, in the presence of the Spirit, enlivening the matters of Jesus in the midst of the assembly, we are drawn into the presence of God.

Our assemblies of the present time should be seen as inheritors both of the sign-description in John 20 and the discourse-meaning in John 13-17. In word and sacrament on Sunday, the risen Jesus shows his wounds and breathes out his Spirit so that sins may be forgiven, and the Spirit proves the world (and much of the religion of the world!) wrong about sin, righteousness, and judgment, reversing what the world might think about the dead Jesus. In all of this, the mercy of God for the misled and misruled world is shown forth (cf. 3:16). Our own assemblies—and not just some ancient assembly in Jerusalem—are the inheritors of this promise. We rightly ask whether we have allowed the Spirit to speak among us by keeping central the things that declare the reversal of the world's judgment, the things of Jesus, the words and meal which are full of his death and resurrection.

The preacher of the day will do well to regard *this* text, and not the Acts account, as the central text of the day. Are not the ruling judgments of our world also in need of being overthrown? Is not our religion also frequently wrong about sin and righteousness and judgment? And could we not be invited to see how the things of Jesus and God, being given away here in our assembly like bread into the hands of the hungry, are the deepest truth about us and God's whole beloved world? Pentecost gives the preacher a remarkable occasion to help the assembly understand the meaning of "church" as a free space in the world, empowered by the Spirit and devoted to the death-reversing judgment of God, for the sake of the life and freedom of the world. When, in the assembly, the things and works of the triune God are present, the Spirit is winning the trial. Such a conception of the resurrection of Jesus and the gift of the Spirit—such a *Johannine* conception—will be experienced as far more profound for our time than an easy reading of the chronology of Luke-Acts.

JOHN 20:19-23 (BCP); 14:8-17 (BCP alt.)

The alternate Gospels in the lectionaries have already played a role in the foregoing reflection on John 15 and 16. The passage from John 20 is the very sign which shows forth the meaning of the Sunday assembly, the risen Christ breathing out the Spirit for the life of the world, sending the church with the forgiveness of sins. The Gospel from John 15-16 functions as discourse to this sign. And the passage from John 14 is the first occurrence of the word *parakletos* in the Johannine literature: "I will ask the Father, and he will give you another Advocate" (14:16). The Gospel from John 15-16 gives further strength to the forensic image "Advocate." But both alternate passages make the trinitarian character of the assembly abundantly clear. And both celebrate that the Spirit which makes alive, establishing the church and saving the world, is the Spirit which vivifies in our midst the words and works of Jesus. Here, too, the preacher will be wise to find in this Gospel, addressed to the present church, the central text of the day.

FIRST READING

ACTS 2:1-21 (RCL); 2:1-11 (BCP/RC)

The account of the day of Pentecost at the outset of Acts arises from a way of presenting reality quite different from the Johannine way. Here, ordered calendars, fifty days counted from the feast of Passover, play a major role. If we get lost in this calendar-keeping, as if the events we are proclaiming here are only being commemorated and not encountered now, we will run the significant danger of trivializing Pentecost. But the deep point in Acts, if we will see it, is actually quite similar to the Johannine argument. By the presence and power of the Spirit in the assembly, the particular story recounted in the first book of Luke, the gospel-book (cf. Acts 1:1), is now made universally available in the world. Indeed, this Spirit is none other than that Spirit promised by the prophet Joel. Only now the Spirit is come in such a way that the Jewish feast which had celebrated the giving of the Law to Israel on Sinai, fifty days after the feast that celebrated the passover and exodus from slavery, is seen as transformed into the sending of the gospel to all the nations everywhere.

BY THE PRESENCE AND POWER OF THE SPIRIT IN THE ASSEMBLY, THE PARTICULAR STORY RECOUNTED IN THE FIRST BOOK OF LUKE, THE GOSPEL-BOOK, IS NOW MADE UNIVERSALLY AVAILABLE IN THE WORLD.

The preacher will need to recall that the assembly of Pentecost (2:1), like the Emmaus assembly (Luke 24:13-35), is best understood as a type and symbol of all of our assemblies. To all of our gatherings in word and sacrament comes the charge to proclaim the gospel in translation, using the many languages of the world. The Spirit poured out in our assemblies, for the enlivening of the "first book" for all the nations, is constantly giving birth to the church.

EZEKIEL 37:1-14 (RCL alt.); ISAIAH 44:1-8 (BCP alt.)

The remarkable First Reading proposed by the RCL gives us the account of the dry bones made alive, "a vast multitude" (37:10). Of course, this account is a significant and symbolic prophetic vision, a magnificent metaphor, not the report or promise of many people raised literally from the dead. The prophet has heard people in exile grumbling, "Our bones are dried up" (37:11).

So God will send the Spirit or the Breath or the Wind, and these "dead," "dried up," and despairing people will live. That is to say, God will cause the exiles to return. Exactly in the same way, Christians hear the news of the vindication of Jesus as the outpoured Breath of God, causing us to live now, not die. And exactly in the same way, this breath, this Spirit, establishes a whole people, local assemblies of witness in touch with other local assemblies of witness, inviting all the world to come home from exile to the good news of life.

The BCP, instead, offers a passage from Isaiah as an alternate First Reading. This passage includes a "trial speech" of Yahweh (44:6-8), in which Israel's God bears testimony in the public court, being vindicated over the other gods and calling the people to be witnesses of this vindication in the world. The passage should be read side by side with the Johannine interest in the "other Advocate" who bears testimony to the vindication of Jesus in the contest with the world and who empowers the assembly as witness. At the same time, the passage includes a rich description of the outpouring of the Spirit on the "offspring" of Israel, including the possibility that other than flesh-and-blood offspring, by the power of that Spirit, may say, "I am the Lord's," and join the company of witnesses. To Christians, this is a precious possibility.

Psalm

PSALM 104:25-35, 37; 33:12-15, 18-22 (BCP alt.)

Psalm 104 celebrates God's creation as a rich and beautiful reality, but one that is entirely dependent on the "face" and breath of God. Singing this psalm today, Christians may celebrate that the intention of the Spirit, poured out in the assembly, includes the renewal of all the beloved world. While sometimes, together with Jesus himself, we may know the "turned away face of God," God's intention for the earth is life. The BCP also appoints Psalm 33 as an alternate, a psalm in which God beholds and creates the people.

Second Reading

ROMANS 8:22-27 (RCL); 1 CORINTHIANS 12:4-13 (BCP); GALATIANS 5:16-25 (RC)

Depending on your lectionary and the choices you (or the competent authority) make in the use of that lectionary, one of these readings may be added to your community's celebration of Pentecost. If so, the reading will take the place of any reading from the Hebrew Scriptures, but the reading from Ezekiel or Isaiah is to be preferred if it is possible. Nonetheless, these readings are all primary Pauline accounts of the Holy Spirit, and they are themselves strong and important. Read next to John and Acts; one or the other of these texts can give yet further depth to the communal celebration of the Spirit of the victory of Jesus Christ, the Spirit who reverses the judgments of the world. This Spirit groans with all the creation and prays underneath the prayers of Christians, already a downpayment on the last day, gathering us into the very life of God (Romans). This Spirit enables the confession of faith, pours out many gifts in the church, and gives the unity of the church in baptism and the sharing of the holy cup (1 Corinthians). This Spirit gives gifts for life that no law forbids (Galatians). In all three cases, the trinitarian and christological work of the Spirit is manifest.

(See First Reading for RCL and BCP alternate readings in Acts.)

IN THE ASSEMBLY

There are many spirits in the world. Pentecost celebrates that, by the mercy of God, the Spirit of our meeting may be a Spirit of life and hope, the Spirit proclaiming the resurrection of Jesus Christ and drawing us into the life of God. Pentecost celebrates the outpouring of the Easter festival into every one of our meetings. Because of the Spirit, our meeting may be a free space in which the judgments of the world—about who is religious and who is successful and what life itself truly is—are reversed and overturned. Paradoxically, that free space is finally meant by the Spirit to be a downpayment on life and hope for all the world, not just for the members. And, paradoxically, sometimes the judgments of our churches have also been the judgments of the world, not the life of the Spirit, and the church itself must be proved wrong and given new life.

Many people have taken the Acts account as the central reading of the day, and regarded the festival as the "birthday of the church." That is not entirely wrong. But even for Luke, the church that is "born" is not just an ancient gathering in Jerusalem, at a datable and now distant event. The church is brought to birth wherever the Spirit is bearing witness, against the conviction of the world, to the vindication of God. The church is brought to birth here, in your assembly. And your assembly, in its very event today, in its songs and words and holy meal, is made part of the court scene, called to testify in the world now: "Do not fear or be afraid . . . You are my witnesses!" (Isaiah 44:8).

HOLY TRINITY SUNDAY

JUNE 18, 2000

REVISED COMMON	EPISCOPAL (BCP)	ROMAN CATHOLIC
Isa. 6:1-8	Exod. 3:1-6	Deut. 4:32-34, 39-40
Ps. 29	Ps. 93 or Canticle 2 or Canticle 13	Ps. 33:4-6, 9, 18-20, 22
Rom. 8:12-17	Rom. 8:12-17	Rom. 8:14-17
John 3:1-17	John 3:1-16	Matt. 28:16-20

HOLY TRINITY SUNDAY ECHOES PENTECOST and, like Pentecost, it sums up the meaning of the whole Easter Feast. The Spirit enlivens the story of the death and resurrection of Jesus in our midst. By the presence of that story—the presence of the name and reality of Jesus Christ crucified—and by the power of the Spirit, we are thus gathered before the very face of God. Indeed, "Trinity" has become the name for the God we encounter in this lively, dynamic way. The Spirit who fills our meeting is God. The One around whose story the meeting is held, the One who shared the lot of the wretched and the dead, is God. The One who sent this "Son" and sends the Spirit, the One to whom our meeting prays, is God. And yet there are not three Gods but one God. The day ought not be taken as an unattached occasion for dogmatic exhortation. Rather, the day gives us words and images for articulating and celebrating how every Sunday meeting is enfolded in the very life of the triune God. The day is a kind of archetypal Sunday.

HOLY TRINITY SUNDAY GIVES US WORDS AND IMAGES FOR ARTICULATING AND CELEBRATING HOW EVERY SUNDAY MEETING IS ENFOLDED IN THE VERY LIFE OF THE TRIUNE GOD. THE DAY IS A KIND OF ARCHETYPAL SUNDAY.

Each of the texts of the day thus presents the active work of the triune God, who enfolds the community and is saving the world. In an echo of Pentecost and of the general pattern of readings in Eastertide, John again provides the primary Gospel of the day, inviting a plural "you" (a whole community, not just Nicodemus) to be born anew from the Spirit and to trust God's love for the world shown forth in the gift of the Son. If baptism is thus implied in this reading, it is made explicit in the alternate Gospel from Matthew 28: people from all the world are to be baptized into that community which is surrounded by the very name and presence of the triune God.

The Second Reading (Romans) then finds the Spirit of God "bearing witness with our spirit" to our adoption as co-heirs together with Christ of all that God has. In every case, "us" and "our" refers to the assembly of the church, and this church is being gathered into the very life of the triune God. And yet, the various possible Old Testament readings all celebrate the awesome holiness of this God, whose presence we may know, whose voice we may hear, and still, surprisingly, not be killed but live (Deut. 4:33). Trinity Sunday holds us before—and *in*—this very awesome God, sending us to the world with burned lips, in a mission of words and love from God's astonishing, embracing, *plural* unity: "Whom shall I send and who will go for us?" (Isa. 6:8).

Gospel

JOHN 3:1-17 (RCL); 3:1-16 (BCP)

The Gospel for this festival day consists of the very familiar dialogue of Jesus with Nicodemus from the Fourth Gospel. The preacher may refresh her or his approach to this text by recalling the structure of the Book of Signs (John 2-12). This text functions as the first full "discourse" in the Fourth Gospel. As such, it is paired with the first two "signs" of the Gospel: new wine replacing the purification water at Cana (2:1-11) and the cleansing of the temple at Jerusalem as a proclamation of the coming new temple (2:13-22). This discourse about "new birth" or "birth from above" and the "lifting up of the Son of Man" is thus meant to say, in thick poetic prose, the same things that those signs say. The signs themselves, of course, lean forward toward the coming "hour" of Jesus' glory (2:4). It is the destruction of Jesus that the cleansing of the temple foreshadows. It is his risen body—indeed, the assembly around and in his risen body—that is to be the new-built temple. And it is his death—and the water and blood which flow from that death—that replaces the purification rituals of all religion.

But now, in John 3, this replacement or "new life" motif is expressed in *discourse*, not sign. A teacher of Israel comes to Jesus by night. That it is night underscores the revelatory character of what follows; the light is to shine in the darkness. That Nicodemus is a teacher prepares us for a new "teaching," like the new temple replacing the old. Only the teaching, like the form of the discourse itself, is surprising, full of *koan*-like turns and gaps. An individual addresses Jesus, but Jesus responds with speech full of reference to a plural *you*. The proposed new birth is, at the same time, a birth "from above"; indeed, the Greek *anothen* is intentionally ambiguous. And more: the "Son-of-Man," the renowned Jewish apocalyptic figure who was expected to come from God, is now "ascending into heaven." And, paradoxically, the form of that ascension is called a "lifting up," in a word that recalls the lifted up goddess-serpent on a pole (Num. 21:4-9) but is now used as a circumlocution for death by crucifixion.

While the leaps and gaps and meanings here still perplex us and leave us breathless, the intention of this mysterious speech in the Fourth Gospel remains clear. It is like the wine of Cana replacing the purification rites of religion and showing forth the hidden glory of Jesus. In spite of the conflict with the "world" throughout John's Gospel, God loves the world and does not hate or condemn it. Jesus in the midst of the world is for the saving of the world, not for an enabled escape from it. Jesus' death, his participation in the deep sickness and horror of the current order, is held before the eyes of faith for the sake of the wholeness and healing of all things, like the raising up of the serpent-pole amid the serpent-bit. And when baptism is no longer a purificatory rite but a new birth into a new community of witness—a new plural *you*—then it may be seen as the action of God's own Spirit, God's uncontrollable Wind bringing new life into the world.

Of course, "water and the Spirit" (3:5) may itself represent the "old" and the "new" of the replacement motif. On this reading, water-birth would be natural birth from a physical, watery womb. Spirit-birth would be the formation of a believer in the community of believers, empowered by the Spirit of God poured out "from above." But because of the ongoing Johannine interest in identifying water and the Spirit (4:14, 23-24; 7:38-39; 19:30, 34), it seems wiser to understand "water and the Spirit" as a typical Johannine pleonasm for the making of a Christian in the world through means that include baptism in water for the purposes of the Spirit. This, then, is water used no longer for the intentions of religious anxiety, for the observance of purity laws as at Cana, but water poured out with the presence of the Spirit, water flowing in the restored *kosmos* of God, as a community is healed in the crucified Christ and made witness to God's love for the world. That this first discourse of the Book of Signs is then immediately followed by Jesus and the disciples *baptizing* (3:22 ff.), then by the *second* discourse—on the living water and worship in the Spirit—with the woman of Samaria by the well (4:5 ff.), seems to confirm this reading.

Hidden within this mysterious discourse of replacement-teaching the preacher may find what the Fourth Gospel has to say about *God*. God is the One who loves the world and is saving it, even though the world is marked by refusal, ignorance, and sin (cf. 1:10, 29). More: God blows as the wind, bringing to birth and to life that which cannot be born in our world—believers, not just religious observers. More: God is encountered as the one who is called, in the language of Jewish hope and Jewish apocalyptic, the "Son." This one nonetheless appears not as a superhuman figure clothed in light, a mythic redeemer, but, astonishingly, with a "glory" and an "ascension" which include our worst sufferings and ignominy. This dynamic presentation of the work of God-as-triune, one of the biblical sources of the later Christian doctrine of the Trinity, will give the preacher of the day occasion to present the vocation of the baptized assembly as a calling to show forth the rich life and love of this God in the world, a life and love which deeply contradict the world's expectations of "God." Here is a day when the sermon is rightly about God and about the assembly as enacted witness to the surprises of God.

MATTHEW 28:16-20 (RC)

This baptismal theme becomes even more explicit in the Gospel used in the Roman lectionary. The final gospel pericope of Matthew sums up the whole narrative with an assertion that the Risen One will always be with the baptizing, teaching, missioning community. That community around the Risen One and in mission to the world is constituted by a washing with water that recapitulates Jesus' own baptism (3:16-17), a washing with the beloved "Son," under the outpoured Spirit, and within the designating voice of the "Father." The church thus becomes a living icon of the presence of the rich, triune mercy of God.

This triune "name," as it is used in Matthew 28:19, ought to be taken as a verbal reflection of the baptismal account with which Jesus' ministry begins. It ought not be understood as a "baptismal formula," or even as a "name," in any ordinary sense. These were not words recited at the baptisms of the Matthean church to make them valid. Rather, Matthew 28:19 confesses that baptism in the presence and power of God—as God is known in the story of Jesus, as God is the one who sent Jesus and the one who enlivens his story—is baptism which makes a loving and witnessing *community*, not a religiously purified *individual*. The community of the one God who loves the world creates the community of the church in mission.

First Reading

ISAIAH 6:1-8 (RCL); EXODUS 3:1-6 (BCP); DEUTERONOMY 4:32-34, 39-40 (RC)

The First Reading proposed by the RCL is the remarkable inaugural vision and call-story of the prophet Isaiah. The initial figure of the Isaian tradition seems to have been a "cult-prophet" or, in any case, a priest or temple functionary. The material of his vision—the winged seraphim carved on ancient Near-Eastern temple facades, the waving fabrics of robes and curtains, smoke and shouts and an altar of burning coals—all may be understood as the physical materials of the temple cult, now transfigured to the purpose of his vision. Within the liturgy of the temple, Isaiah meets God. The temple cult opens onto the cult of heaven itself. In the midst of the action and figures of worship, Isaiah asserts the simple and awesome: "I saw the Lord" (6:1). There follows the overwhelming sense of sin and mortality before the Holy One—anyone who sees God should die—and then the purifying coal and the call of the prophet to go and speak.

Christians have loved this story. The song of the seraphim has reappeared at their eucharistic tables as a central act of praise. The imagery of the coal has been used to interpret the meaning of Holy Communion, preparing Christians themselves as witnesses in the world. And the "thrice-holy" acclamation and even the plural of "who will go for us" have been borrowed, out of their original context, to celebrate the Trinity.

But the primary purpose of this text, on Holy Trinity Sunday, will be to present again before the eyes of the assembly, the awe-full holiness of God. The same purpose is found in the readings of the other lectionaries. The Exodus account has us encountering with Moses the Fire of the burning bush. The Deuteronomy account speaks of the expectation that to hear or to see God is to die.

Still, in all three readings, the beloved ones of God do not die. Rather, they live and are loved and are sent. It is this richness of the mercy of God—this great holiness which yet surrounds and sends a people in love—that provides the deepest links between these readings and the Christian conception of God as triune. And the liturgy of the Christian church ought to be seen like the materials of Isaiah's vision, like the bush that burns with the Triune God's presence.

CHRISTIANS HAVE LOVED THIS STORY OF ISAIAH'S CALL. THE SONG OF THE SERAPHIM HAS REAPPEARED AT THEIR EUCHARISTIC TABLES AS A CENTRAL ACT OF PRAISE. THE IMAGERY OF THE COAL HAS BEEN USED TO INTERPRET THE MEANING OF HOLY COMMUNION, PREPARING CHRISTIANS THEMSELVES AS WITNESSES IN THE WORLD.

RESPONSE

PSALM 29 (RCL); 93 (BCP); CANTICLE 2 or 13 (BCP alt.); 33:4-6, 9, 18-20, 22 (RC)

The texts appointed to receive and respond to these First Readings all variously continue to sing the holiness of God. But they all also continue to find the marvelous condescension of this God in the word or strength or decrees which flow from God to the chosen community. Psalm 29 may stand for the others. It is an overwhelmingly Canaanite description of the holiness of one god

(Baal?) above the other gods, and the voice of this god as a great thunderstorm. It is a primal expression of the general religious experience of powerful holiness. (When the psalm follows Isaiah 6, Christians will hear these other "heavenly beings" to be the seraphim, shouting "Glory!" in the temple, but at their origin, even these figures were "gods.") The psalm becomes explicitly Israelite, expressing the dynamic, saving, biblical God, the God that Christians call the Holy Trinity, when it concludes, in a way made surprising by the rest of the psalm: "May the Lord give strength to his people! May the Lord bless his people with peace!" The whole psalm is thus transformed. For Christians, the "voice of the Lord," with all of its cosmic power, is seen to be the word of the Gospel alive in our midst. This awe-full God is the God *for* us and *for* all the world.

The alternate psalmody appointed in the *Book of Common Prayer* are two separate fragments of the Song of the Three Young Men, the song from Nebuchadnezzar's fire in the apocryphal parts of Daniel. These fragments are found as Canticle 2 (BCP, p. 49) and Canticle 13 (BCP, p. 90). If one remembers the saving act of God in this story, the God who stands in the fire with them, whose appearance was as "a son of the gods" (Daniel 3:25 Aram.), and if one remembers the use of this canticle in the Great Vigil of Easter, then either of these acts of praise may seem a good choice for this day.

Second Reading
ROMANS 8:12-17

The Christian understanding of the Trinity becomes yet more existential, more engaging of the life of the believer, in this passage from Paul. It comes down to this: to cry out to God is to be within God's very triune life. The Spirit empowers our babbling prayers, arising out of the widespread experience of human need. But Jesus Christ, who has shared this same lot of human need and death and is *risen*, is the sign that blessing and life, not death and loss, are God's intention. To cry out to God in the Spirit is to already have the assurance of "inheriting" such life. From now on there is no place so abandoned that Christ is not already there, and the prayer that arises from that place is a prayer in the Spirit together with Christ.

That Paul calls God *abba* in this passage—using what may be the Aramaic word for *papa* or may, more likely, simply be the vocative "O father"—fits with his metaphor of "inheritance" in an androcentric, patrilineal culture. It ought not be taken as apostolic warrant for "father" as the proper name of God. Widespread Hellenistic practice called any chief god "father." Christian practice makes use of the surrounding language, but breaks it to new purpose. Christian tradition knows

God not as a father and a son who are related to each other in the old subordination of patriarchy, but as "three persons, equal in majesty, undivided in splendor" (Preface of the Holy Trinity, *LBW*). What is astonishing in this passage is not calling out to God from a situation of acute need by saying "father!" That would be widespread Hellenistic practice, a human phenomenon in which Christians shared. Rather, the grace-filled surprise, the Christian good news, is the presence of God *in our cries*, in the Spirit and the presence of God *in our very situation of death and need*, in Jesus Christ. The grace-filled surprise is the doctrine of the Trinity. On this Father's Day in North America, preachers may peacefully note that some people still cry for a father in a situation of need, and this cry has sometimes been lovingly answered and sometimes been bitterly neglected by our own fathers. Neither the answer nor the neglect, however, should be made into the Christian doctrine of God. The doctrine of the Trinity presents us with a richer and more gracious word than would be present in a kind of apotheosis of our own family structures.

IN THE ASSEMBLY

Many Christian assemblies begin their Sunday meeting with one or the other trinitarian greeting. "The grace of our Lord Jesus Christ, the love of God, and the communion of the Holy Spirit be with you all" (2 Cor. 13:13) is a common one. The sense of the greeting is that this meeting is convened as an assembly surrounded by the very presence of this triune God. With Isaiah, we may say of our meeting—filled as it is with the surprise of God, with the word and meal of Christ and the deep prayers and groans of the Spirit—"I saw the Lord." With Moses, we may find here the burning bush. Holy Trinity Sunday gives us an opportunity to be explicit about this deep meaning of Sunday assembly, establishing the doctrine of the Trinity as a profound hermeneutical key to all Christian meeting. And the texts appointed for this day provide us with images that the preacher may use to help us understand our meeting. Gathered as a baptized people, born into a new communal life by water and the Spirit, beholding the healing of the world that God sets forth in the crucified Christ, we may learn again to cry out to God for the sake of a needy world. Then, with the burning coal of the Eucharist on our lips, we may learn again to bear witness to our neighbor that God loves the world, is saving the world, does not condemn it. *That* is the festival of the Holy Trinity.

THE BODY AND BLOOD OF CHRIST

JUNE 25, 2000

ROMAN CATHOLIC
Exod. 24:3-8
Ps. 116:12-13, 15-18
Heb. 9:11-15
Mark 14:12-16, 22-26

IN ROMAN CATHOLIC EUCHARISTIC ASSEMBLIES, a second echo of Pentecost and Easter occurs on this day. Corpus Christi, formerly observed on the first available Thursday after Easter's fifty days as a kind of echo of Maundy Thursday, is now transferred to the second Sunday after Pentecost and celebrates the full meal of Christ. This feast, too, may be taken as a way to sum up the whole festival of the death and resurrection of Jesus and to propose that this festival gives the central meaning to all of our weekly meetings. The Eucharist, the feast of the body and blood of Jesus, is one form of the continuing presence of the paschal mystery, of the outpoured Spirit, of the grace of the Holy Trinity in our midst.

The texts for the day provide images for this assertion. The Gospel, Mark's account of the Last Supper, is one of the primary sources for calling the death of Jesus a *paschal* mystery, for it proposes that the meaning of that death may be expressed in terms borrowed from the Passover feast itself, from its roots in the Exodus and from its anticipation of a great eschatological meal of victory and life. The First Reading gives us the text from which the phrase "the blood of the covenant" is drawn, one of the great texts of the very Exodus tradition alive in the Passover celebration. And the Second Reading applies the metaphors "high priest" and "sacrifice" to Jesus' death and, by extension, to the Eucharist which proclaims his death, thus drawing both death and Eucharist into a thoroughly trinitarian theology.

GOSPEL

MARK 14:12-16, 22-26

The Gospel for this feast in Year B is drawn from the gospel book used on most of the Sundays in Ordinary Time in this year, the Gospel of Mark. The text itself provides the Markan account of the Last Supper of Jesus. According to the Markan chronology, followed in the other Synpotics though not in John, this supper occurs on the first evening of the Passover feast, and the preparations for it take place at the same time that the passover lamb—the *pascha*—is being killed. These preparations, like the preparations for the triumphal entry (11:2-6), are made by the disciples at Jesus' word, as if foreordained, mysterious, even miraculous.

It is not useful to debate whether Mark's chronology or John's is "right." Both have symbolic purpose. Both intend to set the death of Jesus—and the meal which proclaims his death—within the context of Passover meaning. Neither is objective history. Nor is it useful to discuss whether Jesus had prophetic foreknowledge of, or a prearrangement with, the person with the jar of water and the house to which this person leads. As with the arrangements for the entry into Jerusalem, this small miracle narratively frames Jesus as a miracle-worker, a *theios aner*. But in Mark, Jesus is a "divine man" whose wonders are most encountered, paradoxically, in his hiddenness and death. The one who enters and is acclaimed is on the way to the cross. The one who keeps the feast speaks of "my blood of the covenant" at the feast of the slain lamb. Both chronology and miraculous preparation are interpretive images for the purpose of the gospel narrative.

THE EUCHARIST, THE FEAST OF THE BODY AND BLOOD OF JESUS, IS ONE FORM OF THE CONTINUING PRESENCE OF THE PASCHAL MYSTERY, OF THE OUT-POURED SPIRIT, OF THE GRACE OF THE HOLY TRINITY IN OUR MIDST.

That purpose includes the intention to show that the death of Jesus and this meal form a single whole. If you want to know what Jesus' death "means"—indeed, what it *is*, still—then eat this meal. There is no place in all four of the gospel-books that as clearly proclaims the meaning of Jesus' death as does the meal on the eve of his execution. In Mark, this meal is a way to join with the ancient freed people of the Exodus, but now through the blood of Jesus poured out for the "many," for the great crowd of sinners and unclean and outsiders with whom Jesus has identified throughout the whole gospel-book. Indeed, this meal is understood, like all authentic Passover celebration, as a foretaste of the great banquet of the reign of God. And this foretaste is also available to the "many." But the reader is astonished to discover, on a repeated reading of Mark, that Jesus'

Nazirite vow of abstinence from "the fruit of the vine" until he drinks it "new in the kingdom of God" (14:25) is only kept until he is dying on the cross, when he is given sour wine to drink (15:36). To the ears of faith, of course, this nearly hidden account of the drinking on the cross is the very "drinking it new" of Jesus' vow. The cross-death of Jesus itself is the arrival of the day of God as a day which welcomes all, especially sinners and the wretched of the earth. And the continued drinking with Jesus in the church is the beginning of the gift of that last day: the resurrection.

It is probably not wrong to see in the house where the supper is held—as also in the image "house" more generally in Mark (cf. 1:29; 2:1 ff.; 2:15; 9:28, 33; 10:10; 14:3)—an evocation of the house churches wherein the Gospel of Mark was anciently read. Then the person with the water who leads the disciples to the house may rightly be taken as an evocation of the way of baptism which has led Christians into the gathering of the house. And then the account of the supper—with its marvelous present indicative verbs: "this *is* my body . . . this *is* my blood of the covenant"—is an account of the present meaning of the Eucharist in those houses of the church, in the time of the evangelist.

And in our time. It would be better if our eucharistic prayers and our distribution of communion made use of those same present indicative verbs. Indeed, the point of Mark's Gospel here is not, like the texts in Paul or Luke, to give us a significant outline of the local celebration, with its bread before the meal and its cup afterward, reinterpreting specific, identifiable parts of the ancient Passover meal (1 Cor. 11:23-26; Luke 22:14-23). Rather, in the midst of the meal, *while they are eating*, Jesus takes bread and cup with thanksgiving, distributing them as the gift of himself in death. These are not rubrics. The sentences are a proclamation, into our present time, of the meaning of the meal in the house, and thus of the meaning of Jesus' death. At least the preacher for the day can proclaim these strong verbs: This *is* my body, my blood, now. And the preacher can help make it clear that this gift is for "the many," the outsiders, the unclean, the sinners. This is not a holy feast for the pure, a reward banquet for the righteous, a passover for the insider chosen ones. Not in Mark. According to Mark, this Jesus is the hidden Messiah, the secret epiphany of God, whose death and resurrection saves an unclean and needy world. The "new wine" of astonishing joy and hope and life and resurrection is still the vinegar of his cross among the wretched. Indeed, it is the blood which flows from that cross.

First Reading
EXODUS 24:3-8

The First Reading provides us with the text from which the Markan account of the Last Supper derives the phrase "the blood of the covenant." It should be remembered that this text occurs within the narrative of the invitation of God to Moses and the elders of Israel to come up on the mountain (Exod. 24:1-11). The "mountain-meal" which follows continues and typifies the tradition of meals with God, before God, which begins with the passover and is woven through the whole Exodus tradition. So, there on the mountain, representing all Israel, these elders behold God and, surprisingly, they do not die but *eat and drink* (24:11). In the person of the elders, Israel eats with God, a sign of life and covenant with God, a sign contradicting death, a tangible manifestation of the whole Sinai covenant. The way the entire people participates in this meal is by listening to the words of the book and by being marked with the thrown "blood of the covenant" which makes them partakers of the altar of God on which the blood has also been poured.

For the Christian preacher on this day, this old, primal religious rite provides imagery for a surprising reinterpretation. At the Eucharist in the church, having heard again the "words of the book," the people themselves—not just the elders—are invited to eat and drink the death-contradicting meal. Jesus' body is our twelve pillars and our oxen. We need no other. And this shared cup is his blood of the covenant, drunk by us, not just scattered upon us. By watching person after person receiving and receiving this gift of Christ —for that is the direction of his "sacrifice"; here God gives to *humanity*, not humanity to God—we can say: "we have seen God and lived!"

Psalm
PSALM 116:12-13, 15-18

This old psalm of thanksgiving, which may have actually been used as accompaniment to the bringing of a sacrifice but which has undergone a whole series of reinterpretations in different eras, has a new role when it is sung in response to the First Reading on this day. Now we bring no offering but our thanksgiving and our willingness to drink the astonishing, life-giving cup which Christ gives us, turning our sorrow into joy, our bonds into freedom, joining us to the people of the covenant. Now Jesus himself is the faithful one who has died and whose death enables us to eat and drink before the face of God. Now the "presence of all the people" is not the Temple sacrifice but the assembly of the church.

SECOND READING
HEBREWS 9:11-15

With this reading, the feast of the Body and Blood of Christ is drawn into a full trinitarian theology. This Sunday's celebration is made to echo last Sunday's meanings as well. The trinitarian character of the feast is made clear by means of the metaphor of "sacrifice," a metaphor that the writer to the Hebrews takes with great seriousness but which we will have to work hard to interpret. Jesus, of course, was no priest at all, and certainly not a "high priest." He was a layman and a teacher. Similarly, his death was no "offering." It was a cruel and murderous execution. But Christian faith has called that death our only sacrifice, as a way to say that it does all that sacrifices intend to do and more. Indeed, for Christians, Jesus' death is the end of sacrifices, cleansing our already burdened consciences from the "dead works" of trying to please or bribe God with such offerings.

JESUS, OF COURSE, WAS NO PRIEST AT ALL, AND CERTAINLY NOT A "HIGH PRIEST." HE WAS A LAYMAN AND A TEACHER. SIMILARLY, HIS DEATH WAS NO "OFFERING." IT WAS A CRUEL AND MURDEROUS EXECUTION.

Jesus gives himself away to others. Then how is that called "offering himself through the eternal Spirit to God"? How is that "entering into the Holy Place with his own blood"? Because the triune God identifies with human need. Because the Holy Place is henceforth where that need is. Because the Spirit is the Spirit of love which binds the Holy Trinity into one, and the love poured out upon the others, the "many," *is* the living service of God.

IN THE ASSEMBLY

Any Christian community is constantly in need of the renewal of images for the meaning of its central actions. This feast of the Body and Blood of Christ can be used by Roman Catholic preachers to invite their assemblies into a renewed and lively biblical sense of the meaning of the Mass. In the texts proposed for Year B—and in keeping with the character of this "Year of Mark"—that sense can be marked by rich tensions and paradoxes. Here is a "sacrifice" that is given away to humanity, to sinners in need. Here is a foretaste of God's great banquet which is given on the cross. Here is the meal in which we see God by seeing Christ give himself away, in the power of the Spirit, in the broken bread of the body, the shared Cup of the blood, to a whole assembly of the needy. Indeed, here is a feast where the participants themselves are, in turn, made into death-contradicting food for the world. Here is Easter and Pentecost and Trinity Sunday made available, Sunday after Sunday, to eat and drink and give away to the hungry.

SUNDAYS AFTER PENTECOST

Introduction

Gordon W. Lathrop

With the great festival of Easter and its echo-feasts behind us, we turn now to the Sundays in Ordinary Time. The forty days of Lent, the Triduum, the fifty days of Easter and the succeeding Trinity Sunday (and, in the Roman Catholic communion, the further festival of the Body and Blood of Christ) interrupted the flow of Sundays through the year—per annum as the Latin texts say—with a cycle determined by the date of Easter, itself determined by the conjunction of the full moon with the spring equinox, the ancient date of Passover. Now we go on, where we left off, with the Sundays through the year, simply counting "after Pentecost" instead of "after Epiphany."

But to state the matter thus is to be misleading. We are not abandoning "festival" in order to fall back into the "ordinary." Indeed, the oldest festival of Christianity is the one that occurs every week. It is the assembly on Sunday. One could put the matter the other way around. The fifty days of Easter are a kind of Sunday to the year. And Easter, Pentecost, and Trinity Sunday are best seen as a communal way of restating, every year, why Sunday is of such paramount importance. As we have seen, these feasts celebrate in a focussed way the themes that matter to every Sunday gathering for word and sacrament—the resurrection, the assembly in the Spirit, the presence of the triune God as *God for us.*

Indeed, these themes give us a hermeneutic for every Sunday. Sunday is the greatest of Christian festivals because it celebrates the resurrection of Christ as present, in the power of the Spirit, to this assembly gathered in the triune name. As we turn now to consider the texts for the next Sundays in this Year B, this hermeneutic will present itself, again and again, as a major tool for our use. Each of the texts will be asked to come into the meeting that is called for this purpose.

In fact, this use of the texts corresponds exactly to the way the Gospel of Mark makes use of pericopes as well. Mark, the principal source for the Gospel readings of the ordinary Sundays in this year, sent the readers of the gospel-book back to the beginning of the book, back to "Galilee" (16:7; cf. 1:14), in order to encounter the Risen One. The absence of a resurrection appearance in Mark 16:1-8 has made clear that the encounter with the Risen One in Mark is the encounter with the whole book. Each of the pericopes is to be read as a revelation of the presence of the crucified and risen Christ in the midst of the assembly reading that pericope. Each of the pericopes has something of the cross and the resurrection within it already. Then this "Book of the Secret Epiphanies of the Son of God," as it has been called, opens up its mysteries to the present assembly in the Spirit of God.

Mark provides our major texts for these following Sundays. The passages of Mark are read more or less continuously, in order, proceeding through the gospel-book. But during five Sundays in the summer, John provides the Gospel. At the place in the Markan order where the pericope on the feeding of the multitude would occur, the Johannine sign of the multiplication of loaves is narrated, then four passages from the Johannine discourse on the Bread of Life are read on succeeding Sundays. The preacher, of course, ought to be forewarned, finding the possibility of variety in approach and nuance for this rich but repetitious series in the various passages from the Old Testament which pair the Gospel readings with a whole chain of Hebrew stories about the meals of God.

But John's Gospel as well, as we have seen, profoundly accords with our "Sunday hermeneutic." The purpose of "sign" and "discourse," in their characteristic Johannine juxtaposition, is to reveal into the present assembly the truth about Jesus and the world, to make faith possible (20:31), to "take what is mine and declare it to you" (16:14), to form the assembly as the dwelling place of the triune God (14:23). Repeatedly, sign and discourse in the Fourth Gospel give us not only a revelation of God but also a characterization of the Christian assembly. That is most evident in the sign of the first- and eighth-day-meeting (20:19-29) and its paired discourse (cf. 15:26—16:16). But it is also true of all the Johannine pericopes. The sign and discourse of the Bread of Life cast light over the Christian gathering to share bread, even if the texts themselves are not explicitly eucharistic.

These primary readings from John and Mark, then, are paired with a diversity of passages from the Hebrew Scriptures, passages which may be taken as the "scripture" itself for which the Gospel reading is a kind of sermon or illustration or interpretation, according to the old Christian principles of "typology." And a psalm is sung as a way of receiving this text and praising the presence of God in the reading. Or, in the case of those congregations or communities that are following the alternate RCL pattern of reading semicontinuously from the Old Testament, these Sundays make use of passages from 1 and 2 Samuel. And the responding psalm is chosen to correspond with this reading. Here, too, however, there is a kind of typology—in broad stroke, not in detail. For if Mark is the book of the secret epiphanies of the Messiah of God, then these stories of David make an interesting match with Mark. "Interesting" is the right word, for the correspondence is not direct. In Mark, Jesus is no David nor is he a son of David (cf. 12:35-37!), even though he is called upon as "son of David" (10:47), breaks the purity boundaries around food like David (2:23-28), and is hailed, in Mark alone, with the words, "Blessed is the coming kingdom of our ancestor David!" (11:10). No, this anointed king is anointed rather only for his burial (14:8) and reigns from the cross. The Markan revelation theme will always be inverting these Davidic texts.

But, then, the church's use of texts frequently inverts or subverts their expected religious meanings, and this subversion seems to be the deepest intention of the Bible itself. If the lectionary continues this intention, it is only being faithful.

Around this juxtaposition—this pairing in tension—of texts from the Gospels and from the Hebrew Scriptures, we also read passages from the old correspondence of the churches. These "epistles" seem to provide, in relation to the other texts, a symbol of our present assemblies: listening to the word, conversing with each other, dealing with real problems, attending to the apostolic preaching. The Second Reading can be taken as a symbol of the assembly in the power of the Spirit, in the midst of which the word of God is being proclaimed. Outside this theme of "church around gospel," any thematic correspondence with the Gospel or the First Reading will be—and frequently *is*—purely serendipitous. For these next Sundays we will read semicontinuously through 2 Corinthians and Ephesians, and the serendipity may indeed be found in the way the paradoxical gospel of the cross in 2 Corinthians and the epiphany of Christ in Ephesians stand beside the Markan epiphanies of the crucified Messiah.

THE EPISTLES SEEM TO PROVIDE, IN RELATION TO THE OTHER TEXTS, A SYMBOL OF OUR PRESENT ASSEMBLIES: LISTENING TO THE WORD, CONVERSING WITH EACH OTHER, DEALING WITH REAL PROBLEMS, ATTENDING TO THE APOSTOLIC PREACHING.

All these diverse voices come into our Sunday assembly. Joining together with the voice of song and prayer in your place, with your voice as preacher and with the visible words of Baptism and the Supper, they speak strongly of the triune God's action for the life of the world.

Again, in what follows, the texts of these Sundays are interpreted, beginning with the Gospel and then proceeding through the other readings and their alternates in the various lectionaries. Priority is given to the Gospel in a way that accords with the clear intention of the lectionaries themselves: although the Gospel is in last place when read in the church, it is in first place when we begin our study, as a hermeneutical key to our Christian undertaking with these texts. But all of the texts, from the various Western Christian and North American sources, are considered, in the hope that preachers will be enriched in their work by knowing the full range of possibilities alive in the churches on this Sunday. In dealing with these texts, current exegesis and relevant critical, literary, and historical possibilities are first briefly discussed, with an accent on the interplay of symbolic images in each text. Then the writing here usually turns to the concern preachers will have to articulate the meaning of Sunday and the Sunday meeting through the terms of each of the texts. The whole complex of readings is then summarized, together, according to one vision of how the texts sound together *in the assembly*, on this Sunday, next to singing and preaching and praying and the eucharistic meal and the sending to service in the world. May this little preparatory work with the texts be one small contribution to your imagination and to your courage to arise in the assembly with the judgment and mercy of God on your lips.

SECOND SUNDAY AFTER PENTECOST

June 25, 2000
Twelfth Sunday in Ordinary Time / Proper 7

Revised Common	Episcopal (BCP)
Job 38:1-11 or 1 Sam. 17:(1a, 4-11, 19-23) 32-49 or 1 Sam. 17:57—18:5, 10-16	Job 38:1-11, 16-18
Ps. 107:1-3, 23-32 or Ps. 9:9-20 or Ps. 133	Ps. 107:1-32 or Ps. 107:1-3, 23-32
2 Cor. 6:1-13	2 Cor. 5:14-21
Mark 4:35-41	Mark 4:35-41 (5:1-20)

The texts of this Sunday present us with the basic mystery of the gospel of Jesus Christ. Jesus, "just as he is," sleeping, seemingly weak, is encountered as the one who holds all death and chaos—represented by the sea—in his hands. This "secret epiphany," hidden away from the crowd, is narrated in the Gospel reading from Mark. The First Reading, with which the Gospel is paired, is the beginning of the great theophany of the Book of Job, in which Job's sufferings have their only answer: the encounter with the awesome creative might of God, the one who holds even the sea in its bounds. Drawn into the tensions of these readings—weakness and suffering together with chaos-holding might—we then also hear of the paradoxical pattern of the Apostle (as both Paul and the readings from the Pauline epistles may be called), a pattern for the church itself: "as sorrowful, yet always rejoicing; as poor, yet making many rich" (2 Cor. 6:10). The assembly of the church this day gathers around these paradoxes.

Gospel

MARK 4:35-41 (RCL); 4:35-41 (5:1-20) (BCP)

After nearly a chapter full of the teaching of Jesus (4:1-34), Mark turns to a section of miracle narratives (4:35–5:43). This schematic presentation of the ministry of Jesus will then be summed up at the beginning of the next section with the acclamation: "What is this wisdom that has been given to him? What deeds of power are being done by his hands!" (6:2). But in Mark's narrative, this wisdom and these deeds of power remain mysterious, evidence of the secret epiphany with which the book is filled. The teaching is all presented as mysterious parables which require private explanation (4:34). And the miracles are either accompanied by the charge to keep the messianic secret (5:43) or they occur away from the crowd (4:36; 5:14, 37, 40). When the news nonetheless breaks out, it occasions both assembly (5:14) and awe, amazement, or fear (4:41; 5:15, 17, 20, 33, 42).

The story of the stilling of the sea, the Gospel for this day, occurs as the first of this series of "deeds of power." And it carries within itself many of the paradoxical traits of Mark's secret epiphanies. The mighty act occurs resolutely away from the crowd, hidden, private. Yet, "other boats were with him" (4:36). The figure of Jesus is in the boat, "just as he was," even asleep. Yet from his word of command comes astonishing power.

One could argue that the "other boats" and the "just as he was" are simple narrative remnants, the first from another stage of the story, when the tale actually did something with the other boats, and the other from the narrative interest to link this story to the beginning of the teaching section, when Jesus gets into a boat (4:1). Even if this is true, however, the evangelist has maintained the "other boats" reference and has kept the "as he was," even though two passages subsequent to 4:1 indicate Jesus moving away from the teaching-boat location (4:10,34b). We have learned that the old characterization of the Markan Gospel as "rough" and "simple," with lots of untied loose ends, is wrong. These little fragments matter, and they matter in Mark's remarkably sophisticated intention.

WE HAVE LEARNED THAT THE OLD CHARACTERIZATION OF THE MARKAN GOSPEL AS "ROUGH" AND "SIMPLE," WITH LOTS OF UNTIED LOOSE ENDS, IS WRONG. THESE LITTLE FRAGMENTS MATTER, AND THEY MATTER IN MARK'S REMARKABLY SOPHISTICATED INTENTION.

For the hearers of the gospel-book, there is room in the story because of those other boats. The hearers, too, are going along, the boats of the churches alongside the boats of the initial disciples. The members of the assembly where this narrative is proclaimed can know that their congregation and its experience of chaos go along in the boats. They have Jesus in the midst of the same experience, even when seemingly asleep. And for the hearers of the gospel-book, *hos en*, "as he was," will be evoked and remembered when they also hear, in the transfiguration story, that after the amazing events the disciples look up to see "no one with them any more, but only Jesus" (9:8). Indeed, for those who have come to hear this gospel-book in faith, "only Jesus" and "as he was" will point to the deeper mystery: a crucified man is the risen Lord. The sleeping, weak, threatened man in the boat foreshadows the Crucified One who "cannot save himself" (15:31). But in the presence of this very weak one, who is with all the threatened others on the sea, there is the very presence of the awesome God. For the commanding of the wind and the sea and the setting of their limits are none other than the work of God. The hearers of the book know that there is an answer to the question "Who is this then . . . ?" The hearers of the book are themselves called to faith. Indeed, the hearers of the book are in on the secret and have been so since hearing Mark 1:1. And, if they have heard the book before, they know the private explanation of the teaching: this book, in all of its parts, is full of the presence of the Crucified-risen One.

The story of the stilling of the storm, then, at least in the purview of this Gospel, ought to be taken as a proclamation of the death and resurrection of Christ, albeit in the wrong words. But since the resurrection is not just the resuscitation of a corpse but the recreation of the world itself, what other words do we have than the wrong words? Neither the stilling of the storm nor the "resurrection" are simply ancient and curious "miracles" for the credulous. They are limping words that proclaim into the present assembly how God has come among our chaos and death in Jesus Christ, and how we are invited to trust God's active intention for peace and life and salvation in the world. In the power of the Spirit, the preacher should invite the congregation to see this—to be honest about all of our deathly chaos and to trust the presence of God's intention for life in the story of Jesus Christ proclaimed here.

The lectionary of the Episcopal church gives the option that the Gospel of the day may continue with the additional reading of the second "deed of power" in this series, the curing of the demoniac. In the context of the stilling of the storm, this reading can be taken as a particularization of Jesus' victory over chaos and as a further call to faith in the Risen One. May all of our assemblies, through the encounter with the Risen One in these wrong words for the resurrection, be baptismally clothed and in our right minds, and then sent to tell our neighbors of God's peace.

First Reading

JOB 38:1-11 (RCL alt.); 38:1-11, 16-18 (BCP)

With the theophany that concludes the poetry of the Book of Job, Job's sufferings have the only answer that they will receive. Job simply sees and hears God, and it is enough. Indeed, after this encounter, and after Job's confession of repentance and faith, *God* points out that the "answers" and rationales provided by Job's comforters and counselors, for all of their impeccable deuteronomic orthodoxy, are far more wrong than Job's ravings (42:7). This tension at the conclusion of the book is one of the great treasures of the Bible. *God*—God *present*—and not any kind of talk about God is the only answer to the question of suffering.

The First Reading for this Sunday is the very beginning of this theophany. The God who is there revealed is the God of creation, and at the core of creation—in virtually every biblical version of the creation story—is the containing of the chaos of the sea, the establishment of its boundaries making human life possible at all, the transformation of its waters into rain and rivers and springs bringing fertility. That the sea thus also stands for *death* is then further revealed in the verses which the BCP lectionary includes. This ancient symbolic meaning of the sea, which threatened ancient life with chaos and death while yet offering traderoutes and the source of rainclouds, probably will need to be taught to the contemporary congregation.

Read on this Sunday, this passage helps to make clear how the Markan narrative about Jesus is also *theophany*. What the assembly and its preacher may find especially moving is that in Mark the Suffering One and the Revealed One are the same. God comes to share the human lot, the lot of Job.

1 SAMUEL 17:(1a, 4-11, 19-23) 32-39; 17:57—18:5, 10-16 (RCL alt.)

If your congregation is following the pattern of using the RCL semicontinuous series for the First Reading, you will unfortunately lose Job. But you will gain David and Goliath. In fact, the account of a young shepherd boy defeating the mighty warrior, for all of its problematic glorification of war, is an interesting reading to set beside Jesus, "just as he was," stilling the storm. Ancient and medieval Christians readily found in this David—who provided food and who fought off lions and bears and giants from the flock—a deep parallel to Jesus as Savior, as the one who comes not with arms but in the name of God (17:45). Our five smooth stones (17:40) could then be seen as the utterly simple, earthy materials of word and sacrament. But Jesus Christ is victor without sling or sword, "just as he was."

The alternate semicontinuous choice is the account of the Saul's evil spirit and David's lyre, and of the origin of the love of Jonathan and David. This account provides a much less useful pair with the Gospel, unless the passage of Mark 5:1-20 is included. David singing in the face of the madness of Saul and Jonathan's love for David may provide us—like the man clothed and in his right mind, and he and Jesus together—with images of peace and order and healthy relationship, in the face of chaos. Two alternates are provided, in a list already over-rich with alternates, simply out of the desire to cover, more or less, the story of David in too few Sundays. If your congregation is using this series, you will have a choice between the imagery of war and the possibility of ancient homosexuality. Either option, of course, is of immense current significance.

Psalm

PSALM 107:1-3, 23-32 (RCL/BCP alt.); 107:1-32 (BCP); 9:9-20 (RCL alt.); 133 (RCL alt.)

Psalm 107, appointed in one or the other editing if Job has been the First Reading, is a communal psalm of thanksgiving for the deeds of God in salvation: Let those who have been redeemed from trouble, say so! Among those so redeemed are those who go "down to the sea in ships" (107:23). The psalm thus receives the theophany from Job and prepares us for the Gospel. If the Goliath text is read, the congregation should use Psalm 9, a song of thanksgiving for God's assistance for the oppressed, against the nations. If the David and Jonathan text is read, then Psalm 133, the unclassifiable but great biblical celebration of love in the community, is the proper choice.

Second Reading

2 CORINTHIANS 6:1-13 (RCL); 5:14-21 (BCP)

The ministry of the Apostle is one that is not characterized by successful "outward appearance" (5:12), but by the paradoxes of God's life, given amid death. The magnificent list of the paradoxes of that ministry (6:4-10) can be seen as drawing the church itself into the form of the secret epiphany we have known in Mark. In the power of the Spirit, it is not just Jesus but the ministry of the church which ought to be able to be characterized "as dying, and see—we are alive; . . . as poor, yet making many rich" (6:9-10). Alternatively, the image of the "new creation" (5:17) is appropriate on a Sunday in which the church is invited to trust again in the one who is able to restrain and transform all chaos into life-giving order.

IN THE POWER OF THE SPIRIT, IT IS NOT JUST JESUS BUT THE MINISTRY OF THE CHURCH WHICH OUGHT TO BE ABLE TO BE CHARACTERIZED "AS DYING, AND SEE—WE ARE ALIVE; . . . AS POOR, YET MAKING MANY RICH."

IN THE ASSEMBLY

The Christian Sunday assembly is an encounter with the story of the death and resurrection of Christ made present by the Spirit for the sake of the life of the world before God. These texts give unexpected images for the powerful relevance of that trinitarian encounter. The preacher ought not get lost in proving old miracles, but ought rather to directly address the death and chaos within which the present world careens. Then the proclamation of the mercy of God can invite the hearer to trust the "Peace! Be still!" of the Risen One, even when God seems asleep. For now, the authoritative yet humble proclamation of the story-as-revelation in the sermon, then the peace shared within the liturgy, the many prayers for people in agonizing need, the Eucharist as a taste of chaos tamed—a taste of the Spirit hovering over the waters, of death made into the food for life—will be an invitation to trust that life-giving God with all that we are and to go in peace to tell our neighbors.

THIRD SUNDAY AFTER PENTECOST

July 2, 2000
Thirteenth Sunday in Ordinary Time / Proper 8

Revised Common	Episcopal (BCP)	Roman Catholic
Lam. 3:22-33 or Wis. 1:13-15; 2:23-24 or 2 Sam. 1:1, 17-27	Deut. 15:7-11	Wis. 1:13-15; 2:23-24
Ps. 30 or Ps. 130	Ps. 112	Ps. 30:2, 4-6, 11-13
2 Cor. 8:7-15	2 Cor. 8:1-9, 13-15	2 Cor. 8:7, 9, 13-15
Mark 5:21-43	Mark 5:22-24, 35b-43	Mark 5:21-43 (5:21-24, 35b-43)

The texts for this Sunday, while honest about death and sorrow, invite us to have faith in God's action for life. The Gospel is the interwoven Markan account of the healing of the woman with the twelve-year-long flow of blood and the raising of the dead twelve-year-old girl. The First Reading sets beside this account one or the other Old Testament assertion that God did not make death (Wis. 1:13) or that God does not willingly afflict humanity (Lam. 3:33). Alternatively, congregations making use of the RCL semicontinuous option may read the lament of David for the death of Saul and Jonathan. In the face of the life-giving mercy of God, the Second Reading (and the First Reading in the use of the BCP) invites the congregation to open-handed generosity with the poor, with those whose lives are always on the brink of death.

Gospel

MARK 5:21-43 (RCL/RC); 5:22-24, 35b-43 (BCP/RC alt.)

The Gospel for this Sunday once again involves one of the secret epiphanies of Mark. In this third and fourth of the series of "deeds of power" which began at Mark 4:35, Jesus and the woman with the hemorrhages are, as it were, hidden in the crowd. Then, only a few disciples—in fact, the very witnesses of the transfiguration (9:2) and of its answering mystery, the garden agony (14:33)—are allowed to come with him, constituting a little assembly of seven persons in the house, and the witnesses are enjoined to tell no one (5:43). But the hearers of the gospel-book, of course, know. We know of the woman's initiative, against all social custom (a woman without a man, alone in a crowd) and against religious law (she is profoundly, irremediably unclean, yet she seeks to touch a man), an initiative which Jesus calls "faith" (5:34)! And we know of the resurrection (the verbs *egeire* and *aneste* are used) of the girl. To those who hear in faith, knowing the whole course of the gospel, the willing uncleanness of Jesus with the "unclean" woman and the hiddenness of Jesus with the dead girl are foreshadowings of the crucifixion. And the conclusion of the woman's problem with bleeding (*he pege tou haimatos autes*, 5:29) and the walking around of the girl are foreshadowings of the presence of the Risen One. Indeed, this story, like last week's stilling of the storm, is an encounter with the resurrection, in the wrong words. The initiative of the woman is the shape of faith for every Christian. The meal to be given to the child is already a taste of the Eucharist of the church.

THIS STORY, LIKE LAST WEEK'S STILLING OF THE STORM, IS AN ENCOUNTER WITH THE RESURRECTION, IN THE WRONG WORDS.

Some lectionaries propose the alternative of reading only one of these two intertwined stories, dealing with the narrative "sandwich" Mark has created as if it were simply an otherwise unimportant, time-filling technique. In fact, the stories make an important pair, with illuminating parallels and contrasts: a woman and a girl; a twelve-year-long malady and a twelve-year-old who has died; the unclean woman and the unclean corpse; the crowd and the house; touching Jesus and being touched by Jesus. Even the physicians and the mourners of the stories seem to play similar roles: they are no help—in fact, they actively hurt —and they do not know the truth of things. Since, in the Gospel of Mark, women understand the revelation far more frequently than men or even the male "Twelve" do, it is not impossible that there is even a profound Markan intention that the woman of a twelve-year disease and the twelve-year-old girl fulfill the ancient faith and witness role of the twelve tribes of Israel far better than have the twelve closest disciples. The listening church, gathered into this epiphany of life-giving mercy by the preacher, is called to be as the woman and the girl: believing, touching, coming alive, eating and drinking in the presence of God.

LAMENTATIONS 3:22-33 (RCL); WISDOM OF SOLOMON 1:13-15; 2:23-24 (RC/RCL alt.); DEUTERONOMY 15:7-11 (BCP)

The RCL and the Roman Catholic lectionary both set a passage beside this Gospel which calls us to faith in the life-giving intention of God. The deutero-canonical, or apocryphal, Book of Wisdom asserts "God does not delight in the death of the living" (1:13) and praises "the generative forces" of God's good earth (1:14). The hope-filled text from the Lamentations—one of the few passages of hope in this dark book—balances lament with a call to patience and hope in God's deepest will. Either reading makes it clear that the Markan account of God's healing and of life amid suffering and death is not a new idea of the New Testament.

Instead of either of these readings, the BCP lectionary gives us the counsel of the Torah regarding giving to the poor. Using this passage from Deuteronomy prepares the assembly to hear the Second Reading for the day, suggesting that such generosity is one way to cast faith into the teeth of all-embracing death.

2 SAMUEL 1:1, 17-27 (RCL alt.)

The alternative, semicontinuous reading from the Old Testament fits less well with the other readings of the day. Still, with some work on the part of the preacher, it too may make its witness. The text is the so-called "Song of the Bow," attributed to David as a lament for the deaths of Saul and Jonathan, with its repeated refrain, "How the mighty have fallen!" (1:19, 25, 27). While honest, painful lament for the dead certainly stands rightly next to the assembly-intention of this day, the difficulties of this text include no reference to God at all and stereotypical roles for men and women: the men do "lovely" battle and lose, side-by-side with their comrades ("your love to me was wonderful, passing the love of women," 1:26); the women either exult or mourn over the deaths of the men, depending on whose army they were in. The preacher may indeed use this text to sketch the human situation into which the gospel comes, but these difficulties will have to be faced head on. Would it be possible to suggest that, in the mercy of God, we do not need to be caught in these roles any longer: the lament of David, which tells a certain kind of truth about the human situation, and the faith of the woman of the Gospel, which turns resolutely towards life, can be values for all of us, boys and girls, men and women.

Psalm

PSALM 30 (RCL/RC); 130 (RCL alt.); 112 (BCP)

The psalm to be sung in response to a First Reading from either Wisdom or Lamentations is Psalm 30, the individual thanksgiving which asserts the beautiful "weeping may linger for the night, but joy comes with the morning" (v. 5). Indeed, this parallel between night/day and death/life or sorrow/mercy is the very parallel found in the Lamentations: the mercies of the Lord are "new every morning" (Lam. 3:23). This very parallel was later used by Christians to make the course of each night-into-day stand as an icon of the resurrection. To sing this song on the Sunday of the raising of the twelve-year-old girl seems especially appropriate. Psalm 130, the great individual lament, can continue David's "Song of the Bow," deepening its absence of theology into Israel's waiting for God. Psalm 112 responds to the passage from the Torah, using an acrostic form to recount the virtues of one who is generous.

Second Reading

2 CORINTHIANS 8:7-15 (RCL); 8:1-9, 13-15 (BCP); 8:7, 9, 13-15 (RC)

The Second Reading of the day includes passages that are part of Paul's appeal to the Corinthians to participate in the great collection for the poor in Jerusalem. The "generous act" or the "grace" of the Lord Jesus becomes both the source and the model for the generosity of the churches. And for Paul, as well, the appeal is rooted in the Torah: he quotes Exodus 16:18. The people of God, dwelling now in all lands, are to bear witness to the life-giving generosity of God by their open-handedness. Elsewhere (1 Cor. 16:2), Paul places this collection on the first day of every week. It is fascinating to find, in the earliest full description of Christian Sunday assembly—found in the First Apology of Justin Martyr from about 150 C.E.—that a collection for the poor was clearly a regular, central part of the assembly. This collection was the forerunner of our current worship "offerings," especially as these are genuinely about help for the poor and hungry.

IN THE ASSEMBLY

The Christian assembly is to be a space of life in the face of death. Today the preacher may be especially encouraged to make use of the texts to tell the truth about our situation of death, including women's sorrows and men's sorrows and sexual sorrows generally, as *belonging to us all.* Indeed, the preacher ought to invite the church to honest lament for the sufferings in the world. But, in the face of those sorrows, the texts of the day do not finally simply send us to healers or to lament poetry or to encounter groups, as useful as these things may be. Rather, the texts, re-presented in the voice of the preacher, may proclaim to us the deep heart of God, the resurrection of Christ, the assembly in the Spirit. The meal of the Eucharist in our midst today is that little meal in the house of the girl made alive. We too are made alive by Jesus Christ, by his cross and resurrection, together with her. And we too may bear witness to the life-giving God through our collections for the needy world and through going in peace to our "unclean" neighbors, together with the woman who religion called "unclean" but Jesus called a woman of faith.

FOURTH SUNDAY AFTER PENTECOST

JULY 9, 2000
FOURTEENTH SUNDAY IN ORDINARY TIME / PROPER 9

REVISED COMMON	EPISCOPAL (BCP)	ROMAN CATHOLIC
Ezek. 2:1-5 or 2 Sam. 5:1-5, 9-10	Ezek. 2:1-7	Ezek. 2:2-5
Ps. 123 or Ps. 48	Ps. 123	Ps. 123
2 Corinthians 12:2-10	2 Cor. 12:2-10	2 Cor. 12:7-10
Mark 6:1-13	Mark 6:1-6	Mark 6:1-6

IN THE READINGS OF THIS SUNDAY, the assembly stands before the mighty prophet who is rejected and unable to work any miracles at all. That is to say, the assembly encounters the Crucified-risen One and the mystery of God's power present under the form of its contrary. The Gospel gives us both the story of the rejection of Jesus in his hometown and the mission of the Twelve which proceeds from that story. Side by side with this Gospel, we encounter the call of the prophet Ezekiel, who is to speak to the people even in the face of rejection, and the paradoxical boasting of the apostle Paul, who treasures his weakness. The lectionary for this Sunday presents us with an inversion of the usual expectations of religion. Almost as an ironic counterimage, the RCL semicontinuous First Reading tells us of the success of David who is acclaimed by all the tribes.

GOSPEL

MARK 6:1-13 (RCL); 6:1-6 (BCP/RC)

The lectionaries share the account of the rejection of Jesus in his hometown as the Gospel reading of the day. Jesus is solidly rejected, becoming the occasion of stumbling and offense, by people who think they know his origin, his ordinary humanity. In a certain way, of course, they are right. Mary is his mother and folks they know are his brothers and sisters. Furthermore, he really is weak. The Markan Greek employs a double negative in a characteristic intensification of the assertion: "he could do absolutely no deed of power there at all," might be a better translation. In Mark, this weakness is not psychologically motivated. Jesus is simply unable.

Except that he is not. Mark makes the intensified assertion, and then says, surprisingly, "except he laid his hands on a few sick people and healed them" (6:5). Here, too, there is no psychological motivation nor, as in Matthew 13:58, any root cause in "their unbelief," as if only "believers" were healed. It is simply that power nonetheless breaks out of the weak Jesus, even in a situation of unbelief. For the hearers of the gospel-book, this is once again a secret epiphany of the Son of God, once again a proclamation of the crucifixion and resurrection in the wrong words. Hidden in the rejection and weakness of Jesus at home is the revelation of the cross. But hidden in the power that nonetheless breaks out to heal the sick, we encounter the resurrection. Indeed, the hearers of the gospel-book find hidden meaning elsewhere in the passage as well. The hearers know that the question, "Where did this man get all this?" (6:2) has an answer: God. They know that calling Jesus "son of Mary" (6:3) implies an unspoken "son of God" (cf. 1:1). It may even be that calling Jesus a "builder" (6:3; a better translation of *tekton* than the common "carpenter") who is "gifted with wisdom" (6:2) is intended to evoke in the hearers the tradition of the "wise builder" who builds the temple or tabernacle, the very house of God (cf. 1 Kings 7:1-2, 13-14; Exod. 35:30-33). To the faith of the Markan community, Jesus risen is indeed the very builder of the new temple of God.

IN SPEAKING OF JESUS' WEAKNESS, THE MARKAN GREEK EMPLOYS A DOUBLE NEGATIVE IN A CHARACTERISTIC INTENSIFICATION OF THE ASSERTION: "HE COULD DO ABSOLUTELY NO DEED OF POWER THERE AT ALL," MIGHT BE A BETTER TRANSLATION.

But these things are only revealed in the midst of an account of the weakness and rejection of Jesus. They break out of the story, calling the hearers, calling unbelievers to faith, just like the healing breaks out of the weak Jesus. Indeed, these themes are revealed exactly like the revelation of the same themes in the Passion account itself. There, too, the narrative presence of the chief priests and elders striking Jesus and calling out "Prophesy!" reveals to faith the presence of the true prophet. The mocking accusation that Jesus said he could rebuild the temple in three days (Mark 15:29; cf. 14:58), when he cannot even raise his hand from the cross, reveals the presence of the true builder. The weak Jesus among his own people, the crucified Jesus among the wretched of the earth, is the risen Christ, from whom now comes—unexpectedly—wisdom and power, the new family relationships (3:33-35), the community of the new temple, the possibility of faith. Was this visit to "Nazareth" (as Luke calls the town) an historical event? It does not matter, no more than do psychological motivations in the intention of Mark. The story is told now to proclaim the cross and resurrection of the one who encounters us in our assembly, our "hometown," and to invite us to faith.

In the form of the Gospel reading in the RCL, Jesus then sends out the Twelve on mission. This mission—described in terms probably borrowed from the patterns used in the earliest missions of the Christian movement, when poor travelling preachers and poor house churches were united in the meal-hospitality at the center of the Jesus tradition—is here presented as another outbreak from the weakness of Jesus. While Jesus is "unable" in 6:5, the disciples sent by him are quite able in 6:13. The mission of the church, in its simplicity and poverty, in its dependence on hospitable meals (6:8), even in whatever success it enjoys, is rooted in the cross of Christ, in the presence of God as little and weak with the little and weak. The preachers of the day will need to understand that their sermons continue that mission only as they are founded in the same place. The business of the sermon will be to show forth the weakness of Christ with us, so that faith and wholeness and the community of the church may break out.

First Reading

EZEKIEL 2:1-5 (RCL); 2:1-7 (BCP); 2:2-5 (RC)

The First Reading sets out the call of the prophet Ezekiel, as that call is recounted between his inaugural vision (1:4-28) and the invitation of God that the prophet should "eat this scroll" (2:8—3:11). The point of the reading, in our use, is the identification of a *prophet*—"they shall know that there has been a prophet among them" (2:5)—and the instruction to the prophet that he should speak "whether they hear or refuse to hear" (2:5, 7). Just so, the hearers of the Gospel reading are invited to know "the prophet" among them and to listen to the word of the judgment and mercy of God that is revealed in his powerful weakness.

2 SAMUEL 5:1-5, 9-10 (RCL alt.)

Congregations using the semicontinuous series of First Readings will need to deal with a certain irony today. The account of David is most certainly not an account of weakness or rejection. David is hailed and anointed (a second time?) as king by "all the tribes of Israel" (5:1). Then, far from dealing with the rejection of a small village, David succeeds in taking Jerusalem as his capital city. The preacher who uses this text will need to point out the expectations of the "anointed one" which such stories of royal ideology create and the ways in which the gospel reverses and subverts these expectations. Jesus, too, was anointed, but it was by the unnamed woman and it was an anointing "of my body beforehand for its burial" (Mark 14:8). Jesus, too, creates a new Jerusalem, but it is the company of the little, the forgiven, the weak, and the redeemed.

Psalm

PSALM 123; 48 (RCL)

The psalm that responds to the call of Ezekiel is the remarkable and humble song of trust in God: "as the eyes of a maid [look] to the hand of her mistress, so our eyes look to the Lord our God" (123:2). Still the rejection of both Ezekiel and Jesus is not far away: "we have had more than enough of contempt" (123:3). The psalm gives us a pattern in which to listen to the Gospel in faith rather than in offense. Psalm 48, a song of Zion, is the appropriate response for those who read about David taking Jerusalem. In that psalm, "David's city" is made into the "city of our God" (48:1), and in such a city God's works may well be astounding (48:5), not the expected at all. These psalms help to bring the First Reading into relationship with the Gospel.

Second Reading

2 CORINTHIANS 12:2-10 (RCL/BCP); 12:7-10 (RC)

This passage of 2 Corinthians is Paul's long resisted "boasting." Here Paul does speak of his visions and revelations (12:1)—the very things that the supposed "apostles" in Corinth are claiming as their authorization—but he does so in the third person ("I know a person in Christ," 12:2). Furthermore, the content of these revelations are things "that no mortal is permitted to repeat" (12:4). They are therefore irrelevant to his apostleship, which is a service of words that must be spoken. What is relevant, rather, is his parallel to the Christ of the Gospel: his weakness, in which the power of God is manifest. We do not know what the "thorn in the flesh" (12:7) was, nor do we need to know. Every mortal being has such thorns. The point is not to laud weakness, but to rejoice in the power of the God whose grace is present amid our mortality.

IN THE ASSEMBLY

The Christian assembly today gathers around the weakness of Jesus Christ, known most profoundly in his sharing the lot of the wretched and rejected of the earth on the cross. In the power of the Spirit, however, the assembly also proclaims the resurrection, the power of God to make the city of God out of the little and weak ones. The Eucharist, a little bit of food which proclaims the death of Christ, the hospitable meal of the house churches, is still today the meal of that Spirit since it is the breaking out of life and healing and community amid our weakness. The preacher today will need to call the church to reliance on this power of God amid weakness rather than its own efforts at ecclesial success, as if these would build the church.

THE EUCHARIST, A LITTLE BIT OF FOOD WHICH PROCLAIMS THE DEATH OF CHRIST, THE HOSPITABLE MEAL OF THE HOUSE CHURCHES, IS STILL TODAY THE MEAL OF THE SPIRIT SINCE IT IS THE BREAKING OUT OF LIFE AND HEALING AND COMMUNITY AMID OUR WEAKNESS.

FIFTH SUNDAY AFTER PENTECOST

July 16, 2000
Fifteenth Sunday in Ordinary Time / Proper 10

Revised Common	Episcopal (BCP)	Roman Catholic
Amos 7:7-15 or 2 Sam. 6:1-5, 12b-19	Amos 7:7-15	Amos 7:12-15
Ps. 85:8-13 or Ps. 24	Ps. 85 or 85:7-13	Ps. 85:9-14
Eph. 1:3-14	Eph. 1:1-14	Eph. 1:3-14 (1:3-10)
Mark 6:14-29	Mark 6:7-13	Mark 6:7-13

The lectionaries for this day contain a basic difference. Congregations using the RCL continue on from last Sunday's Gospel to hear now the account of the death of John the Baptist. Congregations using either the Roman Catholic or the Episcopal lectionaries also continue on, but, because last Sunday they read only the account of the rejection of Jesus in his hometown, this Sunday they hear of the mission of the Twelve. Their lectionaries omit the reading about the Baptist's death. Surprisingly, however, the other readings are the same and work together with either Gospel. In the RCL, John the Baptist stands as a prophet side-by-side with the Amos of the First Reading, both of them challenging the state and the state's religion and, at the same time, both of them serving as images for God's action in Jesus Christ. In these prophets as well as in Christ, God has made known to us the mystery of the divine will (Eph. 1:8-9). In the BCP and in the Roman lectionary, the missionary Twelve stand alongside Amos, and the apostolic preaching of Christ is the revelation of God's will. But in all three lectionaries, the assembly today is gathered around the prophetic revelation of God's mysterious will.

Gospel

MARK 6:14-29 (RCL); 6:7-13 (BCP/RC)

For a discussion of the sending of the Twelve as an outbreak of power from the weakness of Jesus Christ, see the comment on the Gospel reading for last Sunday.

In the RCL, the Gospel reading provides the "sandwich" material between the sending of the Twelve in 6:7-13 and their return in 6:30-32. This sandwich structure is by no means accidental, however. While its retrospective narrative about the death of John does provide a sense of time passing, it also continues to hold before the ears of the hearer the pattern of the weakness and persecution of the servants of God, the very pattern which is the source and basis for the mission of the church. Indeed, the story gives to its hearers an intimation of the fate of Jesus, while at the same time also suggesting both the resurrection and the utterly different meals of the church.

The story itself is horrible. Herod Antipas is religiously fascinated with John, but also threatened by him. In any case, his fascination is not enough to outweigh his own public pride at the all-male reclining dinner party he holds. A young girl (*korasion*, 6:22, 28, the same word used for the girl whom Jesus, by contrast, raises to life and a meal of life in 5:41-42) is used as bait to bring about John's death, dancing during the *symposion*, the part of a Hellenistic banquet which brought women and slaves into the room as an entertainment that was frequently lascivious. And John's head is served then, as if it were part of the food. It is hard to imagine how we can sing "Praise to you, O Christ!" around this story of sexual abuse and murder.

But we *do* so sing because, in the intention of the gospel-book, we also meet here both a foreshadowing of the cross and the truth of the resurrection. The suggestion of the rumors that Jesus himself—and his manifest name (*phaneron to onoma autou*, 6:14)—is John raised (6:14-16) is not true, but this idea does recall to the hearers the resurrection of Jesus. So does the laying of John's body in the tomb (6:29), just as Jesus' body will be so laid. The theme of Elijah (6:15), the forerunner of the day of God, will recur in the book, but always in conjunction with the cross (8:28-31; 9:11-13; 15:35-36): the forerunner suffers just as the bringer of the Day himself comes in an unclean death. Indeed, the very questions and assertions of the rumors establish the general inquiry about the identity of Jesus, an inquiry made urgent for the present hearers of the story and hovering unspoken behind the rest of the narrative.

Then the narrative of the meal, its awful roles for women and men, and its grisly entrée recall something even more profound to the Christian assembly gathered to hear this book. Jesus, too, holds meals. In fact, one of these immediately follows this narrative (6:30-44). Another is at a little further remove (8:1-10), after a debate about eating together with the unclean (7:1-23) and a narrative about an outsider woman getting even more than crumbs

THE NARRATIVE OF THE MEAL, ITS AWFUL ROLES FOR WOMEN AND MEN, AND ITS GRISLY ENTRÉE RECALL SOMETHING EVEN MORE PROFOUND TO THE CHRISTIAN ASSEMBLY GATHERED TO HEAR THIS BOOK.

(7:24-30). Two other meals immediately precede Jesus' own death (14:3-9, 17-26). And then, the most important of these meals, the church's Eucharist, is occurring in the very assembly where this book is being read. In all of these meals there are several radical contrasts with Herod's banquet: crowds are welcome and loved (6:34; 8:2); outsiders are welcome (7:2, 28); women are part of the hungry and fed assembly (7:28; 8:9), not just the entertainment or the servers. Indeed, a woman plays a central role at Jesus' meals as well, like the role of the *korasion* at Herod's banquet, but what she does is *anoint* Jesus' head (14:3), not maim it or have it maimed, proclaiming forever the meaning of his death in love (14:9). And, astonishingly, Jesus also is served as food in the shared bread and the shared cup (14:22-24), but freely, in love, in the risen presence of his living body encountering the community.

The preacher of the day can use this text to help the congregation see the surprising and gracious meaning of the Eucharist as the polar opposite of Herod's banquet (cf. 8:15, "beware . . . the yeast of Herod"): as the end of false authority; as the vanquishing of death, not yielding to its reign; as the forgiveness of sins; as a new possibility for the roles of women and men. Also this text is a secret epiphany of the crucified and risen Lord, present now in the assembly, under the form of a contrary story.

First Reading
AMOS 7:7-15 (RCL/BCP); 7:12-15 (RC)

This text from the first of the written prophets allows us to see the prophet's vision of God's plumb line and the prophet's dialogue with the false authority of Jeroboam and his royally supported religion. Amos is "no prophet" (7:14) in the sense of a professional religious soothsayer, part of a guild of prophets making their living as prophets. He is simply compelled by the word of God, in this case a word of destruction and rebuilding. Similarly, John the Baptist, Jesus, the travelling preachers, and the house churches are compelled by that same word. Indeed, for Christians, Jesus Christ is the plumb line, measuring for the destruction of the wall and the rebuilding of the city.

2 SAMUEL 6:1-5, 12b-19 (RCL alt.)

The in-course selection for the First Reading today gives us the cultic account of the entrance of the Ark into Jerusalem, under David's protection and with David dancing before it. Michal's hatred of David (6:16) is evidence of the purpose of the story in the royal ideology: a cultic legitimation of the Davidic line and an end to the line of Saul. For Christians, the story may suggest joy in worship for the embodied self. Perhaps the feast at the end can suggest the Eucharist again, that meal of a very different sort of king among a people whose treasure is not the localized Ark but the universally available gospel.

Psalm

PSALM 85; 24 (RCL alt.)

Some selection of the verses of Psalm 85 functions as the response to the passage from Amos. A communal lament, this psalm appeals to God for the restoration of the land. For the Christian, righteousness and peace embrace (85:10) in the community of the Spirit, the community alive in the meals of Jesus. Psalm 24, a great cultic celebration of the entrance of pilgrims into the holy city as an image of the very entrance of God, responds to the reading about David and the Ark. The very question of the psalm—"Who is this King of glory?" (24:8, 10)—allows for the surprise of the gospel: the "King of glory" is very different than anything the Davidic dynasty would lead us to expect.

Second Reading

EPHESIANS 1:3-14 (RCL); 1:1-14 (BCP); 1:3-14 (1:3-10) (RC)

These opening verses of the deutero-Pauline letter to the Ephesians are very opaque in their structure and exceptionally florid in their style. They are best understood as a Christian version of the ancient genre *berakah*, a recitation of the praise of God on the grounds of God's deeds. In this case, the central deed for which God is praised is revelation of the divine will (1:8-9), the plan for all things. For Christians, the name of this will or plan is Jesus Christ, and knowledge of this plan comes from participation in the promised Spirit (1:13-14). Set next to the Gospel of Mark, such revelation might be understood as the way the assembly is drawn into the secret epiphanies of God amid the sufferings and need of the world. The Twelve are sent out with the good news of this revelation. The meal of our assembly, intended to be the opposite of the meal of Herod, is a taste of God's plan.

IN THE ASSEMBLY

In many of the coming Sundays, the meal of Jesus will provide the central theme, first with the account of the multitude on which Jesus had compassion, then with an account of the multiplication of loaves and fishes, then with several passages from the Bread of Life discourse of the Fourth Gospel. It is good, therefore, for the assembly today to see the counter-image of that meal: the banquet of Herod. Nonetheless, hidden under that appalling story—and in the preaching of apostles and prophets—the assembly meets the one who is risen, the one whose Spirit tears down walls and re-orders community and authority, the one who in love "gathers up all things" (Eph. 1:10) into unity and wholeness instead of shame and murder.

SIXTH SUNDAY AFTER PENTECOST

JULY 23, 2000
SIXTEENTH SUNDAY IN ORDINARY TIME / PROPER 11

Revised Common	Episcopal (BCP)	Roman Catholic
Jer. 23:1-6 or 2 Sam. 7:1-14a	Isa. 57:14b-21	Jer. 23:1-6
Ps. 23 or 89:20-37	Ps. 22:22-30	Ps. 23
Eph. 2:11-22	Eph. 2:11-22	Eph. 2:13-18
Mark 6:30-34, 53-56	Mark 6:30-44	Mark 6:30-34

In the readings of this day the assembly is gathered together by the great shepherd, the one who has compassion on the scattered and straying flock. This Sunday can be taken as a little "Good Shepherd Sunday" in summer, a little echo of the Fourth Sunday of Easter. Here the "table" which the shepherd prepares (Ps. 23:5) may be taken as the meal of the assembly in the gift of Christ, for the Gospel of this day narrates either the preparation for, or the full account of, the feeding of the multitude in the wilderness, an account with strong eucharistic connotations. On subsequent Sundays in the rest of the summer, we will use the Fourth Gospel to hear further of this Bread of Life. Today, together with this Gospel from Mark, the First Reading tells us of God acting as shepherd for the misled people (RCL, RC), or of God's comforting care for the people (BCP), or of God's refusal of a house in order to be with the people (RCL alternate). The Second Reading, common to all the lectionaries, then gives us an image of the church as a united people, a single temple in Christ. Around the gathering shepherd a new ecclesiology is possible.

GOSPEL

MARK 6:30-34, 53-56 (RCL); 6:30-44 (BCP); 6:30-34 (RC)

The passage of Mark 6 which all three lectionaries hold in common is the narrative of the return of the Twelve from mission, setting the stage for the narrative of the feeding of the multitude. Indeed, 6:30-32 ought to be regarded as part of the feeding story itself: Jesus' care takes the disciples aside; part of that concern is that they be enabled to eat (6:31); they go to a lonely place, *kat' idian* (6:32). These themes—Jesus' compassion, eating, a lonely or wilderness place—all prepare for and are heightened by the story of food for the multitude.

As the missionaries return, their parallel to Jesus himself is made clear. They have taught and done deeds of power (cf. 6:2; 4:1-34; 4:35—5:43). They are weary, perhaps weak (cf. 6:5), and in any case they need to withdraw into isolation and loneliness (cf. 1:35; 4:36) so they can eat (cf. 3:20). To the hearers of this gospel-book, this isolation and hiddenness, of course, function as a narrative reminder of the crucifixion of Jesus, his greatest isolation, where he was most *kat' idian*. But the crowd which streams to this isolated one and the compassion and food which come from him are narrative presentations of the resurrection. Here is the shepherd for the shepherdless people, to use the metaphor for God with Israel so common in the Hebrew scriptures (cf. Num. 27:17; 1 Kings 22:17; Ezek. 34:5-6; Jer. 23:1-4). And the crowd on which Jesus has compassion includes also the present assembly of hearers of the story. Once again, even this fragment of the feeding story is a secret epiphany of the Crucified and Risen One—indeed, an epiphany of the shepherd *God*—present in the midst of the church.

THE CROWD WHICH STREAMS TO THIS ISOLATED ONE AND THE COMPASSION AND FOOD WHICH COME FROM HIM ARE NARRATIVE PRESENTATIONS OF THE RESURRECTION.

The Roman lectionary presents only this introduction to the feeding narrative. The RCL also omits the actual feeding narrative (which both it and the Roman lectionary will instead borrow from the Fourth Gospel and read next Sunday) but continues with a summary report of Jesus' healings amid the crowds (6:53-56), a further sign of the resurrection to the hearers. The Episcopal lectionary continues with the actual feeding narrative itself, in its Markan form. But, in all three lectionaries, the "shepherd's" profound compassion is already the beginning of food for the crowd, a food radically different from anything that Herod served in the immediately preceding narrative.

The preacher for the day may have shown the contrast of Herod's meal and Jesus' meals last Sunday. This Sunday, the sermon needs to be an epiphany of the compassion of God for a leaderless world, a compassion that then fills the vacuum not with dictatorial, patriarchal leadership but with an astonishing *food*: "this is my body . . . this is my blood . . . for many" (14:22, 24). Can given-away, mercy-filled food lead? Yes.

First Reading

JEREMIAH 23:1-6 (RCL alt./RC); ISAIAH 57:14b-21 (BCP)

The First Reading helps us to see this Gospel as a proclamation into our assembly of the shepherding God. The passage in Jeremiah is a set of two oracles that immediately follow the prophet's denunciation of the failures of the kings (21:11—22:30). God announces the judgment of the false leaders and then promises: "I myself will gather the remnants of my flock" (23:3). To this saying is appended the promise concerning God's own shepherds (23:4), which is then further expanded by an oracle concerning a future righteous king (23:5-6). The passage from "Third Isaiah" gives us a rich description of the work of this shepherding God—"I will lead them and repay them with comfort" (57:18)—even without the metaphor "shepherd." Hearing this reading, Christians are invited to encounter the "gathering" work of God in the revelation made in the Gospel, and to call their own pastors to serve that same gathering work.

2 SAMUEL 7:1-14a (RCL alt.)

The semicontinuous series about David continues with God's refusal to allow David to build a "house"—a temple—for the Ark. The purpose of the royal story at this point is to prepare the narrative ground for the legitimacy of Solomon's temple-building (7:13). But the story of Israel's God always has ways of breaking out of the confines of royal ideology. God *willingly* tents with the people (7:6-7). And *God* is finally to be the builder of any lasting house. Read side by side with the account of the compassion for the leaderless people in the wilderness, Christians may understand that Jesus Christ is God's tenting with the people, the cross and resurrection are the announcement that "the Lord is with you" (7:3) given now to all the ragged people and not just to the king, and this odd crowd gathered by the gospel is the house built by the Spirit.

PSALM

PSALM 23 (RCL/RC); 22:22-30 (BCP); 89:20-37 (RCL alt.)

The psalm appointed as response to Jeremiah's proclamation of the judging, shepherding God is, of course, Psalm 23, further helping us see this Sunday as another Good Shepherd Sunday. The Episcopal lectionary appoints the section of praise which concludes the important lament of the cross, Psalm 22. Here, on the grounds of the rescue of the poor one from death—for Christians, on the grounds of the resurrection—"the poor shall eat and be satisfied" (22:26), just as the assembly eats from the compassion of Jesus. A portion of Psalm 89 is appointed to respond to the Davidic story, proclaiming the eternality of the Davidic line (89:29, 36). This particular royal assertion is a significant problem for biblical theology, one that is only paradoxically resolved for Christians by the gospel insight that Jesus both *is* a Davidic Messiah and, significantly, is *not*.

SECOND READING

EPHESIANS 2:11-22 (RCL/BCP); 2:13-18 (RC)

The passage from Ephesians surrounds these readings about the shepherding of God with a remarkable set of images for the church. The church is a union of the far-off and the near, with the wall torn down and the law which divided abolished (2:14-15). It is indeed the ragged crowd of the Gospel. The church is the "household of God," the gathered people, a single body, and yet a new-built temple (2:19-20). This deutero-Pauline epistle thus continues and elaborates a pairing of metaphors known already in Paul himself: a people is the building for the Spirit; the "body" is also the "temple" (cf. 1 Cor. 3:16; 6:19).

IN THE ASSEMBLY

Let the preacher today arise with the very compassion present in the Gospel, loving the motley assembly gathered in the room. And let the sermon announce the judgment of God on false leadership, including the preacher's own, while announcing the gathering, wall-destroying, death-destroying leadership of God, present in the grace, leisure, and life—in the *food*—that is here given away. And let the assembly be a temple for *that* God, for the holy Trinity, the God of boundless compassion.

SEVENTH SUNDAY AFTER PENTECOST

JULY 30, 2000
SEVENTEENTH SUNDAY IN ORDINARY TIME / PROPER 12

REVISED COMMON	EPISCOPAL (BCP)	ROMAN CATHOLIC
2 Kings 4:42-44 or 2 Sam. 11:1-15	2 Kings 2:1-15	2 Kings 4:42-44
Ps. 145:10-18* or 14	Ps. 114	Ps. 145:10-11, 15-18
Eph. 3:14-21	Eph. 4:1-7, 11-16	Eph. 4:1-6
John 6:1-21	Mark 6:45-52	John 6:1-15

WITH THIS SUNDAY, in the use of the RCL and the Roman lectionary, we turn again to the pattern of sign and discourse in John, rather than the pattern of secret epiphanies we have seen in Mark. (It is not wrong, however, to assert that both patterns are intended to convey the same thing: the revelation to faith of the identity of Jesus Christ for the present assembly.) The assembly arrives at the story of the feeding of the multitude as a major sign in the Johannine Book of Signs (John 2-12). This is the narrative for which we have been prepared, in the last two Sundays, by the narratives of Herod's banquet and Jesus' compassion. And this is the narrative which will stand behind the discourse passages in the four Sundays to come.

The BCP lectionary read the Markan version of this narrative last Sunday. It now continues with the Markan epiphany of Jesus at sea on this Sunday and then goes on, together with the other churches, to read the Bread of Life discourse on succeeding Sundays.

Passages from 2 Kings or 2 Samuel give Hebrew Scripture background to the gospel narratives. And Ephesians once again provides an image of the church as assembly in the holy Trinity, around the gospel. The assembly gathers today, as every Sunday, to eat the Bread of Life. But for the next few Sundays that eating will be the explicit theme of the readings.

JOHN 6:1-21 (RCL); 6:1-15 (RC); MARK 6:45-52 (BCP)

The Fourth Gospel has received the earlier, probably Markan accounts of the feeding of the multitude, and reworked them with Johannine theological accents in mind. In John, Jesus takes initiative in the event, as he does in much of this gospel-book. The need for food does not simply happen to him: "for he himself knew what he was going to do" (6:6). The event occurs near the time of Passover, the time of the great meal-memorial of the Exodus. The whole event is called a "sign" (6:14; cf. 6:2). The further additions—the names of the disciples and the presence of the child (*paidarion*, "child," a little boy or girl, not "boy")—seem more likely to be simply additions out of increasing narrative rather than theological interest. Very little should be made of these further additions in the homiletic use of this text, unless it is to note that this *paidarion* plays a very different role than the *korasion* of Herod's banquet. (Indeed, is this the *korasion* of Mark 5:41-42, showing up narratively in a very different, Johannine place, with the food she was given after being raised up?) But what is important is this: Jesus' initiative and the Passover dating all push the sign forward to its primary referent, the Passion account. In his death and resurrection, Jesus becomes the food which serves a far greater multitude than even this one. Then, in a comment which might be compared with Mark's juxtaposition of Jesus' meal to Herod's (Mark 6:17-44) as well as with the Johannine dialogue with Pilate (18:33-38), Jesus refuses kingship (John 6:15). The Crucified One reigns in an utterly new way: by giving away true bread.

JESUS' INITIATIVE AND THE PASSOVER DATING ALL PUSH THE SIGN OF THE FEEDING FORWARD TO ITS PRIMARY REFERENT, THE PASSION ACCOUNT. IN HIS DEATH AND RESURRECTION, JESUS BECOMES THE FOOD WHICH SERVES A FAR GREATER MULTITUDE THAN EVEN THIS ONE.

Preachers need to note further the eucharistic sense that pervades the text. Jesus gathers the assembly in peace, in the greening, eschatologically blossoming wilderness (6:10). He takes, gives thanks, and distributes the food. These notes would already recall the church's meal in the mind of the ancient hearers of the book. But the fact that such a multitude is fed may also have subtly criticized the tendency of any meal to become a closed-door affair, available only to a few. Such a narrative criticism would parallel Paul's argument with the Corinthian church (1 Cor. 11:17-34) and point to the churches' need to use larger spaces than the old Mediterranean dining rooms, *triclinia*, for their assemblies. But then, the assertion that twelve baskets were left over (and protected; 6:12), like the seven baskets similarly left over in the second Markan story (Mark 8:8), would have assured the hearer that the very food given by Jesus is still available and being passed out in the church itself. The local assembly joins the eschatological feast. The bread comes here.

This astonishing note is enough for today, urging us, too, to open our doors to more people and to pass out the apostolic baskets, the holy eucharist, at the center of our meeting. Then, on succeeding Sundays, we will see more of the meaning of the sign: the revelation of a thing which is finally most deeply given away not in the old miracle but in the constant presence of the Crucified-risen One, who in himself is Bread of Life.

The RCL continues by reading also the Johannine form of the narrative of Jesus walking on the sea. For the BCP, the Markan form of this narrative is the only content of the Gospel for this Sunday. In its Markan form, this story is once again a secret epiphany, a proclamation of the death and resurrection of Christ in the wrong words. In John, it is a further sign. In both books, at the heart of the revelation are the words "It is I," *ego eimi* (John 6:20; Mark 6:50), words which ambiguously indicate both the presence of a known human being and the revelation of the mysterious name of God. In the BCP lectionary, the misunderstanding of the loaves (Mark 6:52) connects this Sunday's reading to the Bread of Life sequence of the current several Sundays, and invites the assembly to understand in faith who is at the heart of the meal.

First Reading

2 KINGS 4:42-44 (RCL/RC); 2:1-15 (BCP)

In the RCL and in the Roman lectionary, the brief reading from the Elisha cycle provides a text on which the Gospel story might be taken as a midrash. In Jesus, the presence of the work of God through a prophet has reached unexpected universality. The BCP First Reading gives us the very beginning of the Elisha cycle. As Elijah and Elisha retrace the places and events of the entry into the land, the Spirit and mantle of the one prophet falls upon the other. This event at the water of the Jordan, then, stands beside the Gospel event at the water of the Galilean sea. Here is yet a greater prophet, a greater "share" of the Spirit.

2 SAMUEL 11:1-15 (RCL alt.)

The in-course, Davidic option for the RCL gives us the first part of the narrative of David and Bathsheba. This Sunday's portion recounts the royal sin itself. From the point of view of the royal ideology, the story provides the background for understanding that Solomon was not illegitimate but the child of a marriage, albeit a marriage purified by the judgment of God. But when the Gospel is read beside this account, it is fascinating to note that Jesus refuses to become king. Herod and David kill and take other men's wives, perpetuating a patriarchal culture. Jesus gives away bread.

PSALM

PSALM 145:10-18 (RCL/RC); 114 (BCP); 14 (RCL alt.)

The psalm which responds to Elisha's bread miracle is the famous meal prayer: "The eyes of all look to you, and you give them their food in due season" (145:15). The BCP psalm is a celebration of the crossing of the Red Sea and of the Jordan, the great water-miracles at which God's name was revealed. The psalm responding to the David and Bathsheba story is an individual lament about human sinfulness. On this Sunday, it is important to note that the evildoers, far from giving away food, "eat up my people as they eat bread" (14:4).

SECOND READING

EPHESIANS 3:14-21 (RCL); 4:1-7, 11-16 (BCP); 4:1-6 (RC)

For the readings of the BCP and the Roman lectionary, see the note on the Second Reading in the RCL for next Sunday (p. 124). The RCL reading for this Sunday is the great doxology at the end of the eucharistic and kerygmatic section of Ephesians, before the *parainesis* or exhortations begin. Here the assembly of Christians is presented as thoroughly drawn into the full triune life of God: before the Father, strengthened with the Spirit, with Christ dwelling by faith in their midst, surrounded by all the other holy people, as they all come to comprehend that which is beyond knowledge, the love of Christ.

IN THE ASSEMBLY

The readings today once again give us a set of words with which to understand the meaning of our gathering on Sunday. Our assembly joins that ancient multitude, where Christ is no king but a bread giver. We begin to think that our doors must be more widely open. In so doing, our assembly comes to have a radically different view of the world, in which the usual courses of power do not matter at all. Rather, we begin to taste "the breadth and length and height and depth" (Eph. 3:18) as we are drawn together into the very life of God.

EIGHTH SUNDAY AFTER PENTECOST

AUGUST 6, 2000
EIGHTEENTH SUNDAY IN ORDINARY TIME / PROPER 13

REVISED COMMON
Exod. 16:2-4, 9-15
  or 2 Sam. 11:26—12:13a
Ps. 78:23-29
  or Ps. 51:1-12
Eph. 4:1-16
John 6:24-35

TODAY THE ASSEMBLY GATHERS, like the people of the Exodus, around the true bread of God, enabling the journey to freedom and witness and praise. The point is not simply to "eat your fill" of bread (John 6:25; Exod. 16:3, 12), but to receive in faith the great gift of God, the mercy of God which delivers from slavery, the presence of Christ amid our hungers giving life to the world, the Spirit which makes us one.

As the preacher and the assembly prepare to celebrate the next four Sundays, it will be wise to look ahead. Passages from John's Bread of Life discourse will provide the Gospel on all four Sundays. Four striking Old Testament accounts of the meals of God and the choice of the people will be read as the First Reading. In each case, this First Reading may well provide the best key to variety in preaching, while the Gospel will provide the strong, even scandalous christological center of the message. Today the account of the manna (Exod. 16) is paired with the beginning of the Bread of Life discourse and its reference to the Exodus story. Next Sunday, Elijah's meal of bread and water, in the strength of which he goes to the mountain to see God (1 Kings 19), is paired with the offense at Jesus' identity. Thereafter, Wisdom's meal (Prov. 9) is paired with the necessity of eating and drinking the very flesh and blood of Jesus. Finally, Joshua's challenge to choose the God of Israel (Josh. 24) is paired with the Johannine form of the confession of Peter. Having heard the story of the feeding of the multitude last Sunday, today the assembly begins down this road of further bread stories.

Preachers and assemblies in the discipline of the Roman Catholic and Episcopal calendars and lectionaries should look ahead to the next entry in this book. Since, in this year, this Sunday falls on August 6, those calendars are observing the feast of the Transfiguration. They will take up the Bread of Life series again on the following Sunday.

Gospel
JOHN 6:24-35

The Gospel for this day is the beginning of the Bread of Life discourse. This discourse commences with dialogue, just like the first Johannine discourse, slowly becoming monological with occasional narrative and dialogue interruptions (cf. 3:1-36). The reader needs to recall that the intention of the dialogues is to reveal the same thing that the paired signs have revealed and, together with the signs, to lean forward to the full revelation of the Book of Glory (John 13–20). But, while the sign of the multiplication of loaves had strong eucharistic accents (see above, seventh Sunday after Pentecost, pp. 117–18), this discourse seems at first to go beyond the reference to the Eucharist. The deep question is the identity of Jesus himself. It should be recalled that the signs with which the discourse is paired include the *ego eimi* on the sea (6:20) as well as the feeding miracle.

THE INTENTION OF THE DIALOGUES IN JOHN IS TO REVEAL THE SAME THING THAT THE PAIRED SIGNS HAVE REVEALED AND, TOGETHER WITH THE SIGNS, TO LEAN FORWARD TO THE FULL REVELATION OF THE BOOK OF GLORY.

Through the centuries Christian theologians have spent a good deal of energy in debate about whether or not there is a eucharistic reference in John 6. Given the fact that the great meal of the Passion account in John (13:1-11) includes no reference to bread and wine but, rather, the slave-service of Jesus in the midst of the meal (in the very place that Mark places the bread and cup; Mark 14:22), it is wise to conclude that the gospel-book itself has a critical attitude toward the Eucharist as it was being celebrated in the late first or early second century. No wonder later theologians have found in John the material for a diversity of opinions.

But the critical attitude of John does not mean that the community of the Fourth Gospel had no Eucharist. Rather, the gospel-book urges that community to find the meaning of the church's meal, the content of the feast that many Christians regarded to be a foretaste of the eschatological banquet, in the presence of the crucified Christ, showing his wounds (20:20), serving in love (13:4). The Johannine critique, then, is very much like the Pauline critique of the Corinthian celebration (1 Cor. 11:26). In today's passage, as in the rest of John, it is the Crucified and Risen One who says the amazing "I am" of God (6:35; cf. Exod. 3:14), who is "true bread," "Bread of Life," all that bread points toward and longs to be in human life, and more.

The point for the preacher of the day is not to be pulled into the gnostic possibilities in the text, interpreting "food that endures" as meaning some other-worldly, self-determined nourishment of any vaguely spiritual sort: new-age soul food. Rather, the food that endures, the food that gives life to the world, is quite specific: it is the identity of the Crucified-risen Jesus as the life-giving presence of God. Such is the food that feeds faith. Similarly, the faith that does the work of God, in that astonishing subversion of religious duty (6:28-29), is not just any faith: it is the faith in the one whom God has sent. In a faithfully celebrated Eucharist, influenced and continually reformed by the critique of both Paul and John, this will be the very faith that is confessed. Or, to say the matter the other way, a Eucharist that does not show forth to faith who Christ is and what the crucifixion means runs the danger of being a perishing meal (6:27) or, to use the Pauline critique, a meal that could make us sick or dead (1 Cor. 11:29-30) rather than alive together in love.

Moses gave bread, and the bread of that old miracle to sustain that particular people is now gone, having rotted by God's intention after a day (Exod. 16:19-20). The Father, the one who sends Jesus, gives bread now, and this bread is for the life of all the world. The Samaritan woman asked, "Sir, give me this water" (4:15). Jesus' interlocutors now ask, "Sir, give us this bread" (6:34). In the cross, Jesus is bread and drink for the world. In the resurrection—and in the Eucharist which proclaims this death and resurrection—this bread and drink come here as the end of hunger and thirst (6:35).

First Reading

EXODUS 16:2-4, 9-15

The Torah narrative on which so many of the references of the Gospel depend comes into the assembly as First Reading today. The preacher may note that the people "ate their fill" by the fleshpots of Egypt and will "eat their fill" again of the manna (16:3, 12; cf. John 6:26). Already this text longs for the people to eat another kind of bread: a dependence on the will and work of God that is carrying them through wilderness hardship to freedom. The text itself begins to point toward eating as an active metaphor for faith.

2 SAMUEL 11:26-12:13a (alt.)

The David story of the day, for those congregations following this semi-continuous pattern for the First Reading, is the second part of the David and Bathsheba story, begun last Sunday. Today's reading gives us the parable of Nathan, the unknowing self-condemnation of David, the powerful "You are the man," and David's repentance. Still, Bathsheba is barely on the screen, and the story is full of difficulties if the assembly wants to hold it beside the other readings of the day. If nothing else, the situation of David is a powerful cry for true bread to be available to the men and the women and the children.

Psalm

PSALM 78:23-29, 51:1-12 (alt.)

The psalm that is sung in response to the manna text recounts the manna and quail gift again, this time calling the manna, "the bread of angels" (78:25), and heightening its meaning. One may recall the history of western typological art in which the manna came to be imaged as if they were the small hosts of medieval eucharistic practice. The response to the David story is Psalm 51, the lament which was traditionally put in David's mouth as repentance for the sin with Bathsheba. Now, David's repentance becomes a song for all of us, and the astonishing mercy which, for Christians, includes Bathsheba and David in the ancestry of Jesus (Matt. 1:6) comes also to us sinners. By the use of Psalm 51, the story of a particular sinful king is generalized to become the story of all of us.

Second Reading

EPHESIANS 4:1-16

The Second Reading today begins the exhortation section of the Ephesians letter, basing the imperatives upon the great gifts of God. The gift with which this passage begins is unity. And the maintenance of church unity, given to us already in "one Lord, one faith, one baptism" (4:4), forms the primary exhortation. The many different gifts for ministry in this church are then called to the mature service of the one body. In this passage, the deutero-Pauline writer carries on the body-of-Christ metaphor so important to Paul's writing elsewhere.

IN THE ASSEMBLY

So what would a "mature" assembly be? It would at least be one marked by "the knowledge of the Son of God," in which the diverse ministries "speak the truth in love" (Eph. 4:13-15). The Christ whose identity is to give himself away as bread for the life of the world is the heart of that knowledge. The Spirit who gathers the assembly into the one faith enables that truth. The God who means, in spite of all of our whining, to lead us into life and freedom, is the ground of that love. May the preacher this day speak such trinitarian truth.

THE TRANSFIGURATION

AUGUST 6, 2000

Episcopal (BCP)	Roman Catholic
Exod. 34:29-35	Dan. 7:9-10, 13-14
Ps. 99 or Ps. 99:5-9	Ps. 97:1-2, 5-6, 9
2 Peter 1:13-21	2 Peter 1:16-19
Luke 9:28-36	Mark 9:2-10

According to the calendrical rules observed by the Roman Catholic and Episcopal churches in North America, today is the feast of the Transfiguration. That feast is also observed by the Episcopal Church on the Last Sunday after the Epiphany. In the Roman Catholic Church, the Gospel story of this day is also read on the second Sunday in Lent. But, when August 6, the old date of the feast, occurs on a Sunday in those churches, these readings replace the normal Sunday readings. The texts bear repeating.

GOSPEL

MARK 9:2-10 (RC); LUKE 9:28-36 (BCP)

In Mark, the Gospel of this day is the paradigmatic secret epiphany. It is secret: only the central three disciples are taken, the very three who also witness the agony in the garden (14:33); they are taken apart, *kat' idian,* "by themselves" (9:2); when it is over they see "only Jesus" (9:8); they are charged to tell no one (9:9); and they do indeed keep silent (9:10). But it is also a stunning epiphany: in this hidden location are found not only the great witnesses, Moses and Elijah, but also the very glory and voice of God, identifying Jesus. The suggestion of Gethsemane is not the only detail of the story which invites the hearers to remember the crucifixion. In a passage not included in today's Gospel, as they are going down the mountain, Jesus speaks of John the Baptist's death as if it were the murder of Elijah and a downpayment on his own murder (9:12-13).

In Mark, the Gospel of this day is the paradigmatic secret epiphany.

The BCP lectionary, instead of reading the account from the gospel-book appointed for the year, fixes August 6 as a Holy Day with one set of propers and proposes the reading from Luke. The Lukan story, while de-emphasizing the Markan paradox of the Messianic Secret, does add two interesting details. The disciples are sleepy, perhaps pulling into this story a further narrative note from the story of the agony in the garden (Luke 22:45). And Jesus, Moses, and Elijah discuss the *exodus* (as the Greek has the content of their conversation) which he is to accomplish at Jerusalem (9:31). The NRSV translates this word as "departure," but the ancient paschal connotation of the word should not be lost.

The transfiguration narrative has frequently been called a "resurrection appearance" story that has been introduced into the gospel account of Jesus' life. Whatever the origins of the story, that is exactly the role it plays in the Gospel of Mark. For the hearer of the book, this secret epiphany presents the Crucified-risen One, the very presence of the glory of God, come now in all the stories into the presence of the church. The transfiguration story gives the hermeneutical key for understanding all of Mark. Luke carries on this same intention, helping us to see in faith that the cross and resurrection are the new Exodus for all the world.

First Reading
DANIEL 7:9-10, 13-14 (RC); EXODUS 34:29-35 (BCP)

The Roman lectionary pairs Mark's Gospel with the passage from the apocalyptic visions of Daniel in which the throne of the Ancient One is seen and a figure "like a human being" is given the kingdom. This passage, written in Aramaic, became the source of endless apocalyptic speculations about this mythic human figure in heaven. In Daniel, however, the figure like a human being is contrasted with the four earlier figures, all like various monstrous beasts, who stand for four historical and despotic kingdoms. At last, in the mercy of God, authority is to be given to God's own people, and the humanness of the figure suggests the hope for a recovery of humane rule. For Christians, of course, this "human being" (also termed "son of man") comes to be understood as not just any ruler—all of whom are quite capable of becoming the beasts again—but Jesus Christ, in his paradoxical rule of weakness. The clouds and the glory of the scene—clouds and glory which belong to the mythic reflections on the divine-human figure—link the vision to the Gospel of the day. So does the shining face of the one who speaks with God—Moses—in the First Reading appointed for the Episcopal church. Only now, the shining of Jesus Christ calls us to listen to the one who speaks *for* God (Luke 9:35).

PSALM

PSALM 97:1-2, 5-6, 9 (RC); 99 (BCP)

The psalm which is sung today in response to the First Reading is one or the other of the enthronement psalms, celebrating the rule of Israel's God. In both cases, the clouds which surround the deity play a role in the song, preparing us for the cloud as a sign of God's presence in the Gospel that follows.

SECOND READING

2 PETER 1:16-19 (RC); 1:13-21 (BCP)

The Second Letter of Peter is widely acknowledged as a pseudonymous work from the late first or early second century. Present readers need to understand that such works were not considered duplicitous, but were widely accepted as using a strategic way to communicate important matters. Our passage, then, though it speaks as if it were in the very voice of Peter, telling what he saw upon the mount of the transfiguration, ought to be regarded as the very earliest record we have of the transfiguration text, as it was known in the gospels, being celebrated and made into a text for a further written sermon. With this "Peter," we will do well to pay attention to the word of the transfiguration as to a lamp shining in a dark place (1:19). The "power and coming of our Lord Jesus Christ" (1:16) may indeed be a coming at the end of time, as 2 Peter seems to say, or it may be the Markan intention: the power and presence of God in our midst now. In either case, the word of this secret epiphany is already the beginning of the rising of "the morning star" (1:19).

IN THE ASSEMBLY

The feast of the Transfiguration gives us yet another set of words to interpret the meaning of the Sunday assembly, on any and every Sunday. We may hold the words of this feast together with the words from Easter and Pentecost and Trinity Sunday and all the secret epiphanies of Mark and all the Bread of Life discourse. Let the preacher say this: here, amid the darkness and need of the world, we gather as if we were "apart." But by the power of the Spirit, we encounter here the very Risen One, Moses and Elijah, and all the saints of God bearing witness. And we discover that this Risen One, who has the word of God and is the end of the rule of the despots, is also the one who has shared the worst sorrows of the world. We see light rising ourselves and we are sent to share light with our neighbors.

SUNDAYS AFTER PENTECOST

INTRODUCTION
NEIL ELLIOTT

"GO IN PEACE, to love and serve the Lord."

With these or very similar words, we routinely end our worship services. Significantly, however, we do not end our liturgy. "Liturgy" means, literally, "the people's work." As the words of the dismissal indicate, the work of the faithful does not end when the music stops and the liturgical *ritual* is over. To the contrary! The liturgy that is our lives, the "spiritual sacrifice" of which the apostle Paul spoke in Romans 12, continues. If the ritual accomplishes what it is meant to accomplish, we go out refreshed and strengthened "to do the work God has given us to do."

I have tried to keep that fact very clearly in mind as I write. What follows is not meant as script or director's notes for a performance, so much as it is reflection on what the Scripture readings for each day might mean for people who have gathered to present their lives and labor in offering to God, and who will be sent out to resume that work in God's world.

These are also not primarily exegetical notes. I do not presume that any of the texts discussed in the following pages has one "meaning" that it is the clever interpreter's task to discover or extract, so as to refine it and deliver it as a finished product to the congregation. I consider that any of these texts may require a good deal of spiritual wrestling. If it is part of the work of the Holy Spirit to guide the faithful "into all the truth" (John 14:13), I believe that work will best be discerned, not by seeking "what the text says" alone, but by listening for what *God* wants to say to us as we struggle with the text.

I have nevertheless ventured for each Sunday to provide something of an interpretive "lay of the land." My concern lies not so much with exegesis for its own sake as with the dilemmas, and in some case real perils, facing the homilist with the assumptions, often unconscious, that we routinely bring to these well-known texts. I covet the reader's patience and active reflection, for I intend to *stimulate* the homilist's discernment, not replace it!

IF IT IS PART OF THE WORK OF THE HOLY SPIRIT TO GUIDE THE FAITHFUL "INTO ALL THE TRUTH" (JOHN 14:13), I BELIEVE THAT WORK WILL BEST BE DISCERNED, NOT BY SEEKING "WHAT THE TEXT SAYS" ALONE, BUT BY LISTENING FOR WHAT GOD WANTS TO SAY TO US AS WE STRUGGLE WITH THE TEXT.

A word about organization. Our lectionaries often invite us to follow a particular evangelist's voice for a series of Sundays. The extraordinary "Bread from Heaven" discourse from the Fourth Gospel is the subject of the ninth, tenth, and eleventh Sundays after Pentecost. The following Sundays, the twelfth through the seventeenth, follow a sequence in Mark's Gospel. For the ninth and twelfth Sundays, therefore, I turn first to comment on important issues arising in the Gospel readings, in the conviction that our lectionaries, and the New Testament itself, seek to elicit from us a discerning hearing of the very distinctive voice of each evangelist. The reader should know that I have relied on Kurt Aland's *Synopsis of the Four Gospels* throughout my preparation. I recommend the regular use of this or a similar tool as an indispensable aid to discovering the particular emphases of the several Gospels.

A special word of thanks to Nancy Anderson, who was of invaluable help in organizing this project, and to K. C. Hanson, for his thoughtful guidance and encouragement.

NINTH SUNDAY AFTER PENTECOST

AUGUST 13, 2000
NINETEENTH SUNDAY IN ORDINARY TIME / PROPER 14

REVISED COMMON	EPISCOPAL (BCP)	ROMAN CATHOLIC
2 Sam. 18:5-9, 15, 31-33 or 1 Kings 19:4-8	Deut. 8:1-10	1 Kings 19:4-8
Ps. 130 or 34:1-8	Ps. 34 or 34:1-8	Ps. 34:2-9
Eph. 4:25—5:2	Eph. 4:(25-29) 30—5:2	Eph. 4:30—5:2
John 6:35, 41-51	John 6:37-51	John 6:41-51

WE BEGIN WITH THE EXTENSIVE "Bread of Heaven" discourse that fills most of John 6 and will occupy our attention for these next three weeks. In this first week I want to give sustained attention to several difficult issues that arise in the interpretation of this passage.

GOSPEL

JOHN 6:35, 41-51 (RCL); 6:37-51 (BCP); 6:41-51 (RC)

The Bread from Heaven and the Hunger of the World

"To the hungry give food; and to those who have food, give hunger for justice."

I learned that simple prayer at the bountiful table of two dear friends, John and Anne. Their constant generosity and good cheer to the friends they call together over great food and wine remind me of no one so much as Mr. and Mrs. Fezziwig in Charles Dickens' *A Christmas Carol.*

There is some irony, of course, in reciting a prayer for the hungry as I sit down to feast with friends. As Monika Hellwig points out in her splendid book *The Eucharist and the Hunger of the World*, most Christians in the prosperous North know hunger only abstractly, from a distance. The hungry are those people we see on TV or pass on the streets. We know hunger second-hand; fasting is for most of us a ritual option, not a necessity of life. The poor know hunger as a constant, brutalizing reality that threatens their very dignity as persons.

The Bible speaks often and clearly of the grave dangers of wealth. One great spiritual danger that we, the prosperous of the world, face as we gather for the Eucharist is that we will misunderstand the symbolic portions of food and drink as God's gift to *us,* and nothing more.

As Hellwig observes, the point of this ritualized meal is not to *receive* food, but to *share* food—as the apostle Paul already insisted in his stern admonition to rich Christians in Corinth (1 Cor. 11: 17-22). If the Eucharist does not draw us into Jesus' self-giving for the life of the world, into awareness of the stark human needs around us, then—to borrow Paul's words—"it is not really to eat the Lord's supper" that we have gathered.

"The important and urgent question with which every eucharistic celebration confronts us," Hellwig writes, "is whether we are entitled to discount the earthly, physical, historical dimensions of human suffering which Jesus recalled in explaining the meaning of his mission and of his death, while we claim to be heirs to a 'more spiritual' understanding of our biblical heritage" (p. 19). To say that we do not "live by bread alone" must never distract us from the even more fundamental truth that we do not live without bread (p. 23).

Today's Gospel reading continues a lengthy account from John 6 that begins with a miraculous provision of bread and fish. In contrast to the other Gospels, however, John does not tell us that Jesus gives food out of "compassion" for the multitude (cf. Matt. 14:14, Mark 6:34) or that he "welcomed" them (Luke 9:11). Rather John suggests the crowd has followed Jesus out of unworthy motives—because "they saw the signs that he was doing for the sick" (6:2). Indeed, when on the following day the crowd follows Jesus to the other side of the Sea of Galilee (6:25), he rebukes them for seeking him out, "not because you saw signs, but because you ate your fill of the loaves"—implying that they are less interested in the person to whom these signs point than in filling their stomachs (6:26). Jesus follows this rebuke with a command that decidedly puts their desire for "mere" bread in second place: "Do not work for the food that perishes, but for the food that endures for eternal life, which the Son of Man will give you" (6:27).

Reading this passage at a surface level, we run a dangerous risk. Did Jesus really consider human hunger unimportant? Would Jesus have told the poor and hungry to stop griping and set their minds on "spiritual" realities? Do these words justify our taking a posture of complacency and indifference to human need—alongside those dreadfully misunderstood words at the Last Supper, "you always have the poor with you" (Matt. 26:11; Mark 14:7; John 12:8)? Doesn't Jesus' rebuke suggest that while feeding the poor may be a meritorious act of charity on the part of the rich, it is hardly something to which the poor should feel entitled?

I pose these questions to emphasize important aspects of the context in which today's Gospel will be read and heard. We have all heard attitudes like these expressed in our churches. We all know Christianity's checkered history regarding the plight of the world's poor. And we all know how politically charged these discussions are in our own time. Dom Hélder Câmara, bishop of Recife, Brazil, quipped famously, "When I feed the poor, they call me a saint. When I ask,'why are they poor?' they call me a communist." Before his election as president of Haiti, Jean-Bertrand Aristide declared the global economic system in our day "so corrupt that to ask for a plate of rice and beans every day for every man, woman and child is to preach a revolution. That is the crime of which I stand accused: preaching food for all men and women." Aristide's subsequent removal from the Roman Catholic Salesian priesthood points the issue sharply: Church leaders should confine themselves to speaking of "spiritual" realities. They should encourage the poor to work not "for the food that perishes, but for the food that endures for eternal life."

The observations that follow are intended to guide our reflection on the Gospel and on our responsibility as we dare to interpret it for our congregations.

Bread and Hunger in the Gospel according to John

Hunger is, of course, not a peculiarly modern problem. We know that grinding hunger was a daily reality for thousands of Galilean peasants who had been driven off their land by exorbitant taxation and loan foreclosures. Indeed, as much as three-fourths of the arable land in Judea and Galilee was owned not by the peasants who worked it, but by a tiny but powerful class of urban "capitalists"—the "absentee landlords" of Jesus' parables. In *The Parables as Subversive Speech,* William Herzog III has shown that Jesus spoke many of those parables, not to draw people's attention heavenward, but to reveal the exploitative dynamics of an economy geared to produce poverty and hunger.

AS MUCH AS THREE-FOURTHS OF THE ARABLE LAND IN JUDEA AND GALILEE WAS OWNED NOT BY THE PEASANTS WHO WORKED IT, BUT BY A TINY BUT POWERFUL CLASS OF URBAN "CAPITALISTS"—THE "ABSENTEE LANDLORDS" OF JESUS' PARABLES.

The Gospels give abundant evidence that Jesus drew the poor and disfranchised to himself, in much the same way David attracted the dispossessed of Judea a millennium earlier (see 1 Sam. 22:2). Unlike David, however, who shared meager provisions with his guerrilla band as he led raids on Philistine chieftains, Jesus is reported to have satisfied the hunger around him much more directly and powerfully—by providing bread, abundantly. The Gospels obviously consider this direct action important: they all report the miracle; Matthew and Mark report *two* such events! (See Matt. 14:13-21; 15:32-39; Mark 6:32-44; 8:1-10; Luke 9:10-17; John 6:1-15.) We are also told that such actions immediately stirred up hopes that Jesus would put an end to hunger. The crowd in John's account poses the challenge neatly: "What sign are you going to give us? . . . Our ancestors ate the manna in the wilderness" (6:30-31).

The Gospels also betray considerable ambivalence about this miracle, however. Note that in John's account, strangely enough, the crowd poses their challenge *after* Jesus has satisfied it! He has *already* provided bread, abundantly, so much that his fellow Galileans had concluded, not unreasonably, that he was "the prophet who is to come into the world" (John 6:14). Indeed, they wanted "to come and take him by force to make him king." Yet John presents their response to Jesus' sign as the *wrong* answer, and has Jesus withdraw from them (6:15). On the following day, Jesus responds to their request for a sign not by reminding them they have already seen it, but by impugning their motives for asking. The sense of this rebuke is, "I'm not providing any more bread; and shame on you for expecting it!" For their parts, although Matthew and Luke are content to describe Jesus "welcoming" the crowds out of "compassion," they have both made clear at the very outset of their Gospels that Jesus' messiahship will *not* consist on providing bread on demand—indeed, the expectation is a diabolical temptation! (See Matt. 4:1-4; Luke 4:1-4.)

This ambivalence on the part of the Gospels is, I am convinced, a function of their apologetic need to demonstrate Jesus' identity as Messiah. To the possible challenge that Jesus simply had not made the sort of difference that people expected the Messiah to make, the Gospels are eager to present the feeding miracle(s) as Exhibit A: He fed the hungry. But to the challenge that hunger nevertheless persisted—that, by implication, Jesus had not done anything messianic *lately*—the Gospel writers seem to respond: That is to misunderstand what the Messiah is. Jesus had more important work to do. Furthermore, both Matthew and Luke suggest that Jesus' *disciples* will be carrying on the work Jesus began, feeding the poor themselves (see Matt. 25:31-46; Acts 2:42-45; 4:32-37). And of course, all the Gospels express the firm conviction that human needs such as hunger will be finally satisfied in the world to come, which they expected imminently. If Jesus had not done all that the Messiah was expected to do, he soon would—at his return from heaven.

The Gospel of John's response to these implicit challenges seems, at first glance, to be disparagement. Jesus warns the crowd not to work for "the food that perishes." If this were the Johannine response to the hungry, we would consider it callous. If, on the other hand, this relativizing of "mere" bread and fish is the price Johannine Christianity paid for exalting Jesus as the source of "spiritual" nourishment, we might well consider this cost too great to be sustained.

Several observations qualify that conclusion, however. First, the crowds who have followed Jesus are *not* characterized as seeking material rather than spiritual nourishment. To Jesus' command they readily respond, "What must we do to perform the works of God?" (6:28). To Jesus' announcement that he will provide true bread, they cry, "Sir, give us this bread always." In these respects the Galileans in John 6 nicely parallel the Samaritan woman in John 4, who was ready to receive the water Jesus promised (4:15) and to accept Jesus as a prophet (4:19).

Further, in both instances the Gospel is not so much drawing a contrast between an inferior "literal" or "material" understanding and a superior "spiritual" understanding of Jesus' words, as it is *sustaining a tension between desire and satisfaction.* In John 4 Jesus asks for water, yet never receives any. He promises water to the woman, yet never provides it. The woman readily follows Jesus' redirection of the conversation, speaking of the coming of the prophet or messiah who will bring God's reign. Ultimately the woman leaves, apparently satisfied, *and leaves her water jar behind* (4:28). The effect of the story is to leave the reader thirsty for more! Similarly in John 6, Jesus speaks at length of providing bread that endures; "one may eat of it and not die" (6:50). The crowds readily accept his redirection of the conversation, asking how they may "perform the works of God" (6:29). The Gospel seems less interested in *quelling* appetite than in *arousing* it.

But an appetite for what? We will not understand the Gospel if we do not appreciate the vision of the hard-pressed community that produced it. Raymond Brown's *The Community of the Beloved Disciple* shows how the Johannine community's perception of Jesus had been fatefully shaped by their own historical experience of marginalization and expulsion from their home synagogues and treachery within their own Christian congregations. Despite these trials—or perhaps because of them!—the Johannine community sustained an ethos of unwavering concern for the needy. "How does God's love abide in anyone who has the world's goods and sees a brother or sister in need and yet refuses to help? Little children, let us love, not in word or speech, but in truth and action" (1 John 3:17-18).

As one breathes in the spiritual "hothouse" environment of the Fourth Gospel, with its emphasis on spiritual intimacy with the risen Jesus (see chaps. 13–17), it helps to keep the First Epistle handy, with its clear theological axiom: "Whoever does not love does not know God, for God is love" (4:8). Jesus' sometimes opaque language in the Gospel—about "doing the will of my Father"—is given specificity in the epistle: "The commandment we have from him is this: those who love God must love their brothers and sisters also" (4:21).

Jesus as Bread for the Life of the World

There is little doubt that the unmistakable eucharistic language that predominates in the next three Sundays' readings represents the meditations of the Johannine community on Jesus' significance. Notice that just this eucharistic language is missing from the "Last Supper" scene in this Gospel (where, surprisingly, Jesus does *not* share bread or wine with his disciples). John has transferred the language of Jesus' offering his body and blood as food and drink from the Last Supper scene (chap. 13–17), where the other Gospels lead us to expect it, to the feeding story (chap. 6), where we do not.

One possible theological motive for such a transposition of material is to guard the intimacy of the Eucharist from betrayal. Note that in John 6, Jesus' eucharistic language so "scandalizes" some followers that they fall away (6:66). Note also that John alone removes Judas Iscariot from the Last Supper scene (13:21-30). To the Johannine community, who had suffered schism and possibly betrayal (1 John 2:18-19), it might have seemed more appropriate for Jesus to declare his self-offering for the life of the world away from the treachery of his last night.

Another explanation, however, is that John wanted to connect the language we associate with the Last Supper more closely with the frank satisfaction of hunger in the feeding miracle. The promises made in John 6 are far greater than the words spoken over bread and a cup in the Upper Room. Jesus is "the bread of life," who has "come down from heaven." His flesh is "bread given for the life of the world."

Curiously, John (alone of the Gospels) specifies that the feeding miracle took place around the time of the Passover (6:4)—an association the other Gospels lead us to expect with the Last Supper. While John knows the early Christian perception of Jesus' death as a paschal sacrifice (see John 19:31, 36), he does not present the Last Supper as the Passover meal, nor do Passover themes occur in the farewell discourse (John 13–17). This shift might also represent John's intention to link the language of Jesus' self-offering more clearly with the vital hopes and expectations for deliverance that are appropriate to Passover. Only John links the feeding miracle with the miraculous provision of manna, explicitly citing the Exodus narrative (6:49).

JESUS SPEAKS ALOUD, IN BROAD DAYLIGHT, NOT JUST OF REPLAYING THE EXODUS STORY, BUT OF GIVING HIMSELF "FOR THE LIFE OF THE WORLD"—THAT SAME WORLD THAT CANNOT UNDERSTAND HIM, DOES NOT RECEIVE HIM, AND WILL REJECT HIM AND HIS FRIENDS.

These are surprising moves, especially if the community behind the Gospel was as isolated and marginalized as many scholars suggest. A more natural response to such experience might be to contract spiritually; to try to contain the language of intimacy with Jesus in the close quarters of the Upper Room. Here, instead, Jesus speaks aloud, in broad daylight, not just of replaying the Exodus story, but of giving himself "for the life of the world"—that same world that cannot understand him, does not receive him, and will reject him and his friends.

Something should be said about the objections raised by "the Jews." It is widely recognized today that this is a code phrase in John for "the enemies of Jesus," those who are "from below," "of the world" (8:23), who belong to the devil (8:44). The use of the phrase in John may reflect the tremendous pain and bitterness of the Johannine community toward a wider Jewish community from which they had been expelled—but that hypothesis can only explain, it cannot justify, such stereotypical language. Preachers and teachers should make clear that the phrase represents a theologically loaded stereotype, and must not be taken to characterize Jews in the past or present. "The Jews" are the foils against which Jesus' dramatic self-claims are made.

Note that John's "Jews" can protest that they know Jesus' father and mother (6:41), yet John is not concerned, here or elsewhere, to correct the impression that Joseph and Mary were Jesus' natural parents. (The Gospel prologue, which declares Jesus the incarnation of the eternal Word of God, says nothing of the virgin birth reported in Matthew and Luke.) Similarly the Fourth Gospel's "Jews" can insist that they "know where Jesus is from" (7:27), and that he cannot be the Messiah since he comes from Galilee, not Bethlehem (7:40-42); the narrator never corrects that perception (as we should expect if John knew traditions that Jesus had been born in Bethlehem). Very possibly the Fourth Evangelist did not know the traditions picked up in Matthew and Luke. The Johannine Jesus comes from the Father, simply enough: any other question about his *human* origins is misguided.

Of course, exegetical and historical observations can provide only so much guidance. Much depends on the stance the preacher takes with regard to the characters and realities described in the reading. It would be easy enough to follow some of the Gospel's cues: to speak, for example, of the foolish and misguided perceptions of "the Jews" or of the irrelevance of material want, in order to exalt Jesus as "the bread of life." But as I have explained, I think such decisions would do a grave disservice to the hearers and to people who may stand outside the circle of Christian congregations. I urge the preacher who approaches the "Bread of Life" material in John's Gospel—and those who seek to discern what they hear—to bear one question in mind as they seek to interpret responsibly: Is this, or is this not, "good news for the poor"?

I URGE THE PREACHER WHO APPROACHES THE "BREAD OF LIFE" MATERIAL IN JOHN'S GOSPEL—AND THOSE WHO SEEK TO DISCERN WHAT THEY HEAR—TO BEAR ONE QUESTION IN MIND AS THEY SEEK TO INTERPRET RESPONSIBLY: IS THIS, OR IS THIS NOT, "GOOD NEWS FOR THE POOR"?

FIRST READING

2 SAMUEL 18:5-9, 15, 31-33 (RCL)

"Power tends to corrupt," Lord Acton declared, "and absolute power corrupts absolutely."

Despite a great deal of sentimental preaching concerning David's remorse for his son, the central theme of the passage, and an important theme of the sweeping deuteronomistic epic of David's rise and fall in 1 and 2 Samuel, is the Israelite king's corruption by near-absolute power. Recall that David's adulterous affair with Bathsheba, often the target of homiletical fulminations, was but the beginning of a sordid cover-up that involved the callous murder of Uriah, Bathsheba's husband, and a host of soldiers at the siege of Rabbah (2 Sam. 11). The contrast between Uriah's loyalty to his comrades and his king's indifference to their deaths (2 Sam. 11:25) reveals the depth of David's treachery.

How the mighty have fallen! You may wish to go back and read of the charm and courage of the young David facing the Philistine Goliath (1 Sam. 17); his popularity in Israel (18:6-7), especially among the dispossessed (22:1-2); his unwavering loyalty to his guerrilla band (22:20-23) and his commitment to their common good (22:21-25). Then read again our text and notice the overwhelming self-absorption the tyrant David now displays. Although civil war has sundered David's house—a measure of the catastrophe to which David's "original sin" led—still David is more concerned that his rebel son be treated "gently" than with the survival of the nation, to which his own officers and soldiers are committed. Imagine the popular reaction to his order in v. 5!

The civil war has split the nation as well. Note that "the men of Israel" are ranged against "the servants of David" on the battlefield: the text implies David is arrayed against his own people. We hear that "the slaughter was great," some twenty thousand men killed (v. 7); the report of the battle (vv. 7-8) does not distinguish sides, as if there were any "winners" on this day.

The terrible fate of Absalom (vv. 9-15) means the end of the rebellion against David, interpreted by a Cushite officer as God's vindication of David's cause (v. 31). Yet all David cares about is the fate of his son. The Cushite's response in v. 32 can be read as an ironic rebuke. Does the king regard as nothing the salvation of his kingdom, indeed of his own person?

Although the RCL is simply following a sequence of passages in the deuteronomistic history, these insights into the character of David's kingship may also provide a background for Jesus' avoidance of kingship earlier in the Gospel text (John 6:15).

1 KINGS 19:4-8 (RCL alt./RC)

The lectionary lifts out of its larger context just enough of Elijah's story to provide a connection with the Gospel reading. Just as Elijah was miraculously provided with food in the wilderness, so Jesus miraculously provides the Bread of Life to the crowds. The larger context bears consideration as well, however.

Within the theological history of 1 Kings, Elijah figures prominently as a champion of the Lord against the worship of Baal in early Israel (see chap. 18). It is this opposition that earned Elijah the enmity of the royal house (Ahab and Jezebel, 19:1-3), causing the prophet to despair of his life (19:3-4, 10, 14). At this desperate moment an angel appears, twice (vv. 5, 7), not only to provide food but to rouse Elijah to his work—anointing new leadership for Israel (19:15-18). Here, as in John 6, bread and word are like nourishment (compare John 6:45). God's reassuring word to the prophet is that seven thousand people are preserved "who have not bowed to Baal" (19:18).

An Orthodox icon of the prophet Elijah hangs in my office. The prophet leans upon a great stone to pray, in the familiar posture of Jesus in the Garden of Gethsemane. Elijah is surrounded by the darkness of the cave on Mount Horeb; he receives a piece of bread from a jet-black raven (see 1 Kings 17:4-6). A spiritual symbolism is intended: even in darkness the Spirit of God may minister to us, strengthening us for the struggle.

DEUTERONOMY 8:1-10 (BCP)

Clearly the Episcopal lectionary provides this reading because of the reference to God's miraculous provision of manna in the wilderness (8:3), to which Jesus refers in the Gospel reading (John 6:49). In the temptation scene in the Gospels of Matthew and Luke, Jesus quotes verse 3 in his rebuke of Satan: "One does not live by bread alone, but by every word that comes from the mouth of the Lord." (See comment on the Gospel passage, above.)

There are other, more troubling sub-themes in this passage. The command to conquer and occupy the land of Canaan (8:1) is elsewhere accompanied by the command to destroy the Canaanite population (7:1-2; 20:16-17), a dread legacy in modern histories where conquerors have seen the land before them as "empty." (Note that the promised land is abundant with material blessings, but curiously devoid of inhabitants: vv. 7-9).

Neither should we acquiesce in the image of parental discipline provided by the text. God "humbled you, by letting you hunger, then by feeding you"; thus "as a parent disciplines a child so the Lord your God disciplines you" (vv. 3, 5). We would probably call such parental "discipline" child abuse if we saw it today.

Deuteronomy reveals itself in its last chapters as an extraordinary work of national admonition. Written centuries after the occasion it purports to describe, Deuteronomy projects back into the days of Moses a stringent Yahwism (worship of the Lord) and centralized worship that probably reflect the reforms of Kings Hezekiah and Josiah in the seventh century B.C.E. The "idealized" ideology of covenant and conquest pronounced on the cliffs of Moab probably reflects a seventh-century Israelite "culture war" against "Canaanite" religious and cultural impulses. Israel's founding covenant is presented in terms of an exclusive loyalty to the Lord, and the nation's checkered history is cast as God's punishment for the people's desertion (chap. 28, 29). Note that Moses' speech specifically offers a "second chance" to Israel at a time *after* they have been "scattered" among the nations (30:3-5). Perhaps some of the more troubling aspects of the book may be ascribed to these ancient ideological purposes.

Responsive Reading
PSALM 130 (RCL); 34 (RC/BCP/RCL alt.)

Psalm 130 is a prayer of supplication, expressing an anguish not unlike David's grief over the loss of his son (in the First Reading in the RCL). Psalm 34 includes the line "Taste and see that the Lord is good; happy are those who take refuge in him," long ago appropriated within Christian worship as a eucharistic reference.

Second Reading
EPHESIANS 4:25—5:2 (RCL); 4:(25-29) 30—5:2 (BCP); 4:30—5:2 (RC)

In the early second century, the Roman governor of Bithynia wrote to the emperor Trajan to ask what imperial policy applied in the case of individuals hauled into court on charges of being a Christian. Pliny wrote that he had interrogated the accused, torturing the slaves among them, but had been able to discover nothing more pernicious about them than that they gathered early in the morning to sing hymns, eat a common meal of bread and wine, and "take an oath." Perplexed, the governor reports that this oath—in Latin, *sacramentum*—involved nothing wicked, simply a vow to avoid thievery and violence.

The day's reading from Ephesians brings out this *sacramental* quality of the Christian assembly. The exhortations here are rather unremarkable, simply suggesting the contours of a decent and honest life. They have consequently long been treated in New Testament scholarship under the category "general paraenesis," indicating that they serve to encourage a strong community ethos rather than to avert some specific abuse.

These are specifically *Christian* exhortations. That is, they appeal not to a general sense of "fair play" or "good nature," but to the fundamental change accomplished in initiation into the Christian community. The hearers are reminded that through the Spirit of God they have been "marked with a seal for the day of redemption" (v. 30). There are riches here: not only is loving behavior encouraged within the group, but all falsehood and exploitation in public life is to be renounced (vv. 25, 28) and labor redirected to the needs of the poor (v. 28).

Note that the final sentences, 5:1-2, are often used at the offertory to move us from gathering to hear the Word and pray together (the *synaxis*) into responding to God by presenting our gifts and ourselves (the *anaphora*). Verse 2, describing Christ's loving self-sacrifice as a "fragrant offering" to God, is reminiscent of Paul's language of "spiritual worship" (Rom. 12:2). This passage points to the distinctive and new way of life that we enter in Baptism and to which we rededicate ourselves in the *sacramentum*.

References

Jean-Bertrand Aristide, *In the Parish of the Poor: Writings from Haiti* (Maryknoll: Orbis, 1990).

Raymond Brown, *The Community of the Beloved Disciple* (New York: Paulist, 1979).

Monika K. Hellwig, *The Eucharist and the Hunger of the World*, 2nd ed. (Kansas City: Sheed & Ward, 1992).

William Herzog III, *The Parables as Subversive Speech: Jesus as Pedagogue of the Oppressed* (Louisville: Westminster/John Knox Press, 1994).

TENTH SUNDAY AFTER PENTECOST

AUGUST 20, 2000
TWENTIETH SUNDAY IN ORDINARY TIME / PROPER 15

REVISED COMMON	EPISCOPAL (BCP)	ROMAN CATHOLIC
1 Kings 2:10-12; 3:3-14 or Prov. 9:1-6	Prov. 9:1-6	Prov. 9:1-6
Ps. 111 or 34:9-14	Ps. 147 or 34:9-14	Ps. 34:2-7
Eph. 5:15-20	Eph. 5:15-20	Eph. 5:15-20
John 6:51-58	John 6:53-59	John 6:51-58

WHERE IS WISDOM TO BE FOUND? What does the community that embraces Wisdom look like? Many of us grew up learning that Solomon was the epitome of human wisdom. The biblical view of his reign is more ambivalent, however. Today's texts present a range of interpretations of Wisdom and raise the urgent question: How might the decision to embrace divine Wisdom in our common life change our standing in and toward the world?

FIRST READING

1 KINGS 2:10-12, 3:3-14 (RCL)

The RCL continues a sequence of readings through the deuteronomistic history (Joshua–2 Kings), now dealing with Solomon's rise to power. The lectionary carefully skirts unsavory aspects of the story: Solomon's assassination of potential rivals and opponents, including his half brother Adonijah, and the exile of the high priest Abiathar and his replacement with Zadok (from whom the Sadducees of New Testament times probably derive their name). The lectionary concentrates on God's granting of Solomon's request for wisdom, and the divine assurance that "no one like you shall arise after you" (3:12).

The deuteronomistic history is so called because it recites the history of Israel's kings from the rigid moral perspective laid out in Deuteronomy. Part of that perspective is an insistence that sacrifice to the Lord is to be offered only in Jerusalem (Deut. 12:1-14); thus Solomon is judged for offering incense at the "high places" (3:3). Despite other criticisms—Solomon embraced "foreign women" and their gods (11:1-8)—the history's overall judgment of Solomon is favorable. Solomon "loved the Lord" (3:3); he was rewarded with surpassing wisdom (3:10-14; 4:29-34). Under his rule Israel prospered, reaching its greatest extent (4:20-21), and the Temple of the Lord was built (chap. 5–7). The goal is not to whitewash Solomon's reign, however. His use of forced labor (5:13), continued by his son Rehoboam, provoked rebellion, dividing the kingdom of Israel (see 12:1-19). The deuteronomist is interested in the example of Solomon's aspiration for wisdom as a template for future leaders.

PROVERBS 9:1-6 (BCP/RC)

Wisdom is also the subject of Proverbs 8 and 9, passages in the center of recent debates over the propriety of addressing God as *Sophia*, "Lady Wisdom." It is hard to read either passage as merely metaphorical descriptions of an abstract quality, "wisdom." The Jerusalem and New Jerusalem Bible translations do well to capitalize Wisdom as a proper noun, for Wisdom *speaks, invites, hosts* a banquet, as a person. Indeed, Proverbs is concerned to instruct potential rulers of Israel, particularly men, and to warn them concerning the wiles of the "loose woman" (7:5 and throughout, NRSV). Against the seductions of this "dangerous" character, Proverbs poses the alluring invitation of Wisdom.

Later Jewish writings—the Wisdom of Solomon, the Wisdom of Jesus Ben Sirach (Ecclesiasticus), 1 Enoch—would expand upon the mythic narrative of heavenly Wisdom, who was present at creation and continued to manifest God's glory and enlighten human beings throughout history (Wis. 6–11; Sir. 1:1-10; 24:1-22). Interestingly, early Christian theologians of the Trinity, seeking to demonstrate that the Spirit had been present with God from eternity, regularly relied on just such passages, substituting "Spirit" for "Wisdom."

Wisdom's invitation to a banquet finds echoes in the Bread of Life discourse, which parallels eating the bread of life with being "taught by God" (John 6:45).

RESPONSIVE READING

PSALM 111, or 34:9-14 (RCL); 147, or 34:9-14 (BCP); 34:2-7 (RC)

All the Responsive Readings offer opportunities to connect the themes of God's providing both material security and justice, and spiritual enlightenment and wisdom (see the comments above on the reading from Proverbs).

SECOND READING
EPHESIANS 5:15-20

The "conventional" wisdom of Proverbs and Psalms routinely contrasts the wise life with the foolish life, righteousness with injustice. The paraenesis in Ephesians is more darkly tinged by an eschatological worldview. The contrast between unwise and wise people (5:15) coincides with the contrast between the present "evil days" and the world to come.

Classical literature and painted drinking bowls from ancient Greece give abundant evidence of the drinking and "debauchery" against which Ephesians warned its ancient readers. If the *krater* paintings abound in wild sexual excess, Ephesians is as impressive in its austerity. Roman philosophers liked to rail against the depravity of the art on display in drinking parties as much as our own moralists decry the excesses of Hollywood movies.

THESE READINGS MIGHT PROFITABLY BE USED IN DISCUSSIONS, IN EDUCATIONAL OR OTHER CHURCH FORUMS, AROUND QUESTIONS OF A CONGREGATION'S ETHOS. WHAT DO WE EXPECT OUR SOCIAL LIVES TO LOOK LIKE? WOULD WE LIKE MORE OPPORTUNITIES TO SOCIALIZE TOGETHER IN MORE EXPLICITLY CHRISTIAN CONTEXTS?

The ethos recommended in Ephesians provides something of a criterion for sorting congregations, and perhaps even denominations, today. Some churches quite seriously intend to pull their members away from "worldly" arenas of conviviality (from "happy hours" to dance halls), and into peculiarly *Christian* social gatherings. Other churches adopt a more laissez-faire attitude, seeing much of the surrounding culture as relatively innocuous, and imagining the Christian life as much more engaged in the life of the surrounding world.

Both postures (and the myriad variations between and around them!) can find echoes in Scripture. Ephesians and the Johannine literature clearly describe a more separated ethos, however. These readings might profitably be used in discussions, in educational or other church forums, around questions of a congregation's ethos. What do we expect our social lives to look like? Would we like more opportunities to socialize together in more explicitly Christian contexts?

GOSPEL
JOHN 6:51-58 (RCL/RC); 6:53-59 (BCP)

Today's Gospel reading continues the "Bread of Life" discourse in John 6. See the readings for the ninth Sunday after Pentecost for a more complete discussion of this discourse in the wider context of John's Gospel and early Christianity.

Scholars of the Fourth Gospel are accustomed now to speak of a "two-level drama" within the Gospel narrative. One "level" is the past of Jesus and his followers in Galilee and Judea; the second level—superimposed on the first—is the "present" of the Johannine community that produced the Gospel, and has projected its own historical experience back into the time of Jesus.

The rather jarring juxtaposition of these levels is clear in today's reading. Note first that "the Jews"—again, a stereotyped expression whenever it appears in John—dispute among themselves, just as they "complained" in v. 41. Their "complaining" (or "murmuring," RSV) echoes exactly the blend of ungratefulness and hard-heartedness with which their ancestors turned on Moses in the wilderness (Exod. 16:7; 17:3; Num. throughout). Also, "the Jews" have been *pushed* to this reaction by Jesus' exalted self-claims (compare their initial openness in 6:28, 30, 34). Quite in contrast to the other evangelists, John finds the feeding scene an appropriate occasion to load all the theological opprobrium of the disobedient wilderness generation on the Jews who have rejected his community's christological claims.

Note, too, that Jesus goes far beyond the metaphorical interpretation of Passover bread and wine familiar to us from the Last Supper scene in the other Gospels (Matt. 26:26-29; Mark 14:22-25; Luke 22:15-20). Now he speaks with a shocking literalness of eating his flesh and drinking his blood. To Christians familiar with the eucharistic rite, as the Johannine Christians surely were, this language would have been dramatic; to community outsiders it would have been shocking. The use of this language here may well have been intended precisely to sustain an emotional or psychic distance from outsiders, particularly those whose departure from the Johannine community had precipitated a crisis (see 1 John 2:19).

This drama from a much later time has been put back into the story of Jesus. He speaks, in the synagogue at Capernaum(!), of providing his flesh to eat and his blood to drink. Such striking talk provokes a crisis: some of his disciples, offended, will "turn back" (6:66). We know that pagan observers protested rumored cannibalistic practices among early Christian groups, surely based on literalizing misapprehensions of the language of the Eucharist. The Fourth Gospel almost invites such protests, setting forth its scandalizing claim forcefully: Yes, it *is* the body of Christ that we eat, and his blood that we drink!

The point, of course, is not to invite charges of cannibalism. Since the Reformation this passage has been taken up in heated debates over the precise nature of the real presence of Christ in the Eucharist; but those arguments are foreign to the Gospel's original context. The narrative is not interested in what happens to bread and wine at the Eucharist. The point is rather what has happened to the body of Jesus. Despite the peculiar features of the Passion narrative in John—Jesus' serene control even over his own betrayal (13:21-30) and arrest (18:4-9), his boldness before Pilate (19:11), his Lordly manner even on the cross (19:26-27, 30)—his death remains a very real, bodily death (19:28, 31-34), his wounds tangible even after his resurrection (20:20, 24-29). We know that some Christians in the late first and early second century preferred a spiritual Christ to the mortal Jesus; they may well be the opponents ("antichrists") condemned in 1 John (cf. 2:18-19; 4:1-3).

One reason to stress the physicality of Jesus' body was to strengthen followers who faced persecution and even the threat of death, of which the Johannine Jesus provides clear warning (16:1-4). To "eat the flesh of the Son of Man and drink his blood" (6:53) is to share intimately in his life and work in the world (cf. 15:1-11)—and also his fate.

The Gospel of John begins with a breathtaking hymn to the incarnation of the divine Word, who was present with God "in the beginning." John seems to have drawn on the rich Jewish tradition, described above, which celebrated divine Wisdom as available to those who will receive her, but as frequently rejected. Can we share the Gospel's conviction, that true Wisdom is to be found precisely in following the way of the Crucified One?

ELEVENTH SUNDAY AFTER PENTECOST

August 27, 2000
Twenty-first Sun. in Ordinary Time / Proper 16

Revised Common	Episcopal (BCP)	Roman Catholic
1 Kings 8:(1, 6, 10-11), 22-30, 41-43 or Josh. 24:1-2a, 14-18	Josh. 24:1-2a, 14-25	Josh. 24:1-2a, 15-17, 18b
Ps. 84 or 34:15-22	Ps. 16 or 34:15-22	Ps. 34:2-3, 16-21
Eph. 6:10-20	Eph. 5:21-33	Eph. 5:21-32
John 6:56-69	John 6:60-69	John 6:60-69

"Our hearts are restless," St. Augustine prayed, "until they find their rest in You."

At different times and in different ways, we all experience a hunger for God. In today's Gospel reading, Peter refuses to draw back from Jesus, declaring that he has found in Jesus the source of true nourishment.

In different ways, several of today's readings raise the question: Where do we expect to find God? In sacred buildings? In a "promised land"? In a particular configuration of our home life? How do our expectations of God merely reflect the values of our society and culture?

First Reading

1 KINGS 8:(1, 6, 10-11), 22-30, 41-43 (RCL)

Whereas Saul had reigned over a fragile alliance of tribes, David consolidated his power as king over a nation. He conquered a "neutral" city, the Jebusite Jerusalem, claimed it for his own (2 Sam. 5:6-10), and brought the symbol of the Israelite federation, the Ark of the Covenant, from Kiriath-jearim to Jerusalem in a politically shrewd display of piety ("dancing before the Lord," 2 Sam. 6:1-5). David was prevented from building a temple to the Lord, however. The deuteronomist explains that the Lord considered a temple inappropriate, and offers instead to build *David* a "house," establishing the Davidic dynasty (2 Sam. 7).

The interests of the deuteronomist's theology are evident in today's reading. The Davidic dynasty continues in Jerusalem through David's son Solomon, who installs the Ark of the Covenant in the newly constructed Temple. The author is careful to have Solomon rehearse God's warning that the Davidic line will last only so long as Solomon's descendants observe God's laws (1 Kings 8:25-27; cf. Deut. 17:14-20, which practically reads as a writ of indictment against Solomon!). This theological principle governs the history that extends through the Babylonian conquest of Jerusalem in the sixth century B.C.E. (2 Kings 25). But this theologically construed history also serves as a blueprint for the temple state that would be restored in Jerusalem under Persian sovereignty (see the books of Ezra and Nehemiah).

The author stipulates, in Solomon's sermon inaugurating the Temple, that the Lord's true dwelling is in heaven, not on earth (cf. 1 Kings 8:27, 30). The Lord nevertheless hears the prayers of the people "when they pray toward this place" (8:30). Thus the centrality of Jerusalem, in Solomon's day and in the days of the Persian restoration, is guaranteed.

JOSHUA 24:1-2a, 14-25 (RCL alt./BCP); 24:1-2a, 15-17, 18b (RC)

The "covenant renewal" ceremony has an ancient structure to it. Notice, however, its place within the larger structure of the deuteronomistic history that extends through 2 Kings; a narrative written with perfect theological hindsight, after the establishment, division, and destruction of the kingdom of Israel.

Joshua sets before the people the starkest choice: serve the Lord exclusively, or reject the Lord and accept the gods of the Amorites (i.e., the Canaanites). The people swear loyalty to the Lord, remembering their deliverance from slavery in Egypt (vv. 16-18). So much is the reading in the RC lectionary.

SOME SCHOLARS HOLD THAT JOSHUA 24:18 ("THE LORD . . . DROVE OUT THE AMORITES") BETRAYS THEOLOGICAL EXAGGERATION: AFTER ALL, IF THE AMORITES/CANAANITES HAD INDEED BEEN COMPLETELY REMOVED FROM THE LAND, JOSHUA'S DIRE WARNINGS WOULD HARDLY BE NECESSARY!

The fuller reading in the BCP includes two further aspects of the story left out of the RC selection. First, the people add that the Lord has driven out "all the peoples, the Amorites who lived in the land" (v. 18). This theme has become a considerable theological embarrassment to readers sensitized to the horrors of centuries of conquest and "ethnic cleansing." Some scholars hold that the verse also betrays theological exaggeration: After all, if the Amorites/Canaanites had indeed been completely removed from the land, Joshua's dire warnings would hardly be necessary! We may be reading a later generation's wishful thinking: "if only Israel *had* escaped the seductive influences of Canaanite culture. . . ."

The BCP reading also includes Joshua's even more dire warning of God's judgment should the people disobey (v. 19), echoing Moses' predictions in the last chapters of Deuteronomy. Here again the purposes of a later generation, to explain the catastrophic history of the sixth-century Babylonian conquest, are transparent—though perhaps not as directly edifying to a modern congregation.

Responsive Reading

PSALM 84 (RCL); 16 (BCP); or 34:15-22 (RCL alt./BCP alt.); 34:2-3, 16-21 (RC)

Psalm 84 praises the God who has established Zion, and goes appropriately with the First Reading from 1 Kings in the RCL. Psalm 34 assures the faithful of God's attentive care for the righteous.

Second Reading

EPHESIANS 6:10-20 (RCL)

Facing condemnation in ancient Athens, Socrates compared his work as a philosopher to a military sentinel charged with holding his position at any cost. In the first century C.E., it was common enough among Cynics and Christians alike to speak of self-discipline in the language of preparation for combat (cf. Rom. 6:12-14). As with the widespread appeal to metaphors from athletic training, or *askesis*—the origin of our word "asceticism"—I think what attracts us in the metaphor is the sense of special alertness, the focused awareness and readiness for action. Clearly, the Christian life is not envisioned here as something that mysteriously "just happens."

Ours is no longer a culture imbued with a "work ethic" as it once was. A popular bumper sticker even urges us to "Commit *random* acts of kindness and *senseless* beauty"—as if *intentional, sustained* efforts to do good are somehow too exhausting to contemplate! Ephesians suggests, however, that the moral life is nothing less than spiritual warfare against what the Episcopal *Book of Common Prayer* calls "the evil forces that corrupt and destroy the creatures of this world." What can we do to empower one another for this struggle?

EPHESIANS 5:21-33 (BCP/RC)

Ernst Käsemann wrote that "the history of Pauline interpretation is the history of the apostle's ecclesiastical domestication." I share the view of a number of modern scholars that Ephesians is an early step down the path to the apostle's domestication by a later, more conservative generation of Christians.

Whether or not the letter is regarded as genuine, the "household code" provided in the BCP and RC lectionaries will doubtless provoke immediate discomfort for many readers, and may well cause lectors to balk! (The RCL simply avoids these problems by moving on to a later passage in the letter.) This passage provides the preacher any number of ways to offend *someone*. On the other hand, one isn't likely to avoid offense by simply ignoring the passage in a homily. If it's read, it should be addressed.

The immediate problem, of course, is that the equanimity of the opening line—"be subject to one another"—is not sustained through the passage. What follows are undeniably lopsided exhortations: wives are to "be subject" to their husbands, husbands are to "love" their wives. While the example of Christ's love for the church (vv. 25-27) clearly marks the love commanded of husbands as a serious and costly love, it may reasonably be objected that women are just as capable of such self-giving love, and that the exhortation to "be subject" instead offers insult by implying inequality.

No less offensive for many is the ringing endorsement of Christian slaveholding in the verses that follow (6:5-9), an integral part of the "household code" that has been omitted from all three lectionaries. While one can certainly applaud the decision not to read those later verses in worship, it would be inappropriate to pretend they do not exist, and have not made their own contribution to a woeful history.

The RC lectionary also drops v. 33, ending the reading on the christological note in v. 32: "This is a great mystery, and I am applying it to Christ and the church." This reading implies that the primary point of the passage is the relation of Christ and the church, understood symbolically as that of bridegroom and bride, *rather than* the actual relations of husbands and wives in the Christian community. This "bridegroom" christology has served a key role in official Roman Catholic teaching on the question of women's ordination. It bears notice, however, that in the wider context the author of Ephesians has nothing to say about the relation of Christ to the church. Verse 32 appears rather to be an attempt to make his subordinationist appeal more palatable.

Interpreters have tried to soften the offense of that appeal in several ways. Some suggest that the subordinationist ethic was "necessary" to ensure the church's survival in a hostile climate. Critics have observed that more radical versions of Christianity survived nonetheless, without compromising their understanding of Christian freedom. Some have argued that this passage is a "natural" and appropriate expression of Christian responsibility; but then one should have to ask whether Paul's own more egalitarian ethic (see Gal. 3:28) was any less responsible. Decades ago, John Howard Yoder suggested the Christian household codes expressed a "revolutionary subordination." By encouraging those who occupied the inferior position in social relationships to subordinate themselves willingly, Yoder argued, these codes undercut the coercive balance of power in those relationships and thus generated a nonviolent social "revolution" in Roman society. Notice, however, that this passage and its parallels only address the Christian household. No transformation of wider society is imagined.

I find all of these attempts unsatisfactory. Neither do I think a responsible homilist should feel obligated to "find some good" in such a subordinationist text. It may well be—as feminist theologians have capably argued—that the genuine mutuality of Christian love will require a greater renunciation of privilege of the powerful than this text seems to imagine.

Gospel

JOHN 6:56-69 (RCL); 6:60-69 (BCP/RC)

The "Bread of Life" discourse reaches its climax in this week's reading. The clearly eucharistic themes put into Jesus' mouth have had their inevitable effect within the logic of the Fourth Gospel. "The Jews," initially open to Jesus—calling him "Rabbi" (6:25), asking what they must do to perform the works of God (6:28), asking him to provide the heavenly bread of which he speaks (6:34)—have been put off by Jesus' increasingly provocative claim that "the bread that I will give for the life of the world is my flesh" (6:51). They began to complain (6:41), and to dispute among themselves regarding what appears to them Jesus' nonsensical language (6:52). Curiously, however, we hear no more of their reaction—they seem to fade from the scene—until 7:1, when we learn that the Jews "were looking for an opportunity to kill him."

The narrative shifts to the circle of Jesus' disciples, some of whom "complain" as did the Jews in v. 41. Scandalized by his talk of eating his flesh and drinking his blood, these disciples fall away (v. 66). Again, we should probably see here an oblique reference to Christians in the author's own time, who have withdrawn from the Johannine community (cf. 1 John 2:18-19). Over against these scandalized disciples John poses Peter's almost plaintive cry, "Lord, to whom can we go? You have the words of eternal life" (6:68). This is John's version of the scene the other Gospels place at Caesarea Philippi (Matt. 16:13-20, Mark 8:27-30, Luke 9:18-21).

For John, the confession that Jesus is Christ requires the willingness to "eat the flesh of the Son of Man and drink his blood" (6:53). As I suggested earlier, I do not think John is simply trying to advance a "realistic" view of the Eucharist, to insists that the bread "really is" the body of Jesus. Note Jesus' reply to the scandalized disciples: "What if you were to see the Son of Man ascending to where he was before?" (6:62). These disciples seem as unable to accept Jesus' ascension to heaven as they are to contemplate the grotesque meal of which he speaks.

Despite the apparent dualism of v. 63—"it is the spirit that gives life; the flesh is useless"—the heart of Johannine faith is not any flesh-withdrawn "spirituality." The Gospel declares that Jesus has been bodily raised from the dead (20:20, 27), indeed, that he is "the resurrection and the life" (11:25). A more "spiritual" Christianity sought to understand the resurrection as the survival of Jesus' spiritual essence, or as a metaphor for enlightenment; John will have none of it (cf. 1 John 4:2-3). These are ways of avoiding the dread reality of death. But Jesus has not escaped death, he has overcome it. Therefore he can promise that "the one who eats this bread," who feeds on Christ, "will live forever."

JESUS HAS NOT ESCAPED DEATH, HE HAS OVERCOME IT. THEREFORE HE CAN PROMISE THAT "THE ONE WHO EATS THIS BREAD," WHO FEEDS ON CHRIST, "WILL LIVE FOREVER."

In light of the great hunger of our world—for justice, for dignity, for real bread—we dare not let the Gospel call us only to a particular theory regarding the nature of the bread and wine we share in our eucharistic rituals! A truly "realistic" theology of the Eucharist, the realism John's Gospel contemplates as Jesus offers himself for the life of the world (6:51), is an *eschatological* realism, based upon a shared memory of what God has done bodily in Jesus and upon a shared hope for what God will do in our mortal bodies.

We should not hear Peter's confession of faith as an expression of satisfaction, as if "you have the words of eternal life" were but another way of saying, "Lord, you feed us *spiritually*, and that's enough." If Jesus truly offers himself "for the life of the world," if he offers the Bread that shall end our hunger, then to say with Peter, "To whom shall we go?" is to refuse any spiritual appetite suppressant. To share in Peter's confession is to allow ourselves to feel and know the hunger of our world. "Blessed are they who hunger and thirst for righteousness," Jesus said, "for they shall be filled" (Matt. 5:6).

References on Ephesians

J. Christiaan Beker, *Heirs of Paul: Paul's Legacy in the New Testament* (Minneapolis: Fortress, 1991).

Ernst Käsemann, *Perspectives on Paul*, trans. Margaret Kohl (Philadelphia: Fortress, 1971).

John Howard Yoder, *The Politics of Jesus* (Grand Rapids: Eerdmans, 1972).

TWELFTH SUNDAY AFTER PENTECOST

September 3, 2000
Twenty-second Sunday in Ordinary Time
Proper 17

Revised Common	Episcopal (BCP)	Roman Catholic
Song of Sol. 2:8-13 or Deut. 4:1-2, 6-9	Deut. 4:1-9	Deut. 4:1-2, 6-8
Ps. 45:1-2, 6-9 or 15	Ps. 15	Ps. 15:2-5
James 1:17-27	Eph. 6:10-20	James 1:17-18, 21b-22, 27
Mark 7:1-8, 14-15, 21-23	Mark 7:1-8, 14-15, 21-23	Mark 7:1-8, 14-15, 21-23

Today's lectionary leaves the "Bread of Life" discourse in John's Gospel and resumes a sequence of readings in Mark. The Gospel reading presents Christians with immediate interpretive challenges, for it is much too easy simply to distance ourselves from aspects of Jewish observance described in the text that may seem foreign or alien to us.

Can we set aside our presumptions—especially regarding a place of privilege before God—and hear what God wants to say to us, deep in our hearts?

Gospel

MARK 7:1-8, 14-15, 21-23

I must confess to some unease whenever I read Mark's Gospel. For the last century and a half, a majority of New Testament scholars have held that Mark's was probably the first Gospel written, that indeed "Mark" may have *invented* the Gospel form. This has often led to the tacit assumption—even when interpreters say they know better—that Mark's Gospel is "closest" to Jesus and therefore presents Jesus more accurately than his successors, Matthew and Luke.

Scenes like our reading today give me doubts that Mark is somehow "purer" than the other Synoptic Gospels, or somehow more innocent of a theological agenda. In the following comments I seek only to sketch an interpretive landscape on which the homilist may wish to maneuver.

The scene in Mark 7 is rather common in the Gospels: Jewish opponents, in this case Pharisees, accuse Jesus of violating a matter of ceremonial observance, and Jesus' response effectively sets his disciples at some distance from the standards of Jewish practice. Here the immediate issue is hand-washing before meals—a common enough practice for us, on hygienic grounds, but for the Pharisees of the first century C.E., a matter of *ceremonial* observance. Jacob Neusner has persuaded many interpreters that the Pharisees were concerned to practice, at private meals *outside* the Temple, the level of ceremonial purity that the Torah commanded for priests on duty *within* the Temple. Jesus' disciples do not observe this distinctly Pharisaic practice, which (interestingly) surprises the Pharisees.

This isn't enough for Mark, however, who proceeds (in an editorial comment, which the NRSV puts in parentheses) to explain that a lot of fussiness regarding "the washing of cups, pots, and bronze kettles" is characteristic of the Pharisees, "*and all the Jews.*" This astonishingly superficial and unsympathetic characterization of the religion of Israel can only have been written by a gentile for other gentiles—and these, gentiles who know Jews only from a distance. The Gospel of Mark shows itself here to be light-years removed from the cultural sympathies of Jesus and his followers.

For Mark, in fact, this story is remembered as the time when Jesus relieved his disciples of responsibility for observing the kosher laws. Read vv. 17-20, verses unfortunately excised from the lectionary reading. Here—and only in Mark—Jesus *takes his disciples indoors* to explain to them that food laws are quite irrelevant: as Mark summarizes the teaching, Jesus "declared all foods clean" (v. 19).

This was undoubtedly good news to gentile readers of Mark's Gospel. I imagine it would have baffled Luke, however, who did not know this was Jesus' intent (this whole scene is dramatically curtailed in Luke 11:37-41), and who went to a great deal of trouble in Acts to explain that it took a heavenly vision given to Peter (Acts 10) and an "apostolic council" (Acts 15) to determine what food laws gentile Christians should observe. And how much shorter Paul's letter to the Romans might have been if, instead of the extended argument of chapters 14–15, he could simply have said, "but Jesus declared all foods clean"!

My point is that we are reading the *gentile-Christian* perspective of an evangelist living one or two generations after the events he purports to narrate, and at considerable cultural distance from them. However important it was for Jesus to attack the "human tradition" of the Pharisees (vv. 6–8—a point even clearer in vv. 9-13, also excised from today's reading), Mark seizes the moment to reassure his audience that they need not trouble themselves with what are to them the more perplexing aspects of Torah observance. I think it would be irresponsible and self-serving for a thoroughly gentile church today to let the caricature of Judaism presented here pass without comment, or to use the occasion simply to congratulate ourselves on our good sense in not keeping kosher!

One of the greatest risks confronting the Christian reader of Mark is to point fingers at "those Jews," who couldn't or wouldn't understand the clear moral teachings of Jesus! Indeed, it's easy enough for us to think we see the moral "speck" in the eyes of others (Matt. 7:1-5). In fact, however, Jesus' words in Mark are no new teaching. The notions that obedience to God must come from the heart, and that the disobedient heart is the source of all wicked actions that take us far from God, are at the core of the Old Testament prophets (cf. Jer. 31:31-34). The gospel in Jesus' words for us is that God wants our heartfelt response, our full-hearted obedience.

A final word about the "human heart" from which, Jesus says, all evil things proceed. Jesus is hardly outlining what we might call a complete theological anthropology here. More pointedly, there is no basis here for speaking of the human heart as some intractable, mysterious, lumpen source of evil. I have in mind the way we sometimes retreat from hard public choices when faced by a great, perplexing evil and wearily shrug, "it's human nature." The "heart" is also a *constructed* thing. We are as much a product of our social environments as we are self-aware, creative beings. Recall that Jesus warned that "the eye is the lamp of the body" (Matt. 6:22-23, Luke 11:34-36). What we "take in" does in fact shape the heart!

First Reading
SONG OF SOLOMON 2:8-13 (RCL)

The RCL provides an interesting choice for both the First Reading and the Responsive Reading. Read together, this text from the love poetry of the Song of Solomon, and the hymn to the king in Psalm 45:1-2, 6-9, abound in sensuous imagery—a tone quite distinct from the moral stridency of Deuteronomy and Psalm 15.

The ancient and medieval church read the amorous poetry of the Song of Solomon as an allegory for Christ's love for the Church. This may have been an urgent expedient when mere erotic desire was held in deep suspicion, but few Christian interpreters today will persist in this ancient habit. Still, the text (and its ancient use by Christian homilists) provides a suitable occasion for talking seriously, if not somberly, about the experience of the love of Christ.

In classical Hinduism, *bhakti* describes the "way of devotion" or "way of love," one of the great traditional ways to God (alongside meditative contemplation and ritual action). The ardent love of Lord Krishna for his devotees, expressed poetically in the *Bhagavad Gita* (the "Hymn of the Lord"), is the supreme example of this religious sensibility. Interestingly, it is just this devotional strand of Hinduism that is most open to Christianity, perceiving the gospel of Christ as a clear expression of the way to God through the heart.

This "erotic" approach to Christ is familiar enough to us through the great mystics of the Christian tradition: prophets of the burning Love of Christ, like John of the Cross or Teresa of Avila. Better known to many of us are old hymns such as "Jesus, Lover of my Soul"; "My Jesus, I Love Thee"; "My Song Is Love Unknown"; or George Herbert's beautiful poem "The Call," set to music as a eucharistic hymn:

> Come, my Joy, my Love, my Heart;
> Such a Joy as none can move;
> Such a Love as none can part;
> Such a Heart as joys in love.

Christ's beguiling serenade to the soul may not have been the intent of the author of the Song of Solomon, but it is nevertheless a reality that has attracted great and beautiful expressions of art, music, poetry. If we are reticent to speak of that great love in so ardent terms—*why*?

DEUTERONOMY 4:1-9 (BCP); 4:1-2, 6-9 (RCL alt.); 4:1-2, 6-8 (RC)

Deuteronomy presents itself as an extended sermon, delivered by Moses to the people Israel on the hills of Moab, looking across the Jordan River valley into the land of Canaan. While the book derives its Greek name, literally "second law," from the repetition of commandments occurring in earlier books of Torah, the heart of the book is the urgent exhortation with which Moses calls upon the people not just to hear, but to *obey* the commandments in order to prosper their lives in the land. Today's reading marks the beginning of that exhortation.

THE TWIN MOTIFS OF EXTERMINATION AND SETTLEMENT OF AN "EMPTY LAND" HAVE PLAYED A HORRIFIC ROLE IN THE HISTORY OF NORTH AMERICA, AND ELSEWHERE.

Only the BCP lectionary includes the whole of verses 1-9; the RCL and RC have dropped vv. 3-5, which refer to the Lord's destruction of those Israelites who worshiped the "Baal of Peor" (Num. 25:1-9). These verses may seem objectionable because they portray a destructive side of God. They also are part of a larger theological theme in Deuteronomy, according to which Israel must be obedient to God by exterminating the idolatrous people of Canaan and settling the "empty" land. The twin motifs of extermination and settlement of an "empty land" have played a horrific role in the history of North America, and elsewhere.

That sobering fact bears continued reflection. Many North American congregants will hear, however subliminally, references to their own nation in the words of the text: "Surely this great nation is a wise and discerning people!" and "What other great nation has a god so near to it?"

Since the Mayflower Compact was signed off the shore of New England, notions of being a peculiar covenant people have saturated American political culture. At times, these notions have convinced people that God has given the United States a privileged role in world history as a chosen instrument of the divine will. At other times, other people have concluded that American society must be shaped into a sanctified community, a "city on a hill" evoking praise to God. The challenge for the Christian community, and (more immediately) for the homilist, is to discern at what point such beliefs become idolatrous.

Years ago I asked a young Christian woman from Cambodia to tell me what she considered the most important text in the Bible. She immediately replied that she treasured the book of Deuteronomy, since—as radio broadcasts by American evangelist Pat Robertson had shown her—its logic explained why her largely non-Christian nation had been "destroyed" during the Vietnam War.

Deuteronomy is a theologically loaded text, intertwining theocratic political theory with a theological reading of history as God's judgment realized against "the wicked." One can, of course, simply preach from the text on the importance of obedience to God; but the text says much more—and congregants may *hear* much more. Some careful treatment of what a "nation under God" might mean, and what it might *not* mean, may be appropriate.

Responsive Reading

PSALM 45:1-2, 6-9 (RCL)

As mentioned above, the RCL provides a choice in the Responsive Reading as well as the First Reading. The ardent hymn to the anointed king in Psalm 45, praising the *Messiah's* justice in richly sensuous imagery, is a fitting accompaniment to the reading from the Song of Solomon.

PSALM 15 (RCL alt./BCP/RC)

This psalm, with its emphases on blameless conduct, honesty in speech, and innocence in public behavior and commerce, is appropriate commentary on Jesus' words in today's Gospel about "what comes out of the human heart."

Second Reading

JAMES 1:17-27 (RCL); 1:17-18, 21b-22, 27 (RC)

The Letter of James is a piece of early Christian paraenesis. That does not mean that the *general* nature of the epistle's exhortations originally had no relation to a flesh-and-blood community. To the contrary: the cumulative effect of such general exhortations is to shape a community's way of feeling and behaving, in such a way that members can address specific questions and issues with a strong sense of their own identity and character. Significantly, today's passage addresses those to whom God "gave . . . birth by the word of truth" (1:18). Some scholars read the epistle as an instruction addressed to the newly baptized.

While James often suffers in comparison with the theological grandeur of Paul's letters—recall Luther's damningly faint praise, "epistle of straw"—it is thoroughly Christian. Jesus is the anchor and goal of the life described here (2:1; 5:7-11). This passage shows well the epistle's eminent practicality, and its debt to Israel's prophets, who insisted that true "religion" is expressed in basic justice.

It bears notice that the care for "orphans and widows in their distress" was a rather distinctive concern of Jewish communities in the Greco-Roman world, where orphans were more likely fodder for the slave market, and widows suffered the stripping of any privilege and status their husbands might have enjoyed. Indeed, pagan sources sometimes comment—with considerable perplexity—on the peculiar penchant of the Jews to care even for those without obvious social standing.

Two particular interests of the epistle have been dropped from the RCL reading. When I was a child, James' dire warnings about the dangers of unchecked speech (vv. 19-21a; 3:1-12) were used to keep us quiet during long midweek services. While sins of speech are prominent in the Bible—far more, for example, than the sexual sins that preoccupy our culture—they are especially a concern to James. We vainly imagine that while sticks and stones may break our bones, mere "words can never hurt" us; but James is as aware as any modern communication theorist about the real damage "mere" conversation can do when it systematically excludes, denigrates, and disfranchises our brothers and sisters.

Just as Jesus' words in the Gospel focus attention on what "comes out" of us, our actions, as the true measure of our "purity," so James is concerned that "hearing" find expression in "doing," and that true religion be manifest in concern for others. In what ways do we prefer to offer God our own definitions of "true religion"?

EPHESIANS 6:10-20 (BCP)

(See last week's discussion of this text, p. 149.)

REFERENCES

On the Pharisees in the first century, Jacob Neusner's prolific work has been widely influential, but has been challenged—in my view convincingly—by E. P. Sanders and Anthony Saldarini, among others. Saldarini's article on the Pharisees in the *Anchor Bible Dictionary*, vol. 5 (New York: Doubleday, 1993) 289-303, is instructive. The critical view of Mark's Gospel adopted here owes much to Paula Fredriksen's discussion in *From Jesus to Christ: The Origin of the New Testament Images of Jesus* (New Haven: Yale University Press, 1988) 117-85.

THIRTEENTH SUNDAY AFTER PENTECOST

September 10, 2000
Twenty-Third Sunday in Ordinary Time
Proper 18

Revised Common	Episcopal (BCP)	Roman Catholic
Prov. 22:1-2, 8-9, 22-23 or Isa. 35:4-7a	Isa. 35:4-7a	Isa. 35:4-7a
Ps. 125 or 146	Ps. 146 or 146:4-9	Ps. 146:7-10
James 2:1-10 (11-13) 14-17	James 1:17-27	James 2:1-5
Mark 7:24-37	Mark 7:31-37	Mark 7:31-37

There is probably no single phrase in the Christian vocabulary that annoys more people than the question "Are you saved?"

Today's readings offer an opportunity to explore various dimensions of salvation: healing of the body, healing of the heart, healing of social relations. In what ways is God's multiform salvation at work in and around us? How can we cooperate in the Spirit's saving energies?

First Reading
PROVERBS 22:1-2, 8-9, 22-23

Verses 8-9, attributed traditionally to Solomon, describe the same well-ordered moral universe hymned in Psalm 37, traditionally ascribed to his father David. Psalm 37:25 announces, "I have been young, and now am old, yet I have not seen the righteous forsaken or their children begging bread."

Though not as uplifting, I have always found the observations of Ecclesiastes much more realistic. Consider Ecclesiastes 7:15: "In my vain life I have seen everything: there are righteous people who perish in their righteousness, and there are wicked people who prolong their life in their evildoing."

The point is not to consider which view is more accurate, as if this were a question of the glass being half-full or half-empty. (We are talking about the poor and hungry, not water glasses.) The point is that nothing must hinder our deliberate efforts to lift up and sustain the lives of the poor. This is one of the clearest messages of the Torah. Proverbs admonishes, "Do not rob the poor because they are poor, or crush the afflicted at the gate" (v. 22), referring to the stout fortified entryway to the ancient Israelite city where the elders would gather to adjudicate rival claims and set wrongs right. We could simply translate, "do not injure the poor or afflicted in court or by law." Why not? Because, says Proverbs, they have one very aggressive legal counsel—the Lord, who "pleads their cause and despoils of life those who despoil them" (v. 23).

ISAIAH 35:4-7a (RCL alt./RC/BCP)

This is yet another of the prophet's marvelous, exuberant outcries, heralding the salvation of God as the miraculous recovery of sight, hearing, movement, speech: the bountiful providence of cool water. It is used today to anticipate the miraculous healing of a deaf man in the Gospel. We should pause to notice, however, that neither Isaiah nor any other biblical writer would have regarded these stirring announcements of God's salvation as "delivered in full" in the ministry of Jesus. Isaiah looks to a salvation of the people, indeed, of all the nations, and for that we still pray.

Responsive Reading

PSALM 125 or 146 (RCL); 146, or 146:4-9 (BCP); 146: 7-10 (RC)

Psalm 125 speaks of God's moral recompense to the righteous and the wicked (see the comments above on Prov. 22). Psalm 146 praises the Lord as the champion of the poor, who brings justice for the oppressed, food for the hungry, healing for the blind, defense for the widows and orphans. This language finds strong echoes in James and anticipates the messianic "sign" of Jesus' activity in the Gospel.

Second Reading

JAMES 2:1-10 (11-13) 14-17 (RCL); 2:1-5 (RC)

Christians speak readily of God's "impartiality" toward rich and poor alike. That theme always has a sharp edge in the Bible, however, for it marks the surprising insistence that—contrary to society's standards—God does *not* prefer the interests and stakes of the rich, but always defends the poor against encroachment upon their lives.

In recent decades, the theologies of liberation emerging from oppressed communities throughout the world have insisted that just this God of the poor is the true God of the Bible. This God of the Bible stands in stark contrast to the "God of the status quo," whom those of us who enjoy the vast proportion of the earth's material blessings find much more reassuring.

Liberation theologies have been held in considerable suspicion and are often repudiated for offering a "partial God" in place of a presumed divine impartiality. The liberation theologians seem, at least, to have the Letter to James squarely on their side. (How unfortunate that the RC lectionary this week, and the BCP next week, drop the indictment in vv. 6-7—"Is it not the rich who oppress you? Is it not they who drag you into court?" As if this voice in Scripture could be so easily muffled!)

The great spiritual challenge to a homilist in any economically advantaged church that enjoys the comparative luxuries of central air conditioning and indoor plumbing—let alone a diversified stock portfolio—is to let the words on the page have their say. Can we resist finding some spiritual evasion to the harsh words we read here?

The Roman Catholic bishops in the United States have declared that "work for social justice is a constitutive element of the proclamation of the Gospel." This suggests that *any* evasion of the clear message of James is an evasion of the Gospel.

The RC lectionary selection ends with v. 5, declaring that God has "chosen the poor in the world to be rich in faith." Such a conclusion too readily becomes a romanticization of the poor—as if being congratulated for their faith is a substitute for having their real needs met (cf. vv. 14-17). Just this once, defy the lectionary. Read through verse 17. Urge your congregation to take the whole passage seriously. See what might happen!

JAMES 1:17-27 (BCP)

(See last week, p. 158.)

GOSPEL

MARK 7:24-37 (RCL); 7:31-37 (BCP/RC)

The first part of the reading, dropped by the BCP and RC lectionaries, tells of Jesus trying to escape notice by entering pagan territory, in the region of the coastal city of Tyre. It doesn't work—as so often in Mark's Gospel. The much-discussed "messianic secret" in Mark refers to a set of peculiar narrative motifs, including Jesus' paradoxically growing fame and celebrity despite his efforts to remain hidden or private and the relative success of his mission in gentile territory, compared to the growing opposition he faces in Judea and Galilee.

The Syrophoenician woman approaches Jesus, we presume, as a wonder-worker; nothing is said of her "faith" regarding Jesus. We can marvel at her boldness in pressing her request even after Jesus tries to parry it—and with an ethnic insult that numbers her and her afflicted daughter among "the dogs"!

This is not an attractive side of Jesus. Interpreters have sought to soften the picture, either by suggesting that Jesus is "testing" the woman to prove her faith, or that the woman and Jesus are both consciously engaged in a sort of verbal joust. The text supports neither supposition. The ironic wink is neither in Jesus' eye, nor the woman's; it is Mark who winks at the reader. *Of course* the "food" *belongs* to Israel—"the children" in Jesus' parabolic reply. But Israel is (wink) undeserving, as the plot of the Gospel will show. So Jesus' miraculous gifts may as well be dispersed among the pagans—as in the story that follows.

WE CAN MARVEL AT THE SYROPHOENICIAN WOMAN'S BOLDNESS IN PRESSING HER REQUEST EVEN AFTER JESUS TRIES TO PARRY IT—AND WITH AN ETHNIC INSULT THAT NUMBERS HER AND HER AFFLICTED DAUGHTER AMONG "THE DOGS"!

All three lectionaries include the healing of the deaf man, in the region of the Decapolis—again, significantly, pagan territory. As in the preceding story, nothing is said of the man's faith. Jesus works his wonder (using Aramaic in v. 34, as in 5:41). He orders the crowd to silence, but "the more he ordered them, the more zealously they proclaimed it" (7:35-6). Among the pagans Jesus receives rave reviews—"he has done everything well" (v. 37)—in stark contrast to the continued opposition of the Pharisees (7:1-5; again in 8:11). One way of understanding the so-called "messianic secret" in Mark, I submit, is to recognize that Jesus fairly consistently is recognized and hailed as a wonder-worker by people not his own; at the same time, Jews, even his own disciples, remain "hard of heart" (8:17-21). This pattern may well be the "perfect hindsight" of the (gentile-Christian) evangelist, rather than an accurate journal of events in Jesus' own day.

Both stories, however, undoubtedly give us an accurate glimpse of the popular excitement surrounding this Galilean wonder-worker. Indeed, Mark goes beyond the traditional expectations of the prophets (see Isa. 37) in portraying Jesus' miraculous activity, and especially his casting out of demons, as signs of his messianic identity. (Demon possession seems to have arisen in the Hellenistic period as an affliction perceived, diagnosed, and cured by itinerant wonder-workers—well after the composition of the Hebrew Bible.) The connection probably goes back to Jesus himself, who (according to Mark 3:22-27) defended his exorcism campaign as part of a much larger effort to confront Satan, the "strong man" guarding the "house" of the world, as God's champion (3:22-27).

The Gospels share a predominantly apologetic concern: they aim to focus attention on the extraordinary signs accompanying Jesus to indicate his identity as Messiah. The challenge to modern readers and hearers is related, yet distinct: to identify where in our own world destructive powers distort and deform human lives, and where God's liberating power is being unleashed.

FOURTEENTH SUNDAY AFTER PENTECOST

September 17, 2000
Twenty-fourth Sunday in Ordinary Time
Proper 19

Revised Common	Episcopal (BCP)	Roman Catholic
Prov. 1:20-33 or Isa. 50:4-9a	Isa. 50:4-9	Isa. 50:5-9a
Ps. 19 or 116:1-8	Ps. 116 or 116:1-8	Ps. 116:1-6, 8-9
James 3:1-12	James 2:1-5, 8-10, 14-18	James 2:14-18
Mark 8:27-38	Mark 8:27-38 or 9:14-29	Mark 8:27-35

"There is one hope in God's call to us." So declares the author of Ephesians. But how do we discern God's call? Today's readings suggest that responding to God may be a difficult, costly process, perhaps evident only in the hope stirred up in us.

First Reading

PROVERBS 1:20-33 (RCL)

As we have already seen (comments on Prov. 9:1-6 for the tenth Sunday after Pentecost, p. 143), the figure of Wisdom has a long and rich history in Jewish and Christian tradition. Especially striking in today's reading is the *judgment and rebuke* that Wisdom pronounces upon the "simple ones," the "scoffers" (v. 22) who reject her counsel. Here Wisdom speaks in a tone reminiscent of the books of the prophets, where the Word of God is judgment against those who refuse to obey. Later Christian theology would conflate these aspects of Wisdom and Word in the developing theology of the Holy Spirit, now understood (in the words of the Nicene Creed) as the One "who has spoken through the prophets."

Several aspects of this passage bear special notice. First, references to "the simple" should not mislead us into imagining that some mental deficiency is in view. Wisdom is addressing those who shape public policy: she "cries out in the street, in the squares she raises her voice. . . . At the entrance of the city gates she speaks," that is, at the site of civic judgment (vv. 20-21). Further, the "calamity" and "panic," the "distress and anguish" (vv. 26-27) should not be imagined as personal misfortune; they are communal woes, crises facing society, as in the books of the prophets.

Lastly, notice Wisdom's response, going beyond the anger so often attributed to God in the books of the prophets. She laughs at the turmoil in which those who have rejected her find themselves; she mocks them when panic strikes. Here, as in the prophets, we are brought face to face with the awful possibility that *a whole people turn away from discerning God's will.*

ISAIAH 50:4-9 (BCP); 50:4-9a (RCL alt.); 50:5-9a (RC)

As in the reading from Proverbs, this "Servant Song" from Isaiah (cf. 42:1-4; 49:1-6; 52:13—53:12a) contemplates a disobedient people who ridicule and abuse the one who brings God's message.

Interpreters disagree on the identity of the servant in Second Isaiah: the prophet himself? Israel, among the nations? To an extent this is a false dichotomy. The servant may represent the prophet as he speaks to his people to describe God's vocation for them and the nation as they come to embrace and embody that vocation. One thing is clear: the responsiveness of the servant, who both speaks with "the tongue of a teacher" and listens "as those who are taught" (v. 4), stands in terrible contrast to the people who are themselves his adversaries, who insult and attack him. Indeed, the servant's openness toward God requires a hard defiance toward the disobedient. "I have set my face like flint" (v. 7). Compare God's word to Jeremiah: "I have made you today a fortified city, an iron pillar, and a bronze wall, against the whole land . . . and the people of the land" (1:18).

Both these readings from the Hebrew Bible portray a people who—despite their constant calling upon God—are so out of touch with God's will that the few among them who are truly obedient, who respond to God's call, must be as hard as flint, as unyielding as a bronze wall, in defying the social pressure that surrounds them.

SO MUCH OF OUR RELIGIOUS CULTURE IS GEARED TOWARD THE INSTANT, THE IMMEDIATE, AS IF A RELATIONSHIP WITH GOD WERE AS EASY AS REACHING OUT TOWARD THE TV SCREEN OR READING THROUGH AN EVANGELISTIC TRACT. IS KNOWING GOD AS EASY AS WE THINK IT IS?

These readings—combined with the readings that follow—raise disturbing questions. *Is* it so hard to know God's will? So much of our religious culture is geared toward the instant, the immediate, as if a relationship with God were as easy as reaching out toward the TV screen or reading through an evangelistic tract. Is knowing God as easy as we think it is?

RESPONSIVE READING

PSALM 19 or 116:1-8 (RCL); 116 or 116:1-8 (BCP); 116:1-6, 8-9 (RC)

The best-known part of Psalm 19 is the last verse, "Let the words of my mouth and the meditation of my heart be acceptable to you, O Lord, my rock and my redeemer." The full Psalm announces that God *can* be known. To the discerning, creation itself "pours forth speech," "declares knowledge" (v. 2). Those who walk according to God's will find it a clear, pure, joyous path. Psalm 116 praises God for salvation experienced. Its selection for this Sunday may be due to v. 16: the "servant" echoes the servant theme in the reading from Isaiah.

SECOND READING

JAMES 3:1-12 (RCL)

At first glance the coherence of this passage is elusive. Is the author concerned with the requirements for Christian teachers (v. 1), or with the dangers of a loose tongue (vv. 2-12)? We move through a series of metaphors for self-control and the lack of it—bridling horses (vv. 2-3), steering ships (v. 4), forest fires (vv. 5-6), taming animals (vv. 7-8), poison (v. 8)—and metaphors describing the impossible: fresh and brackish water, salt and fresh water (vv. 11, 12), trees giving mixed fruit (v. 12).

It is important not to get lost in the metaphorical mix! In fact James is amplifying one basic theme, consistent with his strident warning that we must not discriminate against the poor (2:1-18): it is inconsistent to bless God and curse our neighbors who are made in God's image (3:9). This is simply another way of bringing home the moral urgency at the heart of the letter. Doing the word, not hearing, is what matters (1:22). True religion involves care for the needy (1:27). Faith without works is dead (2:17).

In their classic work *The Social Construction of Reality,* sociologists Peter Berger and Thomas Luckmann say that the most powerful medium for reinforcing a shared view of the world is simple everyday conversation. It is no accident that James devotes so much of this jeremiad to the importance of disciplining our speech. How do our daily conversations shape, and limit, our perceptions of the possible? How do the ubiquitous sources of the images and information that floods our minds—TV, radio, internet—determine the way we look upon "the poor"?

JAMES 2:1-5, 8-10, 14-18 (BCP); 2:14-18 (RC)

(See last week, RCL, pp. 161–62.)

GOSPEL

MARK 8:27-38 (RCL/BCP); 8:27-35 (RC)

Having devoted earlier weeks to the "Bread of Life" discourse in John's Gospel, the lectionaries now bypass Mark's account of the feeding of four thousand people and the disciples' subsequent failure to understand Jesus' warning about "the leaven of the Pharisees" (Mark 8:1-21). In today's reading, Mark brings his narrative to a point of crisis: Have the disciples, who have witnessed all Jesus' miraculous works, discerned his identity as Christ?

I doubt any degree of homiletical skill can recover for modern Christian audiences the bewildering oxymoron that this Gospel's first readers would have confronted: a Christ who must die?! Despite the frequent assurances of New Testament writers, nothing in Jewish Scripture would have prepared Jesus' contemporaries to expect a messiah whose career would end in death, let alone a humiliating death by crucifixion. Christians were the first to juxtapose biblical predictions of the messiah's reign with descriptions of the suffering of the just and their hope for vindication. Indeed, many scholars doubt that Jesus predicted his own death with anything like the precision attributed to him here. Did he warn his disciples he would likely be killed for pursuing his chosen path? Probably. Did he expect God to vindicate his cause nevertheless? No doubt. But if he had really given his disciples such a detailed schedule of coming events, why were they so lost when just those events took place?

After more than a decade teaching New Testament courses at private colleges and state universities, I know very well how resistant many Christians are to the suggestion that Jesus did *not* have just this accurate knowledge of his own death and resurrection. I find that resistance more than a little disconcerting. Mark has consistently clued in his readers to a plot that his characters—the disciples—don't yet know. But what do we gain by assuring ourselves *we* know better than the likes of Peter? If we insist on Jesus' ability to know perfectly his own future, don't we at the same time insulate ourselves from the scandal of this proclamation?

The Gospel is that the man on whom the disciples fixed their hopes for a new, just world ended up suffering the ignominious death of a righteous man; and that, by the power of God, this man was raised from the dead *so that those hopes might continue undiminished.* How very different this astonishing announcement is from a complacent reassurance that everything went according to divine plan!

As Mark's story continues, Jesus goes on to warn his disciples about the cost of following him. He does not tell them they must brace themselves to believe an unusual story about God's surprising ways, but that they must be prepared to face hardship, suffering, even death in the hope and struggle for the new world he proclaims.

"Struggle" and "hope" stand side by side here—as they must: Hope that seeks to bypass struggle and conflict is shallow hope. Note that all three lectionaries avoid Jesus' disconcerting pronouncement that some standing in his presence "will not taste death before they see that the kingdom of God has come with power" (9:1). How much easier to reassure ourselves that everything is under control than to orient our lives toward a new order that has remained elusive for two millennia! Does any passage in Scripture better capture the true scandal of following Jesus the crucified?

HOW MUCH EASIER TO REASSURE OURSELVES THAT EVERYTHING IS UNDER CONTROL THAN TO ORIENT OUR LIVES TOWARD A NEW ORDER THAT HAS REMAINED ELUSIVE FOR TWO MILLENNIA!

MARK 9:14-29 (BCP alt.)

The Episcopal lectionary has already used Mark's passage on the "cost of discipleship" (8:31-38) for the second Sunday in Lent. Today the lectionary provides an alternative: Jesus' deliverance of a boy possessed by a demon.

The boy's symptoms resemble a grand mal epileptic seizure, leading to the widely held view that demon possession was often just a primitive misunderstanding of a neurological condition. Of course, such a "naturalizing" explanation of this event requires either that Jesus "actually" relieved the boy's seizure, which the crowd *mistook* as an exorcism, or that the boy's seizure came to an end naturally, and the crowd gave Jesus the credit (and he accepted it). One implication, on either view, is that Jesus is being disingenuous when he tells the disciples they could not cure the boy because "this kind can come out only through prayer" (v. 29).

The healing is obviously important to Mark, who devotes nearly twice as much space to it as either Matthew (17:14-21) or Luke (9:37-43). Mark alone supplies Jesus' pronouncement, that only prayer can deliver people from such afflictions. Of course, this could be taken to imply that those who suffer terrible physical or mental afflictions *just haven't prayed enough*—a view that can too easily become a source of affliction in its own right! Over against this pastoral danger, recall the father's cry earlier in the story, which also appears in Mark: "I believe; help my unbelief!" (v. 24). That verse is a helpful antidote to the toxic notion that God withholds healing until we show "enough" faith.

Mark's real interest is to encourage and guide his community, which continues to seek and to practice healing. Prayer (and fasting, according to some early manuscripts) is required of those who heal in Jesus' name. The Gospel seems to recommend the father's appeal to those who suffer.

Beyond these immediate, "pastoral" concerns, however, Mark also tells us that Jesus understood his exorcising activity as part of a larger and more complex combat against Satan (3:22-27). The story of the Gerasene demoniac (5:1-20), with its peculiar touches—the name "Legion" (5:9), the surprising reaction of the man's neighbors to his healing (5:15-17)—has convinced a number of modern interpreters that Jesus' exorcisms were also healing interventions into destructive social networks and systems.

"Help my unbelief." How often do we regard our doubts and questions as inadequacies, when they may actually be opportunities to give up inadequate, partial knowledge, and grow into a new understanding of God?

Reference

Berger, Peter L. and Thomas Luckmann, *The Social Construction of Reality: A Treatise in the Sociology of Knowledge* (New York: Irvington Publishers, 1980).

FIFTEENTH SUNDAY AFTER PENTECOST

SEPTEMBER 24, 2000
TWENTY-FIFTH SUNDAY IN ORDINARY TIME
PROPER 20

REVISED COMMON	EPISCOPAL (BCP)	ROMAN CATHOLIC
Prov. 31:10-31 or Wis. 1:16—2:1, 12-22 or Jer. 11:18-20	Wis. 1:16—2:1 (6-11) 12-22	Wis. 2:12, 17-20
Ps. 1 or 54	Ps. 54	Psalm 54:3-8
James 3:13—4:3, 7-8a	James 3:16—4:6	James 3:16—4:3
Mark 9:30-37	Mark 9:30-37	Mark 9:30-37

IN THE ANCIENT GREEK DRAMA LYSISTRATA, women organize a "sex strike" to prevent their men from entering on a potentially disastrous war. For centuries, symbolizations of femininity and masculinity, of motherhood and childhood, have been closely intertwined with the ways in which different cultures understand violence and warfare.

Today's readings present "ideal" images of woman and child. How do we assimilate these images into a meaningful and faithful response to the violence that threatens our communities and our world?

FIRST READING

PROVERBS 31:10-31 (RCL)

This text, one of three alternatives provided by the RCL, remains notorious, in part because it's so often been relied upon rather perfunctorily—for example, in weddings—to describe "the biblical ideal" of womanhood. The text seems condescending in places, describing a woman's worth in terms of the value she contributes to the household. Few women will be gladdened by the text's expectation that the ideal wife "rises while it is still night" to get the household's food prepared (v. 15) or that "her lamp does not go out at night" (v. 18)!

On the other hand, the text—deriving from an ancient agrarian society—puts much more power into the woman's hands than did that picture of the always smiling housewife-consumer that was beamed into our living rooms in the 1950s. The "capable wife" of Proverbs runs a household staff (v. 15), conducts her own real estate transactions (v. 16), works out (v. 17), makes charitable contributions (v. 20), holds her own in public discourse (v. 26), maintains a healthy relationship with integrity (vv. 11, 29)—and even gets the credit for her husband's rising status (v. 23)!

Global economists remind us that around the world, women's labor is a vastly underestimated source of economic value. In nation after nation, military budgets deprive women and children of basic necessities of life—and make them bear the greatest burden of warfare. In the United States, women still get about two-thirds of men's wages for the same work; that doesn't count the "invisible" inequity of disparate household responsibilities. The average married couple works harder for their housing than their parents did: paid work outside the home is more a necessity than a privilege for women today. Whatever this text's charms, it provides little basis for romanticizing women's work. A "dynamic equivalence" translation of the last line might well be, "Equal pay for equal work—*period!*"

WISDOM OF SOLOMON 1:16—2:1, 12-22 (RCL alt./BCP); 2:12, 17-20 (RC)

In Mark, Jesus has warned his disciples to be prepared to share the most horrific of fates if they follow him to Jerusalem. The reading from Wisdom (like the alternative from Jeremiah) finds an Old Testament anticipation: The wicked plot the death of the innocent. The cruel taunt in verses 17-20, along with Psalm 22:8, may lie behind the Gospel accounts of Jesus being mocked as he was crucified (Matt. 27:38-43).

The Wisdom text describes the fateful choice made by "the ungodly" (v. 16). Convinced that they have no hope beyond the grave (2:1), they dedicate themselves to the moment's pleasures at whatever cost (2:6-9). With considerable insight, the Wisdom text finds the heart of their relentless antagonism to the righteous: "They reproach us for sins against the law, and accuse us of sins against our training. . . . They became to us a reproof of our thoughts" (vv. 12, 14). A modern psychologist might well say that the antipathy felt by the "ungodly" toward "the righteous" arises because "the righteous" are a reminder of the "disowned self."

A MODERN PSYCHOLOGIST MIGHT WELL SAY THAT THE ANTIPATHY FELT BY THE "UNGODLY" TOWARD "THE RIGHTEOUS" ARISES BECAUSE "THE RIGHTEOUS" ARE A REMINDER OF THE "DISOWNED SELF."

What hopes have our disappointments taught us to discard? Do we resent others who have not yet learned to give up hope?

JEREMIAH 11:18-20 (RCL alt.)

"I was like a gentle lamb led to the slaughter" (v. 19). Those words from Jeremiah's cry of protest to God could easily be read by Christians as a prophetic anticipation of Jesus' suffering and death—the destiny that overshadows today's Gospel reading. But that flattens out prophecy into a rather uninteresting, one-dimensional scheme of prediction and fulfillment. Give Jeremiah the dignity of his own words: *he* is "like a gentle lamb led to the slaughter" because he has boldly confronted the injustices of his own society. If Jesus later shares his fate, it is because Jesus shares his prophetic message.

Responsive Reading

PSALM 1 or 54 (RCL); 54 (BCP); 54:3-8 (RC)

While Psalm 1 extols the blessedness of the righteous, Psalm 54 is the outcry of the righteous to God, out of the depths of persecution. The anticipation of divine vengeance in v. 5, perhaps troubling to modern sensibilities, pervades the psalms; it is conceived as the inevitable consequence of deliverance for the righteous.

Second Reading

JAMES 3:13—4:3, 7-8a (RCL); 3:16—4:6 (BCP); 3:16—4:3 (RC)

The second of the Buddha's Four Noble Truths is that desire, or craving, is the source of all human suffering. James seems to share that view (4:1).

We encourage our children to "use your words" instead of aggressive behavior. Yet in a single week in 1999, we watched the president of the United States admonish teenagers that "violence is not the answer," and admonish their parents that a certain number of civilian casualties—in this case, Kosovar refugees killed by American bombs—were inevitable in warfare.

Violence is a complex and torturous phenomenon, not least because it has such a hold within our culture. To simply blame our "cravings" seems naive. We *learn* violent behaviors—as individuals or as a society—as strategies for satisfying our desires. What are the little links, the everyday decisions, that tend to tie our desires to reliance on force, rather than cooperation?

Gospel

MARK 9:30-37

Responding to a plea from the world's Nobel Peace Prize laureates, the United Nations General Assembly has declared the first ten years of the new millennium a "Decade for a Culture of Peace and Nonviolence for the Children of the World." Lofty thoughts—but nothing more, unless these hopes are translated immediately into adult actions. The UN has called upon its members to teach "the practice of peace and nonviolence . . . at all levels in their respective societies, including in educational institutions."

In today's Gospel, Jesus confronts his disciples, who are as mystified by his warnings about following him on the way of the cross (8:34-38) as they are eager to establish precedence among themselves.

Jesus' answer is not more words, but a potent prophetic action: he draws a child to his side. This is not mere sentimentality. To set the welfare of a child—notice, we don't know "whose" child—at the center of adult attention, at the heart of community decision-making, is a bold move in any society that sets a premium on power and prestige, for children have precious little of either.

In her brilliant discussion of "the discipleship of equals," Elisabeth Schüssler Fiorenza notices that Jesus had little patience for the structures of the patriarchal household, with its children put firmly in their place. Whatever family ties disciples may have left behind in their new community, they find new mothers, brothers, sisters—but curiously, no fathers (Mark 3:34-35; 10:30)! Rather than simply calling men away from their homes, leaving women to bear alone the burden of rearing children, Jesus speaks of a new community in which children are welcome, indeed, central. Schüssler Fiorenza concludes, "the discipleship of equals must be inclusive of children and serve their needs, if the community wants to have Jesus—and God—in their midst."

References

Resolution of the United Nations General Assembly, November 10, 1998.

Elisabeth Schüssler Fiorenza, *In Memory of Her: A Feminist Theological Reconstruction of Christian Origins* (New York: Crossroad, 1988) 140–54.

THE SIXTEENTH SUNDAY AFTER PENTECOST

October 1, 2000
Twenty-sixth Sunday in Ordinary Time
Proper 21

Revised Common	Episcopal (BCP)	Roman Catholic
Esther 7:1-6, 9-10; 9:20-22 or Num. 11:4-6, 10-16, 24-29	Num. 11:4-6, 10-16, 24-29	Num. 11:25-29
Ps. 124 or 19:7-14	Ps. 19 or 19:7-14	Ps. 19:8, 10, 12-14
James 5:13-20	James 4:7-12 (13—5:6)	James 5:1-6
Mark 9:38-50	Mark 9:38-43, 45, 47-48	Mark 9:38-43, 45, 47-48

First Reading
ESTHER 7:1-6, 9-10; 9:20-22 (RCL)

This reading from Esther seems to drop into the lectionary out of the blue. The Jewish festival of Purim, celebrating Esther's deliverance of her people, is half a year away. There are no obvious connections with other readings today.

Any homilist deciding to preach on this passage confronts some interpretive challenges. First, Esther, herself a Jew, has won a place at the right hand of the Persian king Ahaseurus (Xerxes I, 485-464 B.C.E.) through an ancient equivalent of a beauty contest (2:1-18). She has thus replaced Vashti, the Persian queen who refused her husband's order to make an appearance of state (1:10-12) and thus raised the specter of wifely insubordination throughout the empire (1:13-20). As a tale of quiet, accommodating "constructive engagement" with a massive and potentially hostile empire, the Book of Esther held a certain value for countless generations of Jews living in diaspora. It is hardly a tract for women's empowerment, however!

The book ends happily, with the deliverance of the Jews from an impending Persian pogrom. We cannot hear this account without setting it beside the dread subsequent history of violence against Jews, reaching its terrible climax in our own century. To be sure, some Jews look upon the creation of the State of Israel as divine recompense for the catastrophe of the Shoah, or Holocaust; many other Jews, and many official Christian bodies who have addressed the issue, have taken a more nuanced stance. I simply mean to point out how easy it may be for homilists to bite off more than they care to chew!

NUMBERS 11:4-6, 10-16, 24-29 (RCL alt./BCP); 11:25-29 (RC)

I realized one summer evening years ago that for weeks I'd been making summer salads with "Egyptian" ingredients—garlic, onions, leeks, cucumbers, and melons (though not in the same salads!). Since that revelation it's been easier for me to sympathize with the Israelites in this text!

Three homiletically provocative themes converge here. First is the people's grumbling, an important plot motif throughout Numbers. Even with daily sustenance miraculously provided by God, they complain that a steady diet of manna has become unappetizing; they long for the foods they left behind in Egypt. The book's readers know where the long march through the desert is leading, and so are ready to judge the Israelites for their inconstancy and lack of perseverance.

Second, rather surprisingly, the story does not spare Moses. Like the despairing Elijah (1 Kings 19: see the ninth Sunday after Pentecost, p. 139), Moses is ready for God to strike him dead if this is going to be the way things are (v. 15). The Lord responds by pouring out the spirit of prophecy upon seventy elders—at least temporarily (vv. 16-25). Strangely, this does not establish the seventy as a mid-level leadership, as in Exodus 18:13-23. We do not see them adjudicating cases or otherwise alleviating Moses' "burden" (v.14). The seventy prophesy, this once (v. 25), but do not achieve any charismatic "success in the field" like that enjoyed by the seventy sent out by Jesus (Luke 10:1-12, 17-20). Indeed, their endowment with the spirit seems primarily to buttress Moses' authority. The role of the seventy is hardly made clearer by the story's continuation: God provides a bounty of quail, then becomes angered at the people and strikes them with a plague (11:31-35).

The third, and perhaps most intriguing, element in the story is the fate of two elders who had not gone out of the camp with the others, yet receive the spirit and prophesy nonetheless (vv. 26-29). A young man, and Moses' lieutenant Joshua, urge Moses to stop them, but Moses responds, "Would that all the Lord's people were prophets!" Connecting this episode with the "strange exorcist" in the Gospel reading is irresistible.

RESPONSIVE READING

PSALM 124 or 19:7-14 (RCL); 19 OR 19:7-14 (BCP); 19:8, 10, 12-14 (RC)

Psalm 124 is a fitting reprise of themes from the Esther reading: the Lord's constant loyalty when the people were endangered. Psalm 19 has been discussed above (fourteenth Sunday after Pentecost, RCL, p. 167).

SECOND READING

JAMES 5:13-20 (RCL); 4:7-12 (13—5:6) (BCP); 5:1-6 (RC)

Earlier (thirteenth Sunday after Pentecost, pp. 161–62) I noted that the BCP and RC lectionaries had both skirted James 2:6-7, excising the letter's indictment of "the rich" as the source of oppression and injustice. Note now that the RCL skips over the harsh, apocalyptically tinged blast against the rich in 5:1-6; and the BCP brackets them for optional reading.

To be sure, the RCL moves to a significant passage in its own right. James 5:13-20 addresses the important pastoral role of the elders of the congregation in anointing the sick. It is surely more helpful to emphasize the community's role in bearing up one another in prayer than to pronounce as a general rule the letter's hope that "the prayer of faith will save the sick" (5:15).

It would be a sin to let the moral stridency of James 5:1-6 pass without comment. Indeed, the epistle's words have never seemed more timely. Your congregation may already be involved in "Jubilee 2000," the campaign mobilizing thousands of churches and non-government organizations to address the economic strangulation perpetuated around the world by fiscal policies that most benefit Western banks. In 1998, the president of the World Bank addressed the Lambeth Conference of Anglican bishops, assuring them he recognized the tremendous role that international structures like the Bank play in perpetuating cycles of deadly poverty, and seeking common ground for action. Bishops from Africa and Asia pressed, not just for international debt relief, but for debt cancellation, insisting that the wealth torn from their continents by colonial powers more than justified this demand.

IT WOULD BE A SIN TO LET THE MORAL STRIDENCY OF JAMES 5:1-6 PASS WITHOUT COMMENT. INDEED, THE EPISTLE'S WORDS HAVE NEVER SEEMED MORE TIMELY.

Financial speculation—a principal engine in the global economy—comes in for a searing rebuke in 4:13-17. The accumulation of wealth through exploiting the labor of others—a taboo subject in most polite Western conversation—is decried in 5:1-6. So long as the prosperity of a few depends, in part, on the impoverishment and degradation of the many, the wealthy cannot find words of comfort here. We who live in the prosperous West must find constructive ways to respond to the genuinely evangelical message of James, however uncomfortable it makes us!

Gospel

MARK 9:38-50 (RCL); 9:38-43, 45, 47-48 (BCP/RC)

Today's Gospel reading begins with a startling episode. The disciples have seen someone outside their circle casting out demons in Jesus' name. This "strange exorcist" is otherwise unknown to us, but his apparent success contrasts sharply with the inability of Jesus' own followers to cast out a demon (in 9:14-29).

Just as startling is Jesus' response: "Do not stop him: for no one who does a deed of power in my name will be able soon afterward to speak evil of me" (9:39). His words echo Moses' rebuke to those who would have stifled "renegade" prophets in Israel's camp. Would that all God's people were able to cast out demons and work deeds of power!

Too often, however, we invert Jesus' words. Instead of "whoever is not against us is for us," we assume that any who are not already part of our community—our denomination, our ecclesiastical style (evangelical, charismatic, high-church)—are our rivals. "Mission" becomes a matter of religious colonization; we compete to make our neighbors into people who think and feel and pray just as we do.

JESUS' EVANGELICAL CRITERION IS SIMPLE ENOUGH: WHERE IS GOD'S LIBERATIVE WORK BEING DONE? WHERE ARE PEOPLE BEING FREED FROM THE FORCES THAT BIND HEARTS AND CRIPPLE LIVES?

Whatever its numerical success, such a narrow and narcissistic understanding of mission is usually about as productive as the disciples' efforts, as Mark describes them. Notice that they not only fail to cast out a "hard case" demon, they also resent, and try to stifle, someone who can!

Jesus' evangelical criterion is simple enough: Where is God's liberative work being done? Where are people being freed from the forces that bind hearts and cripple lives?

Strangely enough, we often tend to read the dire warnings in 9:42-50 in individualistic terms. But the context in Mark (and in Matthew's parallel, 18:6-9) is communal. What are the habitual practices, the operating assumptions, by which we cause "the little ones" to suffer a shipwreck of faith? What are the precious "appendages" we can't give up, no matter what their cost to others? Those are urgent questions for churches, where appropriate ritual styles and properly devout personalities may be mistaken for the stuff of the Gospel.

Do we dare to set Jesus' command to "Be salty" next to James's damning indictment of those who prosper from exploitation? What creative mischief would listening to these evangelical commands produce in our shared deliberations on mission and stewardship?

SEVENTEENTH SUNDAY AFTER PENTECOST

OCTOBER 8, 2000
TWENTY-SEVENTH SUNDAY IN ORDINARY TIME
PROPER 22

REVISED COMMON	EPISCOPAL (BCP)	ROMAN CATHOLIC
Job 1:1; 2:1-10 or Gen. 2:18-24	Gen. 2:18-24	Gen. 2:18-24
Ps. 26 or 8	Ps. 8 or 128	Ps. 128
Heb. 1:1-4; 2:5-12	Heb. 2:(1-8) 9-18	Heb. 2:9-11
Mark 10:2-16	Mark 10:2-9	Mark 10:2-16 (10:2-12)

FIRST READING

JOB 1:1; 2:1-10 (RCL)

It's hard to imagine a worse example of tearing a passage out of its biblical context. The lectionary presents the "faithful," "patient" Job, long championed in Christian homiletic as a stalwart, stoic sufferer. We get not a hint of the white-hot defiance that burns in Job through the rest of the book!

Some congregants may know the plot of the book of Job best through its popular adaptation in books like Rabbi Harold Kushner's *When Bad Things Happen to Good People.* If you decide to address this reading, keep several fundamental points in mind.

First, the "easy," orthodox answer to suffering provided by Job's "friends"—that Job "must have" sinned to deserve his terrible afflictions (chap. 3–31)—offers no comfort to Job, whose integrity the book never calls into question. God's rebuke of these friends in 42:7-9 shows that they have proven themselves very poor "pastoral theologians," exactly misrepresenting God. Indeed, the text tells us there is *no* divine "purpose" behind Job's suffering, beyond the will to win a heavenly bet (1:2-6)!

Next, notice that even when God answers Job "out of the whirlwind" and causes him to cease his outcry (chap. 38–41), God never declares Job to be sinful or deserving of his plight. Rather God simply denies Job's right to question God's purposes. Those who have delved most deeply into questions of intractable suffering and inexorable injustice may find the book's ending profoundly unsatisfying—but it is surely realistic.

It is more than a little ironic that the lectionary has set this opening passage from Job next to Jesus' words about marriage in Mark. Job would have been better off single than enjoying the "support" his wife offers (2:9)!

GENESIS 2:18-24 (RCL alt./BCP/RC)

This most familiar, much maligned, and often caricatured text appears here to set off Jesus' words about marriage in the Gospel reading. To be sure, there is more than a little patriarchy here: the man enjoys a solitary sovereignty over all other creatures (2:19-20); the woman appears something of a divine afterthought (2:21-22). We shouldn't be surprised: The story derives from the Late Bronze Age!

Still, some fine points bear consideration. As the NRSV translates, God wishes to make for the man "a helper as his partner." The Hebrew does not have the connotations of inferiority that the English "helper" carries. In fact, the word is elsewhere used for God as a "helper" or savior of human beings! Second, despite the peculiar detail that the first woman is drawn from the rib of the man (v. 21), the man clearly recognizes her as an equal—"bone of my bones and flesh of my flesh." Lastly, notice that in contrast to what we should expect in a patrilineal society, but consistent with a matrilineal one, the man is described as leaving *his* parents and "clinging" to his wife. The man is thus put into a position of vulnerability toward the woman, and the text implies this is "very good" (cf. 1:31).

All three lectionaries have (demurely?) stopped before 2:25: "And the man and his wife were both naked, and were not ashamed." That notice, in sharp contrast to the shame Adam and Eve experience after their primordial disobedience (3:7), has fueled Christian meditation on human sexuality for two millennia. Ironically, the text isn't preoccupied with the question; it seems rather content to offer a "myth of origins" to explain "why we wear clothes."

RESPONSIVE READING

PSALM 26 or 8 (RCL); 8 or 128 (BCP); 128 (RC)

In Psalm 26 the righteous proclaim their own innocence and integrity before God—just as Job proclaimed his own integrity in his protest to God. Psalm 8 echoes themes from Genesis as it speaks of the intended glory of the human race, created "a little lower than God" and crowned "with glory and honor," given "dominion over the works of [God's] hands" (vv. 8-9). Verses from this Psalm are taken up in the reading from Hebrews as well. Psalm 128 describes the blessedness of the faithful (man), whose wife and children will be sources of constant blessing (v. 3).

Second Reading

HEBREWS 1:1-4; 2:5-12 (RCL); 2:(1-8) 9-18 (BCP); 2:9-11 (RC)

Several of the most intriguing christological images in the New Testament occur in the Letter to the Hebrews, to which the lectionaries turn this week. Here, in a passage relying upon Jewish Wisdom traditions, Christ is described as "the reflection of God's glory and the exact imprint of God's very being," sustaining all things by his powerful word (1:3). He is hailed for having "made purification for sins" (1:3), and much of the letter is devoted to a typological interpretation of Jesus' death as the perfect antitype to the high priest's sacrifice on the Day of Atonement (2:17). The epistle also shows considerable interest in Jesus' present status as higher than the angels (1:4), even though "for a little while [he] was made lower than the angels" (2:9). Jesus' obedient subjection to God—becoming subject to suffering, testing (2:18), and death—has won him a name higher than that of the angels, a theme that echoes Paul's hymn to Christ in Philippians 2.

The author is not interested in christology for its own sake, but in order to fortify his or her readers in their Christian life. Thus the admonition in 2:1, to "pay greater attention to what we have heard," and the emphasis upon sanctification in 2:11. Remarkably, the author admits that "we do not yet see everything in subjection" to the angels or to Christ (2:8; cf. 1 Cor. 15:25-28). Nevertheless, "we do see Jesus . . . now crowned" with heavenly glory (2:9)! Note also the understanding of the Christian people as "brothers and sisters" of Jesus (2:12).

Gospel

MARK 10:2-16 (RCL); 10:2-9 (BCP); 10:2-16 (10:2-12) (RC)

Churches continue to struggle over divorced Christians. Jesus' words in today's reading, "What God has joined together, let no one separate" (10:9), are pronounced at Christian weddings. They are also frequently taken as a hard and fast prohibition of divorce, as implied in vv. 10-12 (but see 1 Cor. 7:11, 15).

It is instructive to compare this passage with Matthew, where the Pharisees' question is expanded: "Is it lawful to divorce one's wife *for any cause*?" (19:3), and with the commandment regarding divorce in the Torah, where divorce is permitted if the man "finds something objectionable about" his wife (Deut. 24:1, NRSV). Jesus declares the provision in the Torah to be a divine concession to male "hardness of heart": It is contrary to the will of God expressed in creation, where God commands the mutuality of a shared life as "one flesh" (Mark 10:8-9).

We may read this passage most profitably if we put aside the casuistic question, Under what conditions may we divorce? and ask instead, What is the purpose of marriage? Jesus seems less concerned here to prohibit divorce than to encourage the genuine intimacy of heart and soul, the becoming "one flesh," that makes the question of divorce superfluous. It is worth noticing that in Matthew the disciples remain as "hard-headed" as the Pharisees: "If such is the case of a man with his wife, it is better not to marry!" (Matt. 19:10). There Jesus concedes that "Not everyone can accept this teaching," meaning not that some are exempt from the relational requirements of marriage, but that all should discern their gifts, whether for entering into marriage or thriving in the single life, and live accordingly.

JESUS SEEMS LESS CONCERNED TO PROHIBIT DIVORCE THAN TO ENCOURAGE THE GENUINE INTIMACY OF HEART AND SOUL, THE BECOMING "ONE FLESH," THAT MAKES THE QUESTION OF DIVORCE SUPERFLUOUS.

Curiously, the BCP and RC almost divide the passage in Mark evenly—the BCP ending the reading at 10:9 (before the prohibition of divorce in vv. 10-12), the RC making the earlier verses optional, and thus emphasizing what Jesus has to say about children. Mark has joined together a potent *metaphor*—to enter the kingdom of God one must become *like* a little child (v. 15)—with Jesus' very literal declaration that no one should hinder children from approaching him.

As we saw earlier, Jesus sought to realize a community life in which the patriarchal "chain of command" was broken, and new values of mutuality, vulnerability, and genuine interdependence prevailed. How would our family lives, community relations, and social policies be changed if we took these values more seriously?

EIGHTEENTH SUNDAY AFTER PENTECOST

October 15, 2000
Twenty-eighth Sunday in Ordinary Time
Proper 23

Revised Common (RCL)	Episcopal (BCP)	Roman Catholic (RC)
Job 23:1-9, 16-17 or Amos 5:6-7, 10-15	Amos 5:6-7, 10-15	Wis. 7:7-11
Ps. 22:1-15 or 90:12-17	Ps. 90 or 90:1-8, 12	Ps. 90:12-17
Heb. 4:12-16	Heb. 3:1-6	Heb. 4:12-13
Mark 10:17-31	Mark 10:17-27 (28-31)	Mark 10:17-30 (10:17-27)

"Establish justice in the gate," cries Amos (5:15). The prophet speaks of justice within the framework of the covenant, in which God's people are obligated to care for the poor, the orphaned, the widowed, and the elderly. "Go, sell what you own, and give the money to the poor, and you will have treasure in heaven; then come, follow me" (Mark 10:21). Do this and you will live, says Jesus to the man who asks him about eternal life. While, sadly, the man cannot bring himself to sell his possessions and give the money to the poor in order to follow Jesus, Jesus' disciples have left everything to follow him. "What about us?" they ask him. You will be rewarded a hundredfold, says Jesus, in the spirit of the Wisdom of "Solomon" who asked not for power or riches, yet received both. Job protests that he had performed the works of justice, yet received no reward or even justice from God. But Hebrews proclaims access to the throne of grace through Jesus, our high priest. God hears our prayers of lament as well as our confessions of faith. This may be a Sunday on which the sermon develops from a conversation among the readings.

First Reading

JOB 23:1-9, 16-17b (RCL)

Interpreting the Text

In chapter 22, Job has been accused by his friend Eliphaz of being wicked and powerful and of treating badly the weak and the poor. In the verses of chapter 23 omitted by the lectionary, Job protests that he has not departed from God's commandments and has treasured God's words. These verses might be included when the text is read because they accentuate Job's righteous complaint against God. He wishes he could find God in order to have his case adjudicated. He is confident of acquittal precisely because he has been righteous. In spite of the sense of having been abandoned by God, Job professes his faith in the God who "stands alone" (v. 13—one thinks of the confession of the *Shema Israel*).

Responding to the Text

Job has done everything right, yet God has not been there for him. It is God's absence that marks Job's struggle. Yet Job is not an atheist. He believes in a God who is not at his beck and call, a God who is free to give or withhold himself. But this brings Job into a position of solidarity with all who suffer, and he delivers a powerful speech in chapter 24 on the desperate condition of the homeless, the widows, and the orphans. In the wider context of Job 22–24, this First Reading could be correlated with the Gospel for today in which Jesus invites a rich man to experience solidarity with the poor by becoming poor himself—selling all that he has and giving the proceeds to the poor.

AMOS 5:6-7, 10-15 (RCL alt./BCP)

Interpreting the Text

The people of the northern kingdom of Israel were moving in a direction that could only lead them to destruction. Amos has come from the southern kingdom to warn his northern cousins of their need to make a mid-course correction. As a nation they were no longer seeking the Lord, and the affluent were living a comfortable lifestyle by taking advantage of the poor. The pericope ends with an exhortation to "hate evil and love good." Ever concrete in his admonitions to repentance, however, Amos exhorts Israel to "establish justice in the gate" (v. 15), which reflects back on the practice he observed of pushing aside the needy in the gate (v. 12). In the Gospel reading from Mark, Jesus also reminds the rich man of the covenant responsibility to care for the poor.

Responding to the Text

Amos is a prophet whose message is always timely because there are always those who get rich at the expense of the poor. The underlying problem is greed, and it is fueled by the feeling of most people that they never have enough. Certainly the reasons for economic injustice are varied and are rooted in social-economic-political systems that cannot be changed by one person, one congregation, or even by one church body. But many churches are struggling on national and global levels to deal with economic justice for all, and it may be helpful to share the visions of pastoral letters and church statements. Bringing into the sermon political considerations related to economic justice is appropriate in the context of this text because "the gate" was the place where the elders heard legal arguments and rectified civil wrongs.

On the local level we live in a time when we have developed compassion fatigue especially when it comes to dealing with the poor and the homeless. Posters advise those who would respond to beggars not to give cash, which may well feed addictions. But then something else must be done: programs must be established locally to provide for the basic needs of the poor and homeless. The preacher might point out opportunities for volunteer services in overnight shelters, soup kitchens, and job counseling programs.

WISDOM OF SOLOMON 7:7-11 (RC)

Interpreting the Text

The apocryphal book known as the Wisdom of Solomon is an enthusiastic and eulogistic invocation of wisdom written in Greek by a learned, Hellenized Jew of Alexandria, probably after that city's conquest by the Romans in 30 B.C.E. The author encourages his fellow Jews to take pride in their tradition, which he presents in intellectually respectable terms. The tradition of comparing wisdom and material wealth—to the disadvantage of the latter—goes back to Solomon's prayer in 1 Kings 3:6-9. One may regard wisdom as more precious than power or wealth (v. 8), yet Solomon admits that "all good things came to me along with her" (v. 11).

Responding to the Text

Wisdom, in the Jewish tradition, is a personified attribute of God ("the spirit of wisdom" Isa. 11:2). To receive the gift of wisdom is to receive something of God. One cannot receive God through one's own efforts and natural abilities; nor can one receive God's gifts on this basis. Solomon was wise enough to ask for the best gift, but ultimately the gift is God's to bestow. The attitude that "all good gifts come from God" (see James 1:7) may be contrasted with the attitude of the rich man in today's Gospel, who clings to his possessions as though they were actually his own.

RESPONSIVE READING
PSALM 22:1-15 (RCL)

Interpreting the Text

This archetypal psalm of lament begins with the psalmist's sense of abandonment by God (vv. 1-2). While expressing confidence in God at the outset

(vv. 3-5), the psalmist focuses on being mocked and treated like less than a human being (vv. 6-8). In contrast, God is evoked as the midwife who helped him leave the womb and come into the world (vv. 9-10). This image helps the psalmist to transcend suffering by meditating on the God who has a vested interest in the people. Even so, the verses chosen leave the psalmist in the dust of death without getting to the element of thanksgiving and praise at the end of the psalm.

Responding to the Text

Since this is the psalm of the Passion, and its words were on the lips of Jesus on the cross, this psalm could be used in conjunction with the reading from Job to emphasize Christ's identification with those who experience God-forsakenness. Yet it is the Son of God who is abandoned, just as the righteous Job experienced God-forsakenness. The very sense of God's absence, however, implies a remembered and an anticipated presence.

THE VERY SENSE OF GOD'S ABSENCE IMPLIES A REMEMBERED AND AN ANTICIPATED PRESENCE.

PSALM 90 (RCL alt./BCP/RC)

Interpreting the Text

This psalm is a communal lament which anchors human life in the God who precedes all the passing generations (vv. 1-2). It laments the brevity and frailty of human life, which passes as quickly as a watch in the night (four hours) in contrast with the God to whom the millennium seems like yesterday (vv. 3-4). God is the giver and taker of life, which flourishes like grass in the morning that fades by evening (vv. 5-6). In a poetic way, the psalmist reflects on the penalty of humanity for its primal sin: death as an expression of God's wrath (vv. 7-9, 11). The days of our lives are limited to seventy or eighty years, and are full of trouble (v. 10). Even so, the psalmist asks to be instructed so as to use them wisely (v. 12). In a plea for compassion, the psalmist asks God to equalize affliction with gladness (v. 15), to manifest his work among his servants (v. 16), and to "prosper the work of our hands" (v. 17). The petition for instruction "that we may gain a wise heart" (v. 12) links this psalm with the reading from the Wisdom of Solomon.

Responding to the Text

Two basic contrasts dominate this psalm: the contrast between the eternal, everlasting nature of God and the transitory, dying character of humankind, and the contrast between the holy God who reacts with anger to disobedience and humanity with its overt iniquities and secret sins. In spite of this disparity, the psalmist is not led to despair. The psalmist's faith is such that he is bold enough to ask for the eternal and holy God's favor on human endeavor (v. 17).

SECOND READING

HEBREWS 3:1-6 (BCP)

Interpreting the Text

"To the Hebrews" is less a letter than a midrash (spiritual commentary) on texts in the Hebrew Bible.[1] Hebrews 3:1 begins a homily that compares and contrasts Jesus with Moses, just as in chapters 1–2 the author compared and contrasted Jesus with the angels. The christology of Hebrews is less prophecy-fulfillment than supercessionist. Thus, as the author argued for Christ's superiority to the angels, so he argues for Christ's superiority to Moses. Moses was a faithful servant in God's house, but Christ is the faithful Son in God's house who is "worthy of more glory than Moses" (v. 3). As Moses mediated between God and God's people, so Christ is the ambassador of God and "the high priest of our confession" (v. 1) who presents our faith to God as the basis on which we can come before God. Believers should be confident of this. Ever encouraging, the author of Hebrews exhorts believers to hold firm to the hope offered us as we become (like Moses) God's "house" (v. 6). The image of God as builder and God's people as a house could offer some interesting homiletical possibilities.

Responding to the Text

There is a danger of interpreting this text in an anti-Jewish way that will feed anti-Semitism. It may be important to stress that even in contrasting the two covenant-mediators, Moses and Jesus, the author of "To the Hebrews" assumes the framework of the covenant relationship with God established by God for the people of Israel. The work of Christ is interpreted within the whole cultic system of Israel. Even in the supercessionist views of Hebrews, Christians cannot do without the Hebrew Scriptures.

HEBREWS 4:12-16 (RCL); 4:12-13 (RC)

Interpreting the Text

While the entire "Letter" is a midrash on Psalm 110, it appropriately employs other texts of the Hebrew Scriptures to support the main point, since Jews and early Christians treated the Bible as a whole rather than as individual parts. So Hebrews 4:1-13 is a small midrash on Psalm 95, supported by Numbers 14 and a small poem which the author quoted in vv. 12-13 to strengthen his argument. The purpose of the midrash is to contrast the unfaithfulness of the children of Israel in the wilderness with the possibilities of faithfulness by those who follow Jesus, the high priest who identifies with our weaknesses. The warning tone in vv. 12-13 concerning the word of God that pierces and divides is balanced by the positive invitation to "approach the throne of God with boldness, so that we may receive mercy and find grace to help in time of need" (v. 16).

Responding to the Text

The "living and active word of God" (cf. v. 12) should not be identified with a book. What is meant here is the spoken word in all its force—a sharp two-edged sword of a word that cuts and divides such as we hear from Amos and Jesus in the other readings today. This is a word that has the capacity to pierce every soul, bringing challenge or comfort depending on the situation of the hearer before God. The words of warning and invitation in this text were addressed to a Christian community that was tempted to apostasy in the face of persecution (the unpardonable sin in Heb. 6:4). Apostasy is no less a temptation for a church that is not facing persecution, but may be inclined to reduce the demands of its message in order to attract members or appear "relevant" to current interests rather than hold fast its confession.

GOSPEL
MARK 10:17-31

Interpreting the Text

This pericope joins together three units that make a complete message to the church about possessions and discipleship: the question of a man about inheriting eternal life; Jesus' word to the disciples about how difficult it is for the wealthy to be disciples; and Jesus' assurance to Peter about the rewards for those who have left everything to follow him.

The man who approaches Jesus with his question about eternal life has been called "the rich young ruler" by joining together the assumption in Mark that the man was rich because he had many possessions, with Matthew's version where the man was "young," and Luke's version where the man was a "ruler." There may be some value in seeing him simply as a man whose sincerity is expressed by his gesture of kneeling before Jesus and whose confusion is expressed in his question about doing something in order to receive what is essentially a gift (an inheritance). Jesus sets the man before God and reminds him of the commandments, which are randomly quoted (though all from the "second table of the Law" having to do with human relationships). In these responses Jesus is setting the man before God who alone is "the giver of every good and perfect gift" (James 1:17) and also reminds him of his religious tradition. When the man says he has observed this tradition, Jesus tells him to show it by selling what he has and giving the money to the poor and then by following Jesus. Jesus points to discipleship as the logical consequence of observing the law and heeding the prophets.

Because the man could not do this, Jesus explained to his disciples that it is hard for the rich to enter the kingdom of God. When they showed perplexity at this, he generalized by saying that it is hard—period!—to enter the kingdom of God. "It is easier for a camel to go through the eye of a needle than for someone who is rich to enter the kingdom of God" (v. 25). The popular explanation that "the needle's eye" was a small gate in a walled city through which a camel, when kneeling, could barely get through, now seems to be archaeologically dubious. The point Jesus is driving at is that what is impossible for human beings (being saved) is possible with God.

Finally, Peter points out that he and the others have left everything to follow Jesus. Jesus assures the Twelve and the church that those who experience privation for the sake of the gospel will experience vindication both here and hereafter. But the last line of the RCL and BCP pericope, "many who are first will be last, and the last will be first" (v. 31), reminds the Twelve (and us) that admission into the kingdom of God is still an act of grace, no matter what acts of commitment disciples have committed.

Responding to the Text

A number of little details in this narrative are worth pondering. Why was the man running to Jesus? Why was he disposed to flatter Jesus, calling him "Good Teacher"? Why was a man who was such an obvious practitioner of his religious upbringing concerned about Jesus' opinion of his fitness for God's kingdom? These clues indicate that the man's question was serious and that his interest in Jesus' teachings were sincere. This makes the inability of the man to do what was necessary to be a disciple of Jesus all the sadder—for himself and for Jesus.

There are two dangers to be avoided in preaching on this text: one is to spiritualize it and the other is to make the word of Jesus doable. Either approach softens the challenge of this text. Thus, we could point out that renunciation is not an end in itself; it is a means to fuller discipleship—which is true. We could avoid the issue of dealing with our clinging to our possessions by saying that we need to discern what in our lives keeps us from following Jesus—which is also true. But while there may be many things that make it hard for us to practice discipleship, most people would have difficulty with Jesus' directive to the rich man to "sell what you own, and give the money to the poor." One who didn't was St. Francis of Assisi and the "little brothers" and "poor Claires" who followed him. But most of us are not going to become Franciscans. And even the Francises and Dominics compromised: they gave away their silks and satins but kept their broadcloth and sack-

One either follows the radical word of Jesus or takes comfort from the fact that what is impossible for human beings is possible with God.

cloth; they sold the manor house but kept their hut; they stopped eating beef and pork but ate bread and fish. So even giving away riches has its limitations.

Neither should the preacher use this text as a way of beefing up giving to the church (sorry, Jesus' directive is to give to the poor), because this lets the hearer off the hook by believing that there is *something* he or she can do. One either follows the radical word of Jesus or takes comfort from the fact that what is impossible for human beings is possible with God. We can be justified by grace.

NINETEENTH SUNDAY AFTER PENTECOST

October 22, 2000
Twenty-ninth Sunday in Ordinary Time
Proper 24

Revised Common	Episcopal (BCP)	Roman Catholic
Job 38:1-7 (34-41) or Isa. 53:4-12	Isa. 53:4-12	Isa. 53:10-11
Ps. 104:1-9, 24, 35c or 91:9-16	Ps. 91 or 91:9-16	Ps. 33:3-4, 18-20, 22
Heb. 5:1-10	Heb. 4:12-16	Heb. 4:14-16
Mark 10:35-45	Mark 10:35-45	Mark 10:35-45 (10:42-45)

This week some common motifs run through the reading in each of the three lectionaries, which is not always the case for the Sundays after Pentecost. The theme of suffering is prominent in the First Readings from Job and Isaiah. The preacher must deal with the fact that in both cases suffering is allowed by God according to God's own purposes—testing Job's faith and providing a vicarious atonement for sin. The theme of Christ's identification with suffering humanity can be extracted from the Second Readings from Hebrews, which dwell on Christ's priesthood. The challenge to the disciples to embrace a suffering Messiah and to follow him on the way of the cross is at issue in the Gospel.

First Reading

JOB 38:1-7 (34-41) (RCL)

Interpreting the Text

God responds, at last, to Job's complaints. If we thought that God would answer Job's question—which is the perennial human question, "Why do I suffer so?"—we are mistaken. Instead, God cross-examines Job, asking a series of unanswerable questions. If Job cannot answer the questions of how the earth was made, how will he ever understand the mystery of God's providence for humanity? Job must finally reject any cause-and-effect explanation of human suffering and make room for the dimension of mystery.

Responding to the Text

The whole book of Job was written to explore the question: Why does a righteous person suffer? From the outset, Job is an unknowing victim of a contest between God and Satan. Satan the prosecutor contends that if God would remove the protection that surrounds Job in his blessed life, he would curse God. God takes up the challenge and allows Satan to take away everything except Job's life. Neither Job nor his well-intentioned friends know the real reason for Job's suffering, and they fall into the trap of thinking that the cause lies in something Job has done or not done. But when Job finally gets his audience with God, the real reason for Job's suffering is not disclosed. To Job it remains a mystery.

Any sermon on the problem of human suffering must avoid the temptation to unveil the mystery. God did not cause Job's suffering, but God allowed it to happen. This is also experienced in everyday life. In fact, it would seem that the instances in which God acts to prevent human suffering are really exceptional. The reader of Job is left with the impression that God does not share with humanity the reasons for human suffering and also that all our guesses miss the mark. What surely does not miss the mark is the mission of the Son of God to share in our suffering and redeem us *in* it rather than *from* it. The theology of the cross does not explain human suffering, but it makes suffering bearable because in Christ we see God involved in it. The words of Dietrich Bonhoeffer from his prison cell in Nazi Germany still appeal to many: "Only a suffering God can help."

ISAIAH 53:4-12 (RCL alt./BCP); 53:10-11 (RC)

Interpreting the Text

This pericope is a portion of the fourth servant song in Deutero-Isaiah, the song of the suffering servant (Isa. 52:13—53:12). Christians are used to hearing it read on Good Friday. By intention, through the hermeneutic of prophecy-fulfillment, the Gospels apply this song to the Passion of Christ. While the other servant songs (for example, Isa. 42:1-4) clearly apply to the vocation of Israel as a whole, this song is applied to an individual, perhaps in the sense of Israel reduced to one. Verse 5 indicates an atonement theme: the servant is suffering for the sins of others. Verse 10 indicates that his suffering is the will of the Lord. Verse 12 indicates that he shall be vindicated because of his faithfulness. The closing verse of today's Gospel reading clearly echoes Isaiah 53:11-12 in terms of the redemption of "the many."

Responding to the Text

Christians will rush to the christological application of this text; indeed, they are permitted to do so on the basis of the question of the Ethiopian eunuch in Acts 8:34: "About whom does the prophet say this?" But there may be a value on this Sunday, when we do not hear this song of the suffering servant in the context of the Good Friday liturgy, of pointing out the background of Jesus' messianic vocation in this particular prophetic tradition of Israel. While Christians see this text uniquely applying to Jesus, the prophet was not personally aware of the Jesus of Nazareth who would come along five centuries later. The prophet did understand that righteous suffering can be both vicarious and effective: vicarious because it is on behalf of others and effective because it makes a witness to others. Jesus interpreted his messiahship in terms of righteous suffering for the sake of "the many." But if this was a vocation for Israel, it was *a fortiori* also the vocation of the disciples of Jesus, whom he invited to take up their crosses and follow him.

Responsive Reading
PSALM 104:1-9, 24, 35c (RCL)

Interpreting the Text

This psalm is appointed as a response to the First Reading from Job 38. It is a hymn of praise celebrating God's creation of the heavens and the earth. Within this ascription of God's creative powers is his regulation of the waters and setting of their boundary "so that they might not again cover the earth" (v. 9).

Responding to the Text

To the ancient Hebrews, the waters were chaos—the opposite of the order of creation. This psalm, then, is not just in praise of God's creative powers, but also in praise of God's redemptive powers: God sets a limit to that which threatens life. The psalm may serve as a kind of parable of Job's situation. While he suffered every manner of privation, Job's life was in God's hands, even when God seemed not to be responding to his prayers. Job's life was the one thing Satan could not have. This was so whether Job realized it or not.

PSALM 91 (BCP); 91:9-16 (RCL/BCP alt.)

Interpreting the Text

This psalm is appointed as a response to the First Reading from Isaiah 53 in the RCL and the BCP. It is a psalm of trust that may be divided into three sections: a welcome into the sanctuary (vv. 1-2); a kind of homily of encouragement in the face of dangers, given in the sanctuary (vv. 3-13); a final oracle delivered in God's name (vv. 14-16). Verses 5-6 spell out four dangers that occur at different times of the day. In v. 13 the psalmist balances these four dangers with victories over four animal predators (although it is really two animals doubled because of the parallelism of Hebrew poetry). The concluding verses are an affirmation, as from the mouth of God, of God's protection of those who love him.

Responding to the Text

The affirmation that "Because you have made the Lord your refuge. . . . no evil shall befall you" (vv. 9-10—the opening verses in the RCL selection) stands in contrast with the Isaian song in which the servant of God is "struck down by God, and afflicted" (Isa. 53:4) and "it was the will of the Lord to crush him with pain" (53:10). The apparent contradiction is reconciled by remembering that God's servant suffers *in place of* others. The evil that should befall us befalls the Son of God who faces the evil one on our behalf. Recall that Psalm 91 is also appointed on the first Sunday in Lent, the Sunday of the Temptations of Christ.

PSALM 33:4-5, 18-20, 22 (RC)

Interpreting the Text

This psalm is appointed as a response to the First Reading from Isaiah 53 in the RC lectionary. It is a good example of an Israelite hymn, beginning with a thrice-repeated call to worship (vv. 1-3). The affirmation of the reliability of God's word and God's commitment to righteousness and justice in vv. 4-5 sets the tone for the whole psalm. The concluding vv. 18-21 provide a response of the people expressing trust in the Lord for the reliability of God's word and steadfast love to the people within the framework of the covenant. Verse 22 is used as the next-to-last verse in the *Te Deum Laudamus.*

THE AFFIRMATION OF THE RELIABILITY OF GOD'S WORD AND GOD'S COMMITMENT TO RIGHTEOUSNESS AND JUSTICE SETS THE TONE FOR ALL OF PSALM 33.

Responding to the Text

The psalm invites us to be alive in the covenant relationship with God. God has made promises that are reliable. The Lord's faithfulness to his word is the basis of our hope.

SECOND READING

HEBREWS 4:12-16 (BCP); 4:14-16 (RC)

Interpreting the Text

See the commentary on this pericope for last Sunday (pp. 188–89). While the emphasis in that interpretation was on the living and active word of God that is sharper than any two-edged sword (v. 12), the emphasis this week in the context of the other readings should be on Jesus' high priestly role in vv. 14-16 (the RC reading). These verses assert that Christ is worthy to be our high priest because he has shared our humanity. This enables him to sympathize with our weakness. Jesus knows what we go through from his own personal experience. But more than that, he was tested "in every respect" as we are, "yet without sin" (v. 15). We may therefore "approach the throne of grace with boldness" (v. 16) because the one who knows us intercedes for us. The "boldness" of this act is all the more striking if we recall that the term "approach" (*proserchomometha*) is used in the context of the cult of the Temple in Jerusalem, in which only the high priest could approach the altar in the Holy of Holies, and then only on the Day of Atonement (Yom Kippur). In Christ, we can all "approach the throne of grace" at all times to receive forgiveness of sins.

Responding to the Text

The idea in Hebrews of Christ being "sinless" is prompted by the custom of the high priest entering the Holy of Holies in a state of ritual purity in order to offer the atoning sacrifice for the sins of the people. While the New Testament writers share the conviction that Christ was sinless, none took an inventory of what sins Christ might have been tempted to commit. The clue to the meaning of the statement that Christ was "without sin" is found in an examination of the temptation stories in the Gospels. In every instance, his temptation was to abandon his vocation as a suffering Messiah and follow some other path. Jesus' sinlessness therefore means his total obedience to the Father, even to death on the cross.

HEBREWS 5:1-10 (RCL)

Interpreting the Text

Chapters 1–4 of Hebrews, in which Christ is compared with the angels and with Moses, lead up to the comparison in chapter 5 between Christ as high priest and "the high priests chosen from among mortals." The author of "To the Hebrews" also knows that the high priest is not self-appointed, but is called by God (Exod. 28:1; Num. 3:1). This qualification is also applied to Christ, and two Old Testament passages are used to support it: Psalm 2:7, which, for the author, showed that Jesus is designated Son of God, as were Israel's kings; and Psalm 110:4, which showed that the Messiah was also "a priest forever, according to the order of Melchizedek," the mysterious priest-king of ancient Salem who was called directly by God and, like Christ, offered bread and wine.

Royal and priestly traditions are merged here. From the time of Saul and David, the high priest and the king were different people. Only under exceptional circumstances did the king offer a sacrifice (thus Saul in 1 Sam. 13:2-10, and David in 2 Sam. 6:14-18); otherwise this belonged to the office of the priest. After the Babylonian exile, the expectation was that this dual leadership would be restored to the nation: a king from the line of David and a priest from the line of Aaron, or preferably from the line of Zadok (see Zech. 6:9-13). The Hasmoneans who controlled the Second Temple were Levitical priests of the line of Aaron, but descended through Joarib rather than David or Zadok. They had succeeded in restoring (temporarily) the independence of Israel and were given the dual office of both priest and king (see 1 Macc. 14:41 ff.). The prophet who should come in advance of the Messiah was expected to announce the true anointed high priest from Zadok's line and the anointed king from David's line. Many Jews therefore continued to think of the Hasmonean dynasty as a temporary measure.

The author of Hebrews designates Jesus as both king-messiah and "a priest forever, according to the order of Melchizedek" (v. 6), who became such because of his suffering and obedience. Verses 8-9 associate Jesus with the suffering servant of the Lord (a true priest-king) in Deutero-Isaiah. This pericope is an exegetical tour de force in associating the anointed offices in the Old Testament with Jesus as God's Anointed One (both Messiah and High Priest).

Responding to the Text

A sermon on this text might flesh out the characteristics of the priest in Israel's cult as they apply to Jesus. The priest served as the representative of the people before God, and was therefore identified with the people. We recall that by the time of Jesus, the priesthood had been democratized to the extent that priests from various Jewish communities took a two-week tour of duty serving in the Temple as representatives of their communities "back home." Zechariah, the father of John the Baptist, served in this way.

The image of Christ as priest, therefore, is one way of expressing his identification with humanity. It is noteworthy that when the priestly role of Christ was de-emphasized in favor of his royal role as "universal ruler" in both Eastern and Western Christianity after the Age of Constantine, thus stressing Christ's eminence rather than his lowliness, other mediators came into play in the Christian community. Presbyters (elders), for example, became "priests." They were assigned by the bishop to portions of the bishop's flock in scattered parishes and came to be identified with the people of the parish. The image of the "humble parish priest" has been cultivated in many works of literature, such as Alan Paton's *Cry the Beloved Country* and George Bernano's *Diary of a Country Priest*, and personified by the seventeenth century Anglican poet George Herbert. But to the extent that the priest or the bishop was seen as an eminent mediator, the laity themselves expressed the lowliness of the priestly vocation. Within the laity the women assumed the priestly role where the men were rulers.[2]

THE RECOVERY OF THE ROLE OF THE BAPTIZED PEOPLE OF GOD AS A PRIESTLY COMMUNITY HAS EMPHASIZED THE VOCATION OF CHRISTIANS TO IDENTIFY WITH SUFFERING HUMANITY AS A WAY OF LIVING OUT THEIR BAPTISM IN DAILY LIFE.

The recovery of the role of the baptized people of God as a priestly community in the Reformation and in the liturgical movement has also emphasized the vocation of Christians to identify with suffering humanity as a way of living out their baptism in daily life. Christology has, therefore, had some profound practical consequences in the life of the church.

Gospel

MARK 10:35-45; 10:42-45 (RC alt.)

Interpreting the Text

In the Markan narrative structure, Jesus has foretold his death and resurrection for the third time, and for the third time the disciples fail to understand the nature of Jesus' messiahship. This time, the failure to understand is illustrated in the story of the request of the sons of Zebedee, James and John, who have been a part of the inner circle of disciples from the beginning of Jesus' ministry, for positions of honor when Jesus comes into his glory in the messianic kingdom. A possible background image for the request in this pericope is the ceremony by which the Roman Senate appointed Herod King over Judea in 40 B.C.E., in which Herod was escorted by the two powerful Romans, Mark Antony and Octavian (later Caesar Augustus). It still took three years of fighting for Herod to achieve his crown in fact.

To make such a request immediately after Jesus' prediction of his Passion shows a monumental insensitivity to what Jesus has just said, as well as to the nature of Jesus' mission. Jesus counters this ill-timed request by showing that it is also ill-considered: they will have to achieve what Jesus achieved, drink the cup that he drinks and be baptized with the baptism with which he will be baptized. They assert their ability to do this. Jesus surprisingly agrees that they will share his cup of suffering. But it is not his prerogative to say who will occupy places of authority in his kingdom; "it is for those for whom it has been prepared" (v. 40).

A general unrest arises from the other disciples when they hear of this request. But for their benefit and ours, Jesus redefines greatness in the kingdom of God. Unlike the way it is among the gentiles (the way of the world), to be great in God's kingdom is to be a servant (*diakonos*); the highest calling is to be a slave (*doulos*). Verse 45 provides the key to the meaning of Jesus' mission: "For the Son of Man came not to be served but to serve, and to give his life as a ransom for many." This statement transcends its immediate application to the situation described in this pericope. The ransom image is as close as one gets to a theory of the atonement in the Gospel of Mark. According to Mark, Jesus' death sets free those held captive by sin and evil.

Responding to the Text

The failure of the disciples to understand the nature of Jesus' ministry is a central theme of the Gospel of Mark. It remains a perennial temptation of the church to seek the way of glory rather than the way of the cross and to prefer an all-powerful Christ to a suffering Christ. Two tendencies in contemporary American Christianity are countered by this Gospel text: the tendency of the church to hanker after "success," usually measured in terms of "growth"; and the tendency to present an upbeat message that helps people cope with the problems in life. In these ways, the Christian churches in North America reflect and foster what Douglas John Hall calls "the officially optimistic society" which they serve as chaplain.[3]

There has always been and always will be a desire for a Christianity without the cross, and in American Protestantism for a bodiless cross. The tendencies in some quarters of early Christianity to emphasize miracles and preach a docetic Christ, against which the Gospel of Mark may have been written, are still with us. Such a Christianity seems successful because it draws many followers with its offer of an easy faith and a quick fix to all problems. This is evident in the therapeutic approach to preaching and to church life that is so prevalent today, as if the basic problems of human life can be "solved" by applying workable techniques. But Jesus does not ask us to be successful; he asks us to be faithful.

Nor does he call us to a life of comfort; he invites us to share in his baptism of suffering. He does not guarantee us a privileged place in his community of disciples unless we are willing to serve our fellow members.

It is noteworthy that Jesus asked James and John if they could drink the cup from which he would drink and be baptized with the baptism with which he would be baptized. That same question must be put to all would-be disciples of Jesus. The images are sacramental, and we are reminded that we are baptized into Christ's death (Rom. 6:3) and that in the celebration of the Eucharist proclaim his death until he comes (1 Cor. 11:26). The sacraments themselves are signs keeping us on the path of following Christ: the way of the cross.[4]

TWENTIETH SUNDAY AFTER PENTECOST

OCTOBER 29, 2000
THIRTIETH SUNDAY IN ORDINARY TIME / PROPER 25

REVISED COMMON	EPISCOPAL (BCP)	ROMAN CATHOLIC
Job 42:1-6, 10-17 or Jer. 31:7-9	Isa. 59: (1-4) 9-19	Jer. 31:7-9
Ps. 34:1-8 (19-22) or 126	Ps. 13	Ps. 126
Heb. 7:23-28	Heb. 5:12—6:1, 9-12	Heb. 5:1-6
Mark 10:46-52	Mark 10:46-52	Mark 10:46-52

THIS IS ANOTHER SUNDAY with readings all over the biblical map. Yet if the preacher is willing to put the pericope texts into their contexts, certain commonalities appear. Take the clue from the Gospel, which is as much about the unperceptive disciples as about the newly seeing blind Bartimaeus. Job's eyes, too, have been opened to the mysteries of God and he prays for the friends who had wronged him. Jeremiah announces a wonderful promise for Israel's future, but speaks from a Jerusalem with the armies of Babylon literally at the gates and himself placed in "protective custody" by the state as a result of his denunciations of Judah's unfaithful policies. Deutero-Isaiah castigates a people whose path is not straight and who are groping "like the blind along a wall" (Isa. 5:10). The readings from Hebrews 5 and 7 present Jesus as a high priest who can identify with our condition and "go easy" on us, while Hebrew 6 exhorts us to "grow up" spiritually and theologically.

FIRST READING

JOB 42:1-6, 10-17 (RCL)

Interpreting the Text

This is the climax of the story of Job. He has been humbled by God's response and offers to "repent in dust and ashes" (v. 6) for having felt abandoned by God. He admits now that he cannot know all that God knows and must therefore simply trust in God's providence (vv. 2-3). He prays for his friends who had spoken foolishly about God, and the Lord accepts Job's prayer. Job's fortunes are then restored twofold.

Responding to the Text

The result of Job's experiences is that he now recognizes that his insight into the mystery of God's providence deepens what he has been taught. He can now accept as a matter of personal conviction what he had learned as a matter of rote before evil befell him. This is undoubtedly the experience of many in the congregation. The inadequacy of the much-maligned "Sunday School faith" is that it is not deepened by personal experience and reflection on that experience.

JEREMIAH 31:7-9 (RCL alt./RC)

Interpreting the Text

The theme of this oracle of consolation is the reconstitution of Israel. Commentators note the similarities between the four poems in Jeremiah 30-31 and Deutero-Isaiah (Isa. 35, 40-55). Even though only a remnant shall be brought back to the land, their return shall be an occasion of great joy because they shall be a sign of God's fidelity to the covenant. The fact that they come from the "north country" and even "the farthest parts of the earth" (v. 8) may reflect awareness that the people of Israel are scattered from Babylon to Egypt. Their glorious return is described in language that is more like the oracles of Deutero-Isaiah than of Jeremiah. Even those who have trouble walking ("the blind and the lame, those with child and those in labor") will be aided by God with a smooth walk alongside streams of water—the reverse of the hardships the people experienced when they went into exile. The reason there shall be so many children and pregnant mothers is that Jeremiah had told the Jews to increase their number while in Babylon (29:6). The father-son imagery recalls Hosea 11:1-4, yet goes beyond it in calling Ephraim "my firstborn." Parallel with "I have become a father to Israel," "Ephraim . . . my firstborn" suggests Israel's rights and responsibilities.

Responding to the Text

Within Jeremiah, long passages of lament have been turned into songs of rejoicing. In the face of the disaster that Jeremiah correctly predicted, the prophet utters a word of hope. The reasons for hope are not founded on any geopolitical considerations (which were stacked against Israel), but on the faithfulness of God to the covenantal promise. Jeremiah showed his own trust in the promise of God by buying real estate just before the exile.

THE REASONS FOR HOPE ARE NOT FOUNDED ON ANY GEOPOLITICAL CONSIDERATIONS (WHICH WERE STACKED AGAINST ISRAEL), BUT ON THE FAITHFULNESS OF GOD TO THE COVENANTAL PROMISE.

ISAIAH 59:(1-4) 9-19 (BCP)

Interpreting the Text

The optional opening verses of this reading indicate that while salvation is God's work, it may be hastened or delayed by Israel's response. It is because of the iniquities of the people that God hides his face. Verse 9 begins an indictment of the people: "justice is far from us." The people do not walk a straight path; they stumble like blind people (v. 10). They wait for justice and salvation, but there is none (v. 11). "For our transgressions . . . are many, and our sins testify against us" (v. 12). The Lord saw the transgressions of the people and "it displeased him that there was no justice" (v. 15). In this situation God's coming is more to be feared than hoped for, because the Lord will come in judgment to repay the people "according to their deeds" (v. 18). Jeremiah's quiet brook of living water (Jer. 31:9—the RCL and RC First Reading) becomes a rushing stream of vengeance driven by the Lord's wind (v. 19). God "will come to Zion as Redeemer" when "Jacob" (all Israel) turns from transgression (v. 20).

Responding to the Text

This is a text that hits us where it hurts. Caregivers often hear people cry out for justice. "Life isn't fair," some people say. Like the people of Israel, they may long to do right, "but it is far from us." It's like the heart patient who can't give up smoking and therefore experiences no healing. We complain that God is absent from us, and so we grope and stumble through life, longing for deliverance. But without repentance, expressed, for example, in a change of lifestyle, do we really want the God of justice to come to us and give us justice?

Preaching this text as it is to people as we are would be sheer "law." "Gospel" (good news) comes by relating this reading to the Second Reading from Hebrews 6 (BCP) and the Gospel (all lectionaries). Hebrews calls for maturity in faith and practice—in the context of this reading from Isaiah 59, maturity would be a recognition and ownership of our own culpabilities. Blind Bartimaeus in the Gospel reading cries out like the people of Israel for mercy, but he experiences the Savior's real presence.

RESPONSIVE READING

PSALM 34:1-8 (19-22) (RCL)

Interpreting the Text

This psalmody is a response to the First Reading from Job 42. It is a blessing of God who answers prayers and delivers from fears. Verses 5-6 touch on the blind Bartimaeus story in the Gospel. But v. 8, frequently used as a eucharistic antiphon, picks up the theme of experiential wisdom in the reading from Job: "O taste and see that the Lord is good!" Verses 19-22 also picks up the theme of Job by affirming that God is near the righteous in their suffering and will not fail them.

Responding to the Text

The psalm affirms that the faithful experience God being near to them especially in their suffering. This keeps them from falling into the sin of utter despair when calamity strikes. This sentiment will be shared by many in the congregation who have known God's providence in their lives when they were going through hard times.

PSALM 126 (RCL alt./RC)

Interpreting the Text

This psalmody is a response to the First Reading from Jeremiah 31:7-9. The common theme in Psalm 126 and Jeremiah 30-31 is the return of the people of Israel from exile. Verses 1-3 are translated as a past action ("When the Lord restored the fortunes of Zion") and vv. 4-6 as a future event ("Restore our fortunes, O Lord") in all the new translations except the International Commission on English in the Liturgy translation, which understands the whole psalm as a present yet incomplete action. Verse 4 has an interesting image of sudden storms in the desert that fill dry wadis with rush waters. Verse 6 has an image of sowing and reaping in which those who went mourning into exile shall return home rejoicing "carrying their sheaves."

Responding to the Text

It is possible that ancient rites of lamentation at planting time and rejoicing at harvest time have influenced the images in this psalm. But, as is often the case in the Bible, nature themes are transposed into historical themes. In the New Testament these themes of sowing and reaping even become eschatological (see John 12:24ff. and 1 Cor. 15:36ff.). The final "restoration of fortunes" comes in the resurrection of the dead when "we shall be changed" (1 Cor. 15:51).

PSALM 13 (BCP)

Interpreting the Text

Artur Weiser calls this psalm "a simple lament of a sick man,"[5] although there is nothing in the text to clarify what the original situation of the psalmist may have been. It may be a liturgical piece wrought out of the experience of many generations. While allowing the person of prayer to give vent to the feeling of abandonment by God, it also gives expression to confidence in God's faithfulness.

Responding to the Text

As a response to the First Reading from Isaiah 59, the psalm expresses the sense of God's absence but adds thought that God will to save and restore us. An acute feeling of abandonment by God is nevertheless a faith-conviction that there is a God and that God has acted in the past to forgive and heal and can do so again in the future.

Second Reading

HEBREWS 5:1-6 (RC)

Interpreting the Text

See the commentary on Hebrews 5:1-10 for the nineteenth Sunday after Pentecost (pp. 197–98). Perhaps the aspect of this text to emphasize in the context of today's liturgy is the fact that the high priest deals gently with the ignorant and the erring since he himself is subject to these sins, and must offer sacrifice for his sins before he can offer the sacrifice of atonement on Yom Kippur. Because of his humanity, Jesus is also able (*dunamenos*) to deal patiently with the ignorant and the wayward.

THE TEXT IN HEBREWS SUGGESTS THAT DEALING PATIENTLY WITH THE IGNORANT AND THE WAYWARD IS AN ABILITY, A POWER (*DUNAMENOS*), THAT IS NOT GIVEN TO ALL, AND RARELY GIVEN WITHOUT AN AWARENESS OF ONE'S OWN WEAKNESS.

Responding to the Text

I am struck by the fact that the text suggests that dealing patiently with the ignorant and the wayward is an ability, a power (*dunamenos*), that is not given to all, and rarely given without an awareness of one's own weakness. The author of Hebrews presents a Jesus who has experienced human weakness and is therefore able to effectively represent us before God (Heb. 2:17-18). He is able to deal gently (*metripathein*) with those whose weakness he has shared.

HEBREWS 5:12—6:1, 9-12 (BCP)

Interpreting the Text

The author has introduced the idea that Jesus is "a high priest according to the order of Melchizedek"(5:10)—an eternal high priest appointed by God. Before he spells out the christological ramifications of this, he adds a warning or exhortation. (It is typical of the author of Hebrews to alternate theological discussion with warnings.) The warning in this case is to avoid falling away from the faith or committing apostasy (Heb. 6:4-8). We can only imagine why the drafters of this lectionary omitted the verses that get at what the warning is all about.

What we have in the verses provided is a concern on the part of the author that his readers attain greater spiritual maturity. They have been Christians long enough that they should be teaching others instead of needing to be taught the basic elements of the faith. He makes a comparison between infancy and maturity that is not unlike St. Paul's in 1 Corinthians 13:10-11 and 14:20. The author of Hebrews urges his readers "on toward perfection" (6:1). They should grow beyond "the basic teachings about Christ" (6:1), which could be understood either as Christ's initial teachings (subjective genitive) or the beginning teachings about Christ (objective genitive). The items outlined in 6:1b-2 are not a bad list of catechetics. These must be taken down because to fall away from the faith is to forfeit what has been received. In the view of Hebrews, those who fall away cannot go through "repentance" a second time, just as Christ cannot atone for sins a second time. The idea that there is no second forgiveness after baptism was a point of view widely shared in the ancient church (see also *The Shepherd of Hermas* and Tertullian, *On Purity*), even though it did not universally prevail.

After this word of warning, the author injects his first note of affection for his readers, calling them "beloved" (6:9). He does not expect them to fall away, and God will recognize "your work and the love that you showed . . . in serving the saints" (v. 10). The author encourages his readers not to let their zeal flag or become sluggish. Filled with "the assurance of hope" (v. 11), they should imitate "those who through faith and patience inherit the promise" (v. 12). The example of faith and patience that the author provides is Abraham (6:13 ff.), who once encountered "King Melchizedek of Salem, priest of the Most High God," from whom he received a blessing and to whom he gave a tithe (7:1 ff.).

Responding to the Text

The thrust of these verses is to encourage the faithful to move beyond catechetics to constructive theology. Many Christians have not grown beyond what they learned in Sunday school or confirmation class. That kind of elementary faith in our kind of world puts these Christians at risk of losing their faith altogether. It's not a matter of knowing more facts but of integrating facts with experience and moving to a more profound understanding of the reality of God and the role of Christ. This reading could be correlated very well with the reading from Job 42 and Psalm 34, except that it would be mixing lectionary systems. On the other hand, the Gospel story of the "enlightenment" of blind Bartimaeus can also be correlated with this reading.

HEBREWS 7:23-28 (RCL)

Interpreting the Text

This reading comes at the end of an entire chapter devoted to comparing and contrasting the old Levitical priesthood with the new priesthood of Christ, who has arisen according to the likeness of Melchizedek. The mysterious priest-king of ancient Salem, unlike the Levitical priests who must be descendants of Aaron, was "without father, without mother, without genealogy, having neither beginning of days nor end of life, but resembling the Son of God; he remains a priest forever" (7:5). Being indestructible, Melchizedek is superior to the Levitical priests, and Jesus is such a "perfect" priest.

Reginald Fuller lists a series of contrasts between the Levitical priesthood and Christ in this passage:[6] the Levitical priests are many, but Christ is one; they are impermanent, but Christ is eternal; they are subject to death, but Christ is alive forever; they are sinners who had to offer sacrifices for themselves, but Christ is sinless and offers himself as a sacrifice for others; they offer repeated sacrifices, but Christ's sacrifice is once-for-all; they are appointed by law, but Christ is appointed by an oath superseding the law (the oath is Ps. 110:4, quoted in Heb. 7:21).

It is clear that for the author of Hebrews, that which is a part of the old covenant is included in the new. With Jesus there is a new covenant, a new priesthood, and a new sacrifice. Not only is it new, it is better than the old. Angels continue to function in the new covenant, but they are inferior and subordinate to the Son of God. The servant Moses is replaced by the Son Jesus. In place of the Levitical priesthood there is a priesthood according to the order of Melchizedek, established by a later promise that supersedes the first, and confirmed by an oath from God. The view of Hebrews is that Jesus is superior to anything in the old covenant, not in the sense that the old is inferior to the new (that would make it of no value) but in the sense that the old is a shadow (or foreshadowing) of the reality that is the new covenant.

Responding to the Text

The theology of Hebrews was once a staple of Christian devotion, but has been lost in recent years. In part this is because biblical illiteracy renders opaque the Old Testament allusions, citations, and images on which the theology of Hebrews depends. But references to the high priestly ministry of Christ are found in many hymns, such as William C. Dix's "Alleluia! Sing to Jesus" (*LWB* 158).

As within the veil you entered,
Robed in flesh, our great high priest,
Here on earth both priest and victim
In the eucharistic feast.

It is especially in the eucharistic feast that Christ's high priestly role has been meaningful to Christians. For the ancient Christians, Christ was regarded as the high priest of the priestly community, the church, that offers the sacrifice of the new covenant, the eucharistic sacrifice. In his commentary on Psalm 110, for which "To the Hebrews" serves as a midrash, Theodoret of Cyrrhus writes that "Christ is a priest . . . who does not offer anything, but he acts as the head of those who offer. For he calls the Church his body, and through it he performs the office of priest as a human being, while as God he receives the offerings."[7]

Ambrose of Milan saw the Eucharist in more dynamic terms. In his commentary on Psalm 38:25, Ambrose writes:

> We have seen the High Priest coming to us; we have seen and heard him offering his blood for us. We priests follow, as well as we can, so that we may offer sacrifice for the people. Though we can claim no merit, we are honoured in the sacrifice; for, although Christ is now visibly offered, yet he is himself offered on earth, when the body of Christ is offered. Moreover, it is made clear that he himself offers in us, since it is his words which sanctify the sacrifice which is offered.[8]

The eucharistic action is not so much us obeying a command as it is the work of Christ in his people: "he himself offers in us." Such a notion of the eucharistic sacrifice is strongly christocentric because it links the Eucharist with the saving work of Christ.

This idea is carried still further by Augustine of Hippo in *The City of God.* There he writes that

> A true sacrifice is every act which is performed so that we may be united with God in holy fellowship. . . . Although this sacrifice is made or offered by human beings, still the sacrifice is a divine act. . . . The whole redeemed community, the congregation and fellowship of the saints, is offered as a universal sacrifice to God by the great High Priest who offered himself in suffering for us in the form of a servant, that we might be the Body of so great a Head. This form of a servant he offered, in that he was offered; for in this he is mediator, priest, and sacrifice.[9]

There is a sacrifice that Christ offers as high priest besides his offering of himself; he offers his brothers and sisters as an offering pleasing to God the Father.

Gospel

MARK 10:46-52

Interpreting the Text

In this Gospel reading we encounter Jesus, the compassionate high priest like Melchizedek, who is about to enter Jerusalem, the ancient site of

Melchizedek's city (see the readings from Hebrews 5 and 7). The event of the healing of the blind beggar Bartimaeus occurs as Jesus is leaving Jericho to go up to Jerusalem. It is located in Mark's narrative after Jesus' third Passion prediction and the third time that his disciples have responded inappropriately to that prediction. There is no doubt that the evangelist intended this story to be seen as a symbolic counterpoint to the preceding episode, capping the disciples' consistent "blindness" to Jesus' mission. The blind beggar cries out to Jesus. The expression "to cry out" (*krazein*) had been used to express fear and awe at some extraordinary manifestation of power, as when the unclean spirits cried out (1:24; 3:11; 5:7; 9:26) and when the disciples cried out when they saw Jesus walking on the water (6:49). The blind beggar calls Jesus "Son of David," which is the first time in Mark's narrative that this messianic title is used by someone other than a demon. Others rebuke Bartimaeus for crying out (and presumably for using this title), but Jesus asks him: "What do you want me to do for you? (v. 51). This is the same question Jesus had just put to James and John (10:36). The simple answer of Bartimaeus, "Master, I want to see," stands in contrast to the ambitious request of James and John for positions of power in Jesus' kingdom. They are blind to the nature of Jesus' suffering messiahship and to their overconfidence that they can do anything. Mark indicates no healing gesture (as in Matt. 20:24), but rather emphasizes the man's faith: "your faith has made you well" (v. 52). This faith is an openness to God's saving power. Jesus' assessment of the man's faith is confirmed by the report that "Immediately he regained his sight and followed him on the way" (v. 52). The way is both up to Jerusalem and the climax of Jesus' ministry, and the way of discipleship.

THE BLIND BEGGAR CALLS JESUS "SON OF DAVID," WHICH IS THE FIRST TIME IN MARK'S NARRATIVE THAT THIS MESSIANIC TITLE IS USED BY SOMEONE OTHER THAN A DEMON.

Responding to the Text

The clearly symbolic location of this story within the Markan narrative suggests the possibility of developing a sermon that uses the structure of the Gospel rather than the text itself as the point of departure. This will serve as a review of the sequence of Sunday Gospel readings and help the congregation to see the Gospel's dramatic development and point of view. During the Sundays after Pentecost we have been following the central section of the Gospel of Mark as Jesus journeys from Caesarea Philippi to Jerusalem. This journey-section is framed by two healings of blind men: the blind man at Bethsaida (8:22 ff.) and the blind Bartimaeus. In between, Jesus foretells his death and resurrection three times. Each time the disciples respond in an inappropriate way: Peter rebukes Jesus for offering himself as a suffering servant and Peter is rebuked by Jesus; the disciples argue which of them is the greatest; and James and John ask for positions of power when Jesus comes into his glory. In spite of all that they have heard and seen, the disciples remain blind to the impending reality of Jesus' suffering, death, and resurrection. They have remained ignorant of the purpose of Jesus' mission. Hence, they will not be found at the cross when Jesus comes to the climax of his mission, and they will miss the significance of the resurrection as a vindication of the whole mission of Jesus.

In contrast to the blindness of the disciples, the two blind men who frame this section see, and the blind beggar Bartimaeus follows Jesus on the way. As Werner Kelber has suggested, "the disturbing but profoundly religious truth Mark conveys in the central section of his Gospel" is that "those who are closest to Jesus and claim to know best of all may be furthest from the truth, while those who are spatially and temporally removed from Jesus may spiritually and in the conduct of their lives be very close to him."[10] It would be foolhardy of the preacher to attempt to identify who does or does not really know and follow Jesus. That is ultimately God's judgment call. But who can resist the feeling that Mark is offering a judgment on the leaders of the church who may be triumphantly processing behind Jesus with no awareness of the cross ahead and the cost of discipleship, while many who are on the margins (and perhaps occupying the pews) are quite aware of what it costs them to follow Jesus in their daily lives and who have experienced the same mercy from Jesus in their lives as the blind Bartimaeus? The fact that Mark explains the name Bartimaeus as "son of Timaeus" indicates that it was written for a gentile community—outsiders who are meant to draw comfort from the ministry of Jesus, even at the expense of the insiders.

REFORMATION SUNDAY

October 29, 2000

Revised Common
Jer. 31:31-34
Ps. 46
Rom. 3:19-28
John 8:31-36

Reformation Day is an observance unique in the Lutheran calendar, although it is also celebrated in some other Protestant churches. Its actual date in the calendar is October 31, which commemorates Martin Luther's posting of the ninety-five theses on the door of the Castle Church in Wittenberg in 1517. This event is usually taken to be the beginning of the Reformation. In actual practice the Festival of the Reformation is usually observed on the Sunday preceding October 31. The readings are those assigned for Reformation Day in *Lutheran Book of Worship.* They highlight several of the doctrinal themes of the Reformation: the new relationship between God and God's people made possible by the forgiveness of sins (Jer. 31); justification by faith apart from the works of the law (Rom. 3); the freedom of the Christian (John 8). The nature of this observance as an historical commemoration suggests that the preacher will want to highlight aspects of the Reformation in terms of their contemporary applicability to church and society. Far from being an opportunity for anti-Roman Catholic polemics, the Festival of the Reformation may now be an occasion to apply the doctrines of the Gospel to the ongoing need for the reform of the church and the renewal of society.

First Reading

JEREMIAH 31:31-34

Interpreting the Text

This prose oracle is clearly eschatological: "Behold the days are coming . . ." Uttered by the historical Jeremiah on the eve of the Babylonian exile, it envisions a second chance for God's people in a renewed Israel. With a certain earnestness, "Thus says the Lord" occurs four times in these six verses. Of the sixteen verbs in the passage, "the Lord" is the subject of ten of them. The Lord will bring about a new covenant on his own initiative just as he brought about the old one. The new is contrasted with the old covenant given on Mt. Sinai, which the people broke though God was faithful to them ("though I was their husband"). This new covenant will effect a change of minds among the people because it will be internalized. An inward transformation of the heart will allow people to do God's will (what the Law requires). Hence, no instruction will be necessary for anyone in the community of any age, for all will know the Lord. The condition that enables the new covenant to come about is God's forgiveness of the sins of the people. The slate will be wiped clean and a new relationship will begin.

Responding to the Text

How are we to envision the promise of a new covenant? Robert Carroll regards it as "a pious hope rather than a programme of social organization, and it may be described quite fairly as utopian."[11] "Utopia," of course, means "no place." It's no place that we have yet experienced. Yet Christians have experienced a new relationship with God, brought about through the Holy Spirit, by which sinners are forgiven and reconciled to God for Christ's sake. Thus, as John Bright put it, "We must go beyond Jeremiah's word, and beyond B.C. We must follow Jeremiah's word ahead to the gospel."[12]

Far from being an individual relationship between God and the forgiven sinner, the new covenant occurs in community and through outward means just as the old covenant did. The word of Jeremiah is heard in the institution of the Eucharist (Luke 22:20; 1 Cor. 11:25). Matthew specifies that the new covenant celebrated in the Eucharist is an appropriation of Jesus' sacrifice: "for this [cup] is my blood of the (new) covenant, which is poured out for many for the forgiveness of sins" (Matt. 26:28). The forgiveness conveyed through the sacrament is not only "for you;" it is also "for many."

FAR FROM BEING AN INDIVIDUAL RELATIONSHIP BETWEEN GOD AND THE FORGIVEN SINNER, THE NEW COVENANT OCCURS IN COMMUNITY AND THROUGH OUTWARD MEANS JUST AS THE OLD COVENANT DID.

Forgiveness was a dynamic concept for Martin Luther. He wrote in his *Small Catechism*, "where there is forgiveness of sins, there is also life and salvation." But for the reformer, forgiveness, new life, and salvation are received through *means* of grace. Most specifically, forgiveness is received through the social institutions of the sacraments. Forgiveness is, in fact, a social concept; it is only needed where relationships must be mended and renewed. Therefore there is a place in which to experience the promised new covenant that has been accomplished through the sacrifice of Christ on the cross: in the sacramental life of the church.[13]

RESPONSIVE READING

PSALM 46

Interpreting the Text

This psalm is selected because it served as the inspiration for Martin Luther's hymn, "A Mighty Fortress Is Our God," the so-called "battle hymn of the Reformation." The psalm is therefore not really a thematic response to the First Reading. Luther's hymn might be sung as the psalmody for this day, if it is not used elsewhere in the liturgy.

It has been assumed that Psalm 46 is a song celebrating God's victory in Jerusalem; but neither Zion nor Jerusalem is mentioned. If the "city" (vv. 5-6) is Jerusalem, then the "river" would have to be related to an apocalyptic vision. It is easier to take the geographic details of "waters" and "river" (vv. 4-5) as descriptions of the headwaters of the Jordan at Dan. The psalm then takes on cosmological, even mythological, as well as historical features as God's victory over the subterranean waters of chaos (vs. 3-4) and also over Israel's enemies (vv. 7-10).[14] The psalm thus celebrates God's protection from cosmic and historical forces arrayed against God's people. The ICEL translation has: "the Lord of cosmic power, Jacob's God, will shield us" (vv. 2, 7).

Responding to the Text

The combining of the mythological and the historical is reflected in Luther's hymn "Ein feste Burg ist unser Gott." The historical context in which he wrote his greatest hymn is not known for sure. One possible inspiration was the Diet of Speyer in 1529 at which the German princes protested against the revocation of their liberties to oversee the church on their territory, thus giving rise to the name "Protestant." But it may also reflect the persecution of Luther's followers, such as the burning at the stake of his friend Leonhard Kaiser in 1527. Thus, there were historical contexts that would account for the use of the psalm's battle (and embattled) images the hymn. But Luther understood that behind the attacks on the Reformation stood "the old satanic foe," the devil. The devil was real for Luther (recall Luther's bout with the devil at the Wartburg—a "fortress" in which Luther was kept in safety from his enemies). To a great extent he saw the struggle for the reform of the church as the battleground between God and Satan.[15]

How seriously do we today take the forces of evil that may be arrayed against the church and that prevent genuine reform and renewal from occurring? How much confidence do we have in the power of God's word to thwart "the old satanic foe" that assails the church and Christians in insidious ways?

Second Reading
ROMANS 3:19-28

Interpreting the Text

This is the classic text that sets out what became the heart of the sixteenth century Reformation. Major theologians, from Martin Luther to Karl Barth, have also weighed in with commentaries on the Letter of Paul to the Romans. Faithfulness to Scripture requires that we try to understand what Paul was saying in this text and why he was saying it. In this day and age, we are newly aware that Paul's message must be understood within the apostle's own Jewish background and his sense of the mission of the church.

Paul is saying that the righteousness of God that is attested in the Law of Moses and by the prophets has been disclosed apart from the Law. That righteousness is now manifested through faith in Christ. The term "righteousness" (*dikaiosune*) is itself ambiguous, since it is used in several different ways in the Hebrew and Greek Scriptures. It can be used in an ethical sense of being "upright," but also in a forensic sense of being "made right." Rudolf Bultmann showed that the more Jewish thought became eschatological, the more "righteousness" took on a forensic sense as the condition for receiving "life" or salvation.[16] There is therefore no difference between Paul's understanding of "righteousness" and the understanding in eschatological Jewish thought. The difference is that what Jewish thought posited in the future, Paul posited in the present as the fruit of the saving acts of God in Christ. God has acted in Christ to save humanity because all human beings have sinned and fall short of God's standards. In Christ, God has provided the sacrifice of atonement that covers sin, and now God justifies those who place their faith or trust in what God has done in Christ. God did this to show his own righteousness, by forbearing with sins previously committed against him. Salvation (eschatological justice) therefore becomes a free gift of God: God justifies those who have faith in Jesus. Paul did not believe that this concept of justification as a free gift of God was new; Habakkuk had said centuries earlier, "The righteous live by their faith" (Hab. 2:4). Paul goes on at length in Romans 4 to show that both Abraham and David were justified by faith. Now, Paul claims, God is offering that same salvation to both Jew and gentile ("there is no distinction"); God's salvation is universally available ("for all who believe").

The scandal of Paul's position is that he argued that since righteousness can be manifested by faith apart from performing the works of the Law, the gentiles can be brought into a renewed Israel on the basis of faith in the saving act of God in Christ apart from observing the Law of Moses. Luther used texts such as this to argue that the new relationship between God and humanity is based on trust in God's promise of salvation in Christ rather than on meriting grace through performing good or religious works. Krister Stendahl, however, makes a strong argument that Paul's doctrine of justification by faith (developed first in the polemical Letter to the Galatians, in which Paul contended against "Judaizers" in the church, then in the more irenic Letter to the Romans, addressed to a church with both Jewish and gentile members) was really an ecumenical principle to enable Jews and gentiles to live together in one renewed Israel.[17]

Responding to the Text

This was the central text of the Reformation. To v. 28, "For we hold that a person is justified by faith apart from works prescribed by the law," Luther added the word *alone* (*sola*). Justification by faith alone became, in the view of the Lutheran Reformation, "the article on which the church stands or falls." According to one interpretation, it was a "proposal of dogma" to the universal church at the Diet of Augsburg.[18]

The preacher may draw upon Stendahl's interpretation that "justification by faith" was an ecumenical principle for Paul to show how it was first proposed as a gospel principle in the Augsburg Confession for the reform of the church, and is now serving as the most significant step forward in Lutheran-Roman Catholic relationships since the sixteenth century with the signing of the Joint Statement on the Doctrine of Justification by the Vatican and the Lutheran World Federation. Together Lutherans and Roman Catholics now confess: "By grace alone, in faith in Christ's saving work and not because of any merit on our part, we are accepted by God and receive the Holy Spirit, who renews our hearts while equipping and calling us to do good works."[19]

TOGETHER LUTHERANS AND ROMAN CATHOLICS NOW CONFESS: "BY GRACE ALONE, IN FAITH IN CHRIST'S SAVING WORK AND NOT BECAUSE OF ANY MERIT ON OUR PART, WE ARE ACCEPTED BY GOD AND RECEIVE THE HOLY SPIRIT, WHO RENEWS OUR HEARTS WHILE EQUIPPING AND CALLING US TO DO GOOD WORKS."

By this agreement, the Lutheran and Roman Catholic Churches acknowledge that they do not presently disagree about salvation in Christ and the justification of sinners by faith, that the Lutheran insistence on "Christ for us" and the Roman Catholic teaching of "Christ in us" are more properly complimentary than contradictory, and that the mutual condemnations of the sixteenth century do not apply to our respective teachings today. If the Lutheran and Roman Catholic Churches do not disagree on the article on which Lutherans have said that "the church stands or falls," then the Roman Catholic Church cannot be regarded as a "fallen" church. It follows from this that we must seek reconciliation with the Roman Church, in spite of the immense obstacles that still lie on the path to Christian unity. But if we can only imagine a Lutheran Church going on and on in history somewhat as it is now, we are not really serious about Christian unity.

If we are serious about unity, then the starting place for our quest must be repentance—a change of attitude. It was proposed several years ago that Reformation Sunday should be renamed Reconciliation Sunday. Rather than simply rehearse Luther's rage against the corruptions in faith and practice in the late medieval Western church, or even say nice things about Roman Catholics because we've gotten to know them better, we should reflect on our reluctance to make the sacrifices of thought and habit that will enable us to follow the Spirit's lead into one, holy, catholic, and apostolic church.

As the world becomes less Christian and other religions grow rapidly, we have to make some clear and dramatic choices for the sake of the mission of the gospel. We can either become immersed in perpetuating past conflicts and maintaining the present structures of schism, or we can do what our truth tells us is our only hope as sinful human beings: throw ourselves on the mercy of God who justifies us because of his own righteous forbearance rather than because of our own righteousness, which, as Luther rightly said, is but "a filthy rag."

Gospel

JOHN 8:31-36

Interpreting the Text

"The truth will make you free" is on the list of frequently abused biblical statements. It is often quoted out of context in academic addresses. But it was already misconstrued by "the Jews" who heard Jesus speak. The dialogues in John all proceed on the basis of misunderstanding. In v. 33 the Jews misquote Jesus, leaving out his references to "continuing in my word" and to "know the truth." So they need to ask Jesus what he means by saying that they will be made free, since "the truth" is the reality on which freedom depends. They have also lost the meaning of their history, boasting that they have never been the slaves of anyone. Yet the Passover (a pivotal concept in the Gospel of John) is an annual reminder that "We were once slaves in Egypt." Without the memory of slavery and of God's liberation in the exodus, these Jews cannot understand Jesus' meaning. The household imagery in vv. 35-36 illustrates a new relationship with God in Christ: our place in God's eternal household is assured by Jesus' sonship. If the Son, who exercises the Father's authority, sets you free, you are no longer slaves but are free indeed.

"The Jews who had believed in him" is a problematic designation in this text. Are they former Jewish believers who have fallen away, or Jewish Christians who held to views different than those of the Johannine community? We cannot know. Since Jesus and his disciples are also Jews, it is probably best to simply understand "the Jews" as a dramatic device used to propel the argument of the Gospel through the literary device of misunderstanding and include ourselves among those who are corrected by Jesus. We Christians are just as likely to complacently presume that the status quo is acceptable to God.

Responding to the Text

The dialectic of freedom and slavery characterized one of Luther's best treatises, *On the Freedom of the Christian*. He placed two paradoxical axioms at the beginning of this treatise: "A Christian is a perfectly free lord of all, subject to no one. A Christian is a perfectly dutiful servant of all, subject to all."[20] The Christian is free in the inward life, and cannot be coerced in his or her relationship with God. Luther was one of the most anti-legalistic persons in the history of Christianity. At the same time, the Christian's relationship with God in Christ compels him or her in the outward life to serve the neighbor. Luther is reported to have said that "God has taken care of my salvation. I am therefore free to take care of my neighbor."

In discovering the liberating word of the gospel, Luther experienced the freedom to criticize everything that was not of the gospel. He could even criticize the very faith that had brought him "thus far" as mere credulity and not a living relationship with God in Christ. He could criticize the church and all its offices and institutions that were no longer teaching and promoting the gospel. He could criticize any human authority that taught people to rely on *it* rather than on God's promises. This is not the freedom of someone clamoring for his or her rights, but a freedom founded on truth that shows itself by caring deeply for the needs of others—for their faith, their community of support, their right to hear the gospel preached and taught, and to be protected and provided for by the state and church that serve, respectively, as the "right" and "left" hands of God. Some Christians can bask in their relationship with God without worrying about anyone else's relationship. Reformers cannot leave well enough alone because they care for their brothers and sisters in the household of faith. Reformers care deeply about community.

All of the topics addressed by the readings for Reformation Day—forgiveness of sins, justification by faith, Christian freedom—have been treated by preachers in individualistic ways. Those who listen to sermons are used to hearing calls for personal reform. They are not used to hearing calls for the reform of the church. Lutherans especially may not take kindly to the idea that there may be something amiss in Lutheran church life, because our church life is the product of reform. We can be as complacent about our status before God, and the status of our community, as "the Jews" in today's Gospel. Yet Reformation Day is precisely about the reform of the church. It was, in fact, a motto picked up by the Reformation that "the church must always be reformed."

Freedom comes from knowing the truth that is proclaimed in a word of God that is truly liberating. That's the circular argument embedded in the Gospel reading. "Continuing in my word" is also the basis of the freedom to reform the church. The word of the gospel proclaims a truth that calls into question all that is not right with the church, and gives us the freedom—the authorization— to make corrections. We celebrate a reform that took place at one time in history. But the church today is also in need of reform because it is subject to the sin of unbelief. We really do rely on human works to renew and grow the church, rather than the divinely-instituted means of grace. Today the preacher should affirm the power of God's word alone to accomplish God's purposes. We believe that when the word is truly preached and the sacraments rightly administered, the Holy Spirit works to create or awaken faith and to call, gather, enlighten, and sanctify the church and keep it in union with Jesus Christ. To that end, the holy ministry has the authority of Christ to preach the word and administer the sacraments, and the laity has the authority of Christ to see that this is being done. "Lord, keep us steadfast in thy word."

ALL SAINTS DAY

November 1, 2000

Revised Common	Episcopal (BCP)	Roman Catholic
Isa. 25:6-9	Sir. 44:1-10, 13-14	Rev. 7:2-4, 9-14
or Wis. 3:1-9	or Sir. 2:(1-6) 7-11	
Ps. 24	Ps. 149	Ps. 24:1-6
Rev. 21:1-6a	Rev. 7:2-4, 9-17	1 John 3:1-3
John 11:32-44	or Eph. 1:(11-14) 15-23	Matt. 5:1-12a
	Matt. 5:1-12	
	or Luke 6:20-26 (27-36)	

The church, like other societies, has venerated its heroes. Festivals of all the martyrs who had witnessed to Christ during the age of persecution were celebrated in the Eastern Churches already in the fourth century on different days in different local churches, although usually during the paschal season. A similar observance was set on May 13 in the Roman Church by Pope Boniface IV in 609, the date on which a pagan temple, the Pantheon, was turned over to the Church of Rome by the Emperor Phocas and rededicated to the Virgin Mary and all the martyrs. Our Festival of All Saints on November 1 originated in the churches of Britain and Ireland and is attested to in the middle of the eighth century. This was a time of the year when, in pre-Christian views, the spirits of the ancestors were thought to roam the land, and jack-o'-lanterns were used to frighten away malignant spirits (shades of Halloween). The church countered these pagan customs with a celebration of all the saints. In 835 Pope Gregory IV requested the Emperor Louis the Pious to establish this festival throughout his realm. In 1430 Pope Sixtus IV established the custom throughout the Western Church of celebrating All Saints for eight days. This octave was abolished in the Roman Calendar of 1969. However, in Lutheran and some Protestant practice, All Saints Day is observed on the Sunday after November 1 (that is, within the octave).

It's a very human custom to remember our dead. Nations have memorial days. The idea for a day commemorating all the faithful departed may have originated in the directive of Bishop Isidore of Seville (d. 636) to his monks to celebrate a Mass for all the faithful departed on the day after Pentecost. The idea caught on and was observed on different dates in different places. All Souls' Day, as we know it, was probably established in 998 by Abbot Odo of Cluny. In effect, the Lutheran All Saints Sunday has been merged with All Souls Day because it is used in many congregations as an occasion to remember all the faithful departed of the past year.

The lives of the saints may serve as texts for this memorial day as well as the Scripture readings. A sermon could be given on these lives as evidence of grace and examples of faith.

First Reading
ISAIAH 25:6-9 (RCL)

Interpreting the Text

This passage is sometimes called the "Isaian apocalypse." It looks past the time of pain and suffering to the joyous banquet God will provide on his mountain (Mount Zion, the site of God's rule) for all peoples (v. 6). In the ancient Near East it was believed that gods met humans on mountains, and temples replicated these "high places" of encounter with the sacred. The feast of fat things and well-aged wines suggests a new quality in the communion between God and God's people. In this deepened relationship, God will destroy whatever separates the people from himself, even death itself (v. 7). In ancient Hebrew thought, death was regarded as the conclusion of any relationship with God, as alien to the divine nature and no part of God's original intention for his creation. No wonder there are tears of sorrow when death occurs. When death's powers are finally neutralized, God will take away the "disgrace" of the people (v. 8). This disgrace may be the inability of the soul (*nephesh*) to praise God (Ps. 103:1).

Responding to the Text

Though the cholesterol-conscious and calorie-counters may demur at being served "a feast . . . of rich food filled with marrow" (v. 3), and though tee-totalers or those who would never spend more than five dollars for a bottle of table wine may protest being served "well-aged wines strained clear" (v. 3), surely no one would want to be excluded from the extravagant feast that Isaiah envisions God serving all peoples. Many people might object to being served such a banquet, saying that they are not worth all the fuss. Many people live such a cramped lifestyle on earth that they cannot imagine the luxurious provisions of heaven. In the Danish film, *Babette's Feast*, a French chef escaping from the revolution in Paris is given shelter by a strict Scandinavian Pietist sect. In return she becomes the cook for the patriarch of the sect and his daughters. Years later, Babette wins the lottery and decides to blow the whole amount on an extravagant French dinner for this household, to show her gratitude for their care of her. As the delicacies are brought into the house and the preparation of the meal begins, the eldest daughter says that the group must honor Babette by eating the feast, but they must not enjoy it. Yet as the meal proceeds they do begin to enjoy it, and in the gracious ambience of the table old animosities melt, as must be the case in God's kingdom when many shall come from east and west and north and south to dine at the feast of salvation.

WISDOM OF SOLOMON 3:1-9 (RCL alt.)

Interpreting the Text

The other option for the First Reading in the RCL is from the deuterocanonical or apocryphal Wisdom of Solomon, written in Greek probably in the mid-first century B.C.E.

It was written to the Jews of the Diaspora, especially in Hellenistic Egypt, to strengthen their faith and to apply the tradition to their circumstances. It dealt with age-old questions such as: Why do the just suffer, especially when the wicked seem to prosper? The book begins with an exhortation to righteousness (1:1-15) and reviews life as the ungodly see it (1:16–2:24). In chapter 3 it deals with the destiny of the righteous and the ungodly, reminding the righteous (in the pericope for today) that "the souls of the righteous are in the hand of God, and no torment will ever touch them" (v. 1) The torment in this context refers to the punishments of the afterlife. The author is vague as to the precise timing and character of the afterlife. While the author may have been influenced by Greek ideas (for example, the immortality of the soul), his ideas are still Jewish. He may have envisioned a temporary abode of all souls in Sheol until the final judgment, as in 1 Enoch 22. And the idea of being "disciplined a little" before receiving "a great good" (v. 5) is the basis of the concept of purgatory. But the future brilliance of the righteous and their co-reign with God over the nations (vv. 7-8) is a common idea in Jewish apocalyptic (see Dan. 7:22; 12:3; 2 Esdras 9:97; 1 Enoch 104:2; Testament of Abraham 1-4).

Responding to the Text

People are greatly interested in ideas about the afterlife. Funeral services are not appropriate times to engage in such speculation. But occasions like All Saints/All Souls may provide an opportunity to compare and contrast ideas of immortality and resurrection. The term "immortality" used in this text is not used in earlier Jewish literature. But it was a common term in Greek usage, and was also used by Paul in 1 Corinthians 15, which is otherwise devoted to the expectation of the resurrection of the dead. The Jewish twist on the Greek notion of "immortality" does not imply an indestructible spark in the human being, but God's gift to the just

THE JEWISH TWIST ON THE GREEK NOTION OF "IMMORTALITY" DOES NOT IMPLY AN INDESTRUCTIBLE SPARK IN THE HUMAN BEING, BUT GOD'S GIFT TO THE JUST PERSON.

person. The idea of immortality gained ascendancy in Christian thought once Christianity was loosed from its Semitic moorings and at sea in the Hellenistic world.

People raise many questions related to the afterlife. Are we to be with Christ at the point of death, or do we sleep in Christ awaiting the resurrection of the body and the last judgment? Should we pray for the dead? How will God deal with those who have not heard the gospel or who have only seen it badly lived? Hard and fast answers cannot be given to such questions. Yet the pastoral preacher cannot responsibly avoid at least probing the theological tradition to explore the answers that have been given.[21] Once in a while the books of systematic theology need to be dusted off and consulted!

SIRACH 44:1-10, 13-14; 2:(1-6) 7-11 (BCP)

Interpreting the Text

In Jewish rabbinic tradition through the eleventh century, this book was referred to as "The Book (or Instruction) of Ben Sira." In the Christian tradition the book has been referred to as "Ecclesiasticus" (Vulgate), or "The Wisdom (or Book) of Jesus, Son of Sirach" (most Greek and Old Latin manuscripts.). Manuscript discoveries at Masada, Qumran, and in the Cairo synagogue "storeroom" have restored about two-thirds of the Hebrew text. Written by Ben Sira, a teacher in Jerusalem who wrote between 200–180 B.C.E. during the time of the Seleucids in Syria wrested control of Judea from the Ptolemies in Egypt, Sirach reflects Ben Sira's assessment of the threat to the Jewish way of life mounted by Hellenism, but that threat is not addressed directly. Today's pericope is a portion of a long poem eulogizing the great leaders who have led the people of Israel during their long history. The title "Hymn in Honor of our Ancestors" is included in the Greek text. The examples that Sirach evokes are not only national leaders and great warriors; they include sages, prophets, composers, poets, the famous and the forgotten, to whom the Lord apportioned "great glory" (Sir. 44:2). The alternate reading speaks of the testing of those "who fear the Lord."

Responding to the Text

Sirach 44 provides an opportunity to honor the saints who have gone before us. The preacher might develop a sermon on the kind of examples provided by the faithful departed, both in the history of the global church and in the history of the local church. In keeping with the categorization of heroes in the reading, the preacher might make reference to different categories of saints: for example, martyrs, confessors, teachers, and so forth. Sirach 2 provides an opportunity to speak of the trials of the saints.

REVELATION 7:2-4, 9-14 (BCP)

Interpreting the Text

This reading offers a consoling vision of the future vindication that awaits the saints who have endured trial and persecution from the powers of evil that rule in the present world order. Revelation is an apocalyptic work written toward the end of the first century C.E. by the prophet John of Patmos to the seven churches in Asia Minor who were facing hostility from the Jewish synagogues, civic suspicion, and sporadic persecution by the Roman government that could result in imprisonment, exile, and even execution. John's vision of the ultimate triumph of the Lamb of God over the forces of evil is meant to strengthen Christians whose faith might be wavering in the face of persecution.

The prophecies of Revelation unfold in sevens: letters to seven churches, seven seals, seven trumpets, seven vials. Chapter 7 is inserted between the opening of the sixth and seventh seals and recounts the sealing of the 144,000 of the redeemed of Israel (12,000 from each of the 12 tribes of Israel). This allegorical number is held up as a symbol of completion. Even so, "a great multitude that no one could count" (v. 9), gathered from all the nations and dressed in white robes with palm branches in their hands, was arrayed before the throne of God and the Lamb, acclaiming the victory of the Lamb and worshiping God. These persons who have "come out of the great ordeal" and whose robes are "washed" and made "white in the blood of the Lamb" (v. 14) are undoubtedly martyrs who have experienced the baptism of blood. However, only Christ is directly called a martyr in Revelation; he is "the faithful witness" (*ho martys ho pistos*) in 1:5.

Responding to the Text

This reading portrays a vision of the heavenly worship that is probably a reflection of the liturgy of the earthly church. At the same time the liturgy of the earthly church should be a reflection of the heavenly worship. At several points the earthly church joins the heavenly worship, as when it sings the canticle "Worthy is Christ the Lamb who was slain" and the Sanctus hymn in the Great Thanksgiving along with "angels and archangels and all the company of heaven." It is plausible that the "sealing" of the servants of God on their foreheads in the name of God and the Lamb and their vesting in white robes in Revelation (Rev. 7:3) also reflects the liturgy of baptism in the earthly church. The reverse reflection also pertains here: the liturgy of the Holy Baptism is the beginning of the liturgy of Christian death and resurrection. This connection is symbolized by the lighting of the paschal candle at both baptisms and funerals. A sermon on this reading could develop the idea of the liturgy of the earthly church as an anticipation of the heavenly worship in which all the saints of God will participate.

Responsive Reading

PSALM 24 (RCL/RC)

Interpreting the Text

This is a hymn to the Creator in three parts: an identification of Israel's Lord as Creator of all things (vv. 1-2); an entrance and purificatory rite for believers (vv. 3-6); and a welcoming shout to the "King of glory" who returns victoriously to the Temple (vv. 7-10).

Responding to the Text

This psalm is a piece of liturgy rather than of instruction, complete with an acclamation of the entrance of the King of glory into the sanctuary. Worshipers are invited to participate in the triumph of God in ordering creation out of chaos and saving the people.

PSALM 149 (BCP)

Interpreting the Text

This is a hymn with two parts: praise of the Lord as Creator and King of Israel who has led the people to victory (vv. 1-4), and an invitation to the people to join in the victory celebration by singing for joy "on their couches"—that is, by feasting—(vv. 5-6a), and by taking vengeance on the defeated enemies (vv. 6b-9).

Responding to the Text

The martial traditions of the Bible that belong to the theology of holy war are not in vogue today. However, it is worth pointing out that the victory and vengeance themes refer to the salvation of the people of God and the punishment of the enemies of God. These themes are recast in the New Testament, where it is emphasized that "the weapons of our warfare are not merely human" (2 Cor. 10:4). They include the word of God and the sacraments of Christ.

Second Reading

REVELATION 21:1-6a (RCL)

Interpreting the Text

A new heaven and a new earth, a new Jerusalem, all things new, are promised in this reading (see also Isa. 65:17; 66:22). In Jewish thought the renewal of creation constitutes the final eschatological event. Belief in a heavenly counterpart to the earthly Jerusalem was common to both early Judaism and early Christianity (see Gal. 4:26; Phil. 3:20; Heb. 11:10, 14-16). Images of God making his home with humankind belong to the Feast of Tabernacles and the incarnational Christology of John 1. Such a vision gives hope to our present situation and the promise of a future free of death and its sorrows.

Responding to the Text

Against all "apocalyptic" forebodings of calamity for the earth and the eventual extinction of the universe itself, the real apocalypse envisions a wonderful consummation and a new beginning. Chaos (represented by the sea) is tamed and the city's gates remain open day and night. It is crucial to remember that this vision of the end of things was not offered to the persecuted Christians of Asia Minor as some "pie in the sky" placebo, but as an encouragement to do faithful witnessing in very trying circumstances. It should also be noted that the final state of things in the otherwise private vision of John of Patmos is a city made holy by the presence of God. It is, finally, a social vision that has ramifications for how we live in this world day by day.

JOHN'S VISION OF THE END OF THINGS WAS NOT OFFERED TO THE PERSECUTED CHRISTIANS OF ASIA MINOR AS SOME "PIE IN THE SKY" PLACEBO, BUT AS AN ENCOURAGEMENT TO DO FAITHFUL WITNESSING IN VERY TRYING CIRCUMSTANCES.

EPHESIANS 1:(11-14) 15-23 (BCP alt.)

Interpreting the Text

This reading may have been chosen because of the reference to "all the saints" in v. 15. "Saints" (*hagioi*) are mentioned nine times in the Letter to the Ephesians, by which the Pauline author means the baptized members of the church. Verses 11-14 come at the end of a long Trinitarian thanksgiving that focuses in three parts on the work of God the Father, Christ, and the Holy Spirit. This reading begins with the third part, the work of the Holy Spirit. Verses 11-12 describe how the Jewish tradition, of which Paul is a representative, "first hoped in Christ," "so that we might exist for the praise of God's glory." The "you also" in v. 13 refers to the gentiles who also heard the good news and believed that they were also sealed with the Holy Spirit as a kind of down payment on their final redemption, again "to the praise of God's glory." Verses 15-23 move from thanksgiving to supplication as Paul prays for the church's growth in wisdom and knowledge. He looks to the risen and ascended Christ for the power to foster this growth, since Christ has been exalted to a position of authority at the right hand of God above all other powers. Paul asserts that God has made Christ "the head over all things for the church, which is his body" (v. 23).

Responding to the Text

It's worth dwelling on a couple of phrases in this reading. "Marked with the seal of the promised Holy Spirit" (v. 13) refers to a kind of branding, such as is done with animals so that the rancher knows which ones are his or hers when they're all mixed together for grazing. There was a long tradition of using this image in Judaism before Paul came along. Ezekiel spoke of those faithful to the Lord being marked on their foreheads so that the Lord would recognize and claim them on the last day. In the Christian tradition the newly baptized have been sealed or branded with the sign of the cross on their foreheads, using the oil of chrism. It's like God stamping his own so that he can claim them at the Last Judgment.

The phrase, "the pledge of our inheritance toward redemption as God's own people" (v. 14), is difficult to translate because the inheritance is ours but the redemption is God's. A more literal translation would be: "this [sealing with the Holy Spirit] is the pledge that we shall enter upon our inheritance when God has redeemed his own." The downpayment on our redemption has been made. On the last day God will claim what he has purchased and take us home.

We may worry that a lot can happen between the downpayment and the final delivery. But the reading also speaks of Christ's enthronement at God's right hand—the position of clout, as they say in city hall. The great powers that come and go in history are placed under his feet; Christ the King will triumph over all forces of evil for the sake of his body, the church. Because we are claimed by God, and God has appointed a champion to subdue those powers that might steal us away from God, we can claim the glorious inheritance of the saints with confidence.

1 JOHN 3:1-3 (RC)

Interpreting the Text

The First Letter of John was written to combat heresies that were afflicting the churches (of Asia Minor?) at the end of the first century. This heresy may have been a form of docetism or gnosticism. In any event, it involved a denial of Christ's humanity and therefore a false understanding of Christian life. The false teachers presented a view that we are already perfected and therefore do not need to make any moral effort. Against this, the author of 1 John injects the sense of the "not yet" into Christian life: "what we will be has not yet been revealed" (v. 2). The love of God given to us has already made us children of God. But this is only the first installment of our final salvation. The final state of the Christian is still a matter of hope. In the meantime, we should purify ourselves from sin as Christ is pure. This emphasis on purity is actually a counter to those who believe they are already perfect, since the author of 1 John assumes that we do sin and need to make confession and receive forgiveness (1 John 1:8-10).

Responding to the Text

We often think that at death all we are is completed. This is why eulogies seem appropriate at funerals. There is nothing further to be added to a person's life after death. So we may now present the complete picture of the departed.

This passage from 1 John is a subtle critique of this tendency to fix and solidify what is in flux. It suggests that even in death we are not yet what we shall be. All we can know for sure is that we are children of God, and when God is finally revealed we shall be like him. In the meantime, since God is pure, the more we strive to be pure ourselves the more we shall be now what we shall be revealed to be in the resurrection to eternal life. This quality of purity has sometimes been seen in those who are officially designated as "saints." But even of the greatest saints it must be said that there is more to be revealed when we behold them in the presence of God.

GOSPEL
JOHN 11:32-44 (RCL)

Interpreting the Text

This reading is the story of the raising of Lazarus from the dead, which occurs as a climax of the longer sign-story in chapter 11. To say it is a sign-story means that Jesus acts according to his "time," and not just in response to requests (see John 2:4; 11:6). It also means that Jesus performs a revelatory act in which the purpose of his mission is disclosed. Here it is not only that Jesus' mission brings new life, but that it leads to his own death (11:45-57). Neither Mary nor Martha could know the price Jesus would pay for raising their brother. But the reader knows, since clues are given all along: the weeping; Lazarus' tomb in a cave covered by a large stone; the stone rolled away; the loud cry; the mention of the grave clothes. Because this is a sign-story, the reader knows that we are not dealing just with the trauma in Bethany but with the crisis of the human race; not just with the death and resurrection of Lazarus but with the death and resurrection of Jesus Christ.

Responding to the Text

The scene is the home in Bethany that has been brought to mourning by the death of Lazarus. But it could be any home where death has intervened to cancel hopes and terminate relationships. This is the context in which Jesus enters the scene and acts to bring the beloved Lazarus back into the lives of his loved ones. But by doing this, Jesus will seal his own fate with the chief priests and Pharisees, who now join forces to arrest him. The evangelist is developing, with dramatic skill, the story of Jesus entering his own grave in order to conquer death so that all the sisters and brothers of Lazarus might have eternal life.

Embedded in this story, although not in the reading, is one of the grandest and most comforting statements in the New Testament: "I am the resurrection and the life. Those who believe in me, even though they die, will live, and everyone who lives and believes in me will never die" (vv. 25-26). Jesus affirms the conviction of the Pharisees that the dead will be raised in the flesh on the last day. But he adds something new: resurrection in the body will be realized through belief that *he* is the resurrection and that new life has already begun in him. This gives us all the more reason to remember the faithful departed who lived and died in Christ. They even now live in Christ and will still be raised on the last day.

LUKE 6:20-26 (27-36) (BCP alt.)

Interpreting the Text

This Gospel reading is Luke's "Sermon on the Plain," which should be compared and contrasted with Matthew's "Sermon on the Mount" (see below), the traditional Gospel for All Saints' Day. Originally, beatitudes were congratulatory declarations of a happy state that an individual or a group had achieved. In the apocalyptically-charged atmosphere at the time of Jesus, beatitudes became declarations of future happiness even though the present time may be one of suffering for the individual or group. The Beatitudes in the Gospels are blessings in which Jesus announces to his disciples the kind of people who will find the kingdom of God favorable to them. The word "blessed" (*makarios*) means more than "happy," as it is rendered in some translations; it suggests people who are the privileged recipients of God's gifts. Especially in the Gospel of Luke, Jesus is not saying "Be this way"; rather he is saying, "There are people who are this way; lucky for them when the kingdom comes."

The categories delineated in the Lukan Beatitudes are not virtues that can be cultivated, as in the Matthean Beatitudes, but conditions of life in which some people find themselves: the poor (*hoi ptochoi* = the economically disadvantaged in Israel, most of whom were small farmers or tradespeople) as well as the hungry (see Luke 1:53), those who mourn (see Matt. 5:4; Ps. 126:6; Isa. 61:2-3; Isa. 65:18-19), and those who are defamed (Acts 5:41; 9:16). Luke shows special concern for the poor. Because of the demands of making a living, these people did not have the luxury of the more prosperous Pharisees of carrying out the minutiae of the religion of the Law. But they observed the spirit of the religion of Israel, a condition that Matthew caught by having Jesus bless "the poor in spirit" (Matt. 5:3).

We note that these beatitudes are addressed to Jesus' disciples, a category which Luke distinguishes from the apostles (vv. 12-16), and also from the crowds (vv. 17-19). These people could very well be from among the lower classes who followed Jesus and whose spiritual needs were as great as their economic needs. Jesus consoles them with the promise of "great reward" which is contrasted with the woe (*ouai*) directed to the rich who do not rely on God because they have already received their "consolation." Thus Luke gives us four contrasts between those on whom blessings and woes are pronounced: poor/rich, hungry/filled, weeping/laughing, persecuted/honored. These beatitudes continue the themes already announced in the beginning of the Gospel of Luke, specifically in Mary's song (1:52) and in Jesus' inaugural sermon in the synagogue at Nazareth (4:18, 21, from the text of Isa. 61).

In vv. 27-36, which are optional in this Gospel reading, Jesus speaks about the response of his community to persecution. They are to practice principles of nonretaliation and nonviolence. They are also to be generous to beggars, follow the Golden Rule, lend without expecting anything in return, and be merciful as God is merciful. Again, Jesus assures his disciples who follow his precepts that "your reward will be great" (v. 35). They will be regarded as "children of the Most High" because they are showing their kinship with God by practicing the kind of generosity that God shows even to "the ungrateful and the selfish" (v. 35).[22] Because of the lifestyle of godliness advocated in these verses, they should be included in the Gospel reading for All Saints' Day.

Responding to the Text

While many might regard the blessings in this reading as applying to those whose practice of faith is extraordinary, the blessings Jesus pronounces are really for ordinary believers who do what they are able to do to witness by their lives and conduct to the coming reign of God, but must rely on the grace of God. Are ordinary people capable of practicing the values of the kingdom? "Love your enemies" really worked in the town of Capernaum, which had been the center of Jesus' Galilean ministry. When the Roman legions came through in 66 C.E. on their way to Jerusalem, the townspeople showed hospitality to the legions and the town was spared to become the archaeological gold mine that it is today. The kind of neighborliness envisioned in these teachings is reflected in our own ideal of small-town life in which people help one another rather than practice the "scratch my back and I'll scratch yours" attitude that one finds in business arrangements and aldermanic turf wars in big cities. If this strikes us as an ideal that could be practiced in the small towns of Palestine but would

THE BLESSINGS JESUS PRONOUNCES ARE REALLY FOR ORDINARY BELIEVERS WHO DO WHAT THEY ARE ABLE TO DO TO WITNESS BY THEIR LIVES AND CONDUCT TO THE COMING REIGN OF GOD, BUT MUST RELY ON THE GRACE OF GOD.

not be applicable to big city life, remember that Luke addressed his Gospel to the Graeco-Roman world in all its urbanity. This Gospel reading offers an opportunity to focus on the *community* of saints here and now. Luke would not have had in mind any saints but ordinary ones to receive the rewards of the kingdom of God.

MATTHEW 5:1-12a (BCP/RC)

Interpreting the Text

The Beatitudes form the opening of the Sermon on the Mount in the Gospel of Matthew. Matthew's purpose in locating this sermon on a mountain is that he understands Jesus to be a new Moses, giving his disciples a new Torah, corresponding to the commandments Moses received on Mt. Sinai. Each of the Beatitudes falls into two parts. The first part describes the humiliations of the present; the second announces the glory to come. It is noteworthy that in Luke's version (6:20-23) the blessings are directed to the disciples: "Blessed are you." In Matthew this is the case only in the last one. Perhaps it was a way of indicating the category by which the disciples would join those who will receive the blessings of the kingdom: persecution on account of Christ. While the Lukan Beatitude blesses the poor, the Matthean Beatitude blesses the poor in spirit—the ones who realize that they are spiritual have-nots, who have no righteousness of their own, and therefore hunger and thirst for God's righteousness (perhaps like Matthew the tax collector). Along with desiring righteousness (v. 6), there are other categories of activities that receive the blessing of the kingdom: mourning that includes repentance from sin (v. 4), and showing mercy and kindness to others (vv. 5, 7). The Matthean Beatitudes are different from the Lukan in that they extol several virtues that can be cultivated rather than conditions of life that are a given: meekness, mercy, purity of heart, and peacemaking.

Responding to the Text

There's a lot of concern about teaching values today. The former U.S. Secretary of Education, William Bennett, has written a best seller, *The Book of Virtues: A Treasury of Great Moral Stories*. The book is an anthology of stories and poems which Bennett has put together "to aid in the time-honored task of the moral education of the young."[23] Some of the stories are about real historical figures; most of them are fictional. They are told to illustrate virtues which Bennett holds up as the values that should be taught to our young (and which we might be reminded of as we read these stories to our children, which is also a value Bennett would hold up). The stories are gathered into ten sections to illustrate the virtues of self-discipline, compassion, responsibility, friendship, work, courage, perseverance, honesty, loyalty, and faith. As an active Roman Catholic layman, Bennett acknowledges that faith is one of the three theological virtues, along with hope and love (or charity). He does not hesitate to include stories from the Bible in his anthology. He has collected these stories because he knows that among the several paths that lead to virtue, the most obliging is the way of imitation. He wants to give children examples they can emulate. Before we become doers, we must be spectators. We must watch and imitate other people. Stories are memorable ways to communicate. We remember what the heroes did in the stories, and that might inspire us to act in similar ways.

In a scene in Dostoevsky's *The Brothers Karamazov*, shortly before Father Zossima dies, the aged monk gathers his fellow monks and friends in his cell for a final conversation. As a child he had owned a book with beautiful pictures, entitled *A Hundred and Four Stories from the Old Testament and New Testament.* From this book he had learned to read, and as an old man he still keeps it on his shelf. Father Zossima remembers many stories from his book as well as the lives of other holy men and women: stories about Job and Esther and Jonah, the parables of Jesus, the conversation of Paul, the lives of Saints Alexei and Mary of Egypt. These stories plant a tiny mysterious seed in the hearts of men and women which grows up into virtues. Some of these "sacred tales," like the story of Job, Father Zossima cannot read "without tears." Like a bright spark amid darkness, these accounts lodge indelibly in his memory. In these stories of God's people, says Father Zossima, "one beheld God's glory." He advises that the priests should gather the children for an hour a week and read these stories to them. "The priest will reach people's hearts with these simple tales." People need the word of Christ, he said, but "what good is the word of Christ without an example?"[24]

Just so! We don't have only teachings in the New Testament without examples. We don't have only abstract virtues; we have the lives of saints who exemplified the virtues of God's kingdom. Butler's *Lives of the Saints* is the church's book of virtues.[25] And unlike Bennett's *Book of Virtues*, they don't stop with faith but go on to hope. When the Orthodox venerate icons—pictures of the historical Jesus, the Mother of God, and the saints—these believers are not just remembering the past; they are envisioning the future. The icons are windows through which we glimpse eternity. The lives of the saints build on the tradition of providing examples to emulate, but they enrich that tradition by showing a pattern of holiness—a way of belonging to God—worked out over a lifetime and culminating in the life of the world to come. The sermon might include stories of saints who demonstrated the beatitudes, even from among the faithful departed in the parish, who are remembered on this All Saints Day.

TWENTY-FIRST SUNDAY AFTER PENTECOST

NOVEMBER 5, 2000
THIRTY-FIRST SUNDAY IN ORDINARY TIME
PROPER 26

REVISED COMMON	EPISCOPAL (BCP)	ROMAN CATHOLIC
Ruth 1:1-18 or Deut. 6:1-9	Deut. 6:1-9	Deut 6:2-6
Ps. 146 or 119:1-8	Ps. 119:1-16 or 119:1-8	Ps. 18:2-4, 47, 51
Heb. 9:11-14	Heb. 7:23-28	Heb. 7:23-28
Mark 12:28-34	Mark 12:28-34	Mark 12:28b-34

THE RCL BEGINS A TWO-SUNDAY READING of the story of Ruth, and all the lectionaries continue the readings from the Letter to the Hebrews. All of the other readings, however, converge on a single issue: the heart of the Law. The Gospel reading contains the earliest tradition of the Great Commandment, in which Jesus combined Deuteronomy 6:4-5 (in the First Reading) with Leviticus 19:18 to place love of neighbor on an equal basis with love of God. Psalm 119, with its prayer for the capacity to know the Law and live by it, is an appropriate response.

FIRST READING

RUTH 1:1-18 (RCL)

Interpreting the Text

The book of Ruth is a short story dealing with family affairs that is placed after Judges in the Christian Bible because of the location of the story "In the days when the judges ruled." But it is placed among the Writings in the Jewish Bible. Scholars differ widely on the date of the composition of Ruth. But the story of this Moabite women who became the grandmother of King David would seem to address the problem of maintaining the purity of the Jewish people during or after the Babylonian exile when the idea of opening up the covenant blessings to gentiles who were interested in the religion of the Jews was being considered. The idea of family continuity motivates all the characters in the story. Within this concern it develops the concept of *chesed* or "steadfast love" typical of Yahweh's covenant with Israel and the marriage covenant. Ruth's mother-in-law Naomi invokes the God of the covenant in 1:8, "May the Lord deal kindly with you." Ruth's touching pledge to stay with Naomi also expresses *chesed.*

The preacher who wants to use this story would do well to retell it to the congregation in more colloquial terms. A family living in Bethlehem moves east of the Dead Sea to Moab because of famine. The family's two sons take Moabite wives. The father dies and ten years later the two sons die. The mother Naomi, hearing that conditions are better in Bethlehem, decides to return with her daughters-in-law Orpah and Ruth. But on the journey Naomi advises her daughters-in-law to return to Moab where they can seek the help of relatives and perhaps re-marry among their own people. Orpah does so, but Ruth pledges to stay with Naomi and claims as her own Naomi's people and her God. To be continued next Sunday.

Responding to the Text

The book of Ruth tells the story of fidelity which at first seems to be faithfulness to the memory of a dead husband manifested in devotion to his mother. But within the context of the whole biblical story it is about the Lord's fidelity to his people. It raises the question of what it means to be a member of God's people. Is that limited only to Jews? The book of Ruth apparently thinks not, since Ruth declares her willingness to accept Naomi's God as well as her people. This Moabite woman becomes the mother of Jesse, the grandmother of David, and the ancestor of Jesus, who opened the faith of Israel to "all nations."

The idea of conversion in this story is an interesting one, since it involves a new relationship not only with God but also with God's people. Ruth forsakes her own people and culture and takes on an entirely new way of life as a proselyte incorporated into the covenant between Yahweh and Israel. What more expressive way would there be, especially in our day when religion is so regarded as a "private matter," for a new member joining a church than to stand before the congregation and say, in the words of Ruth, "your people shall be my people, and your God my God"?

WHAT MORE EXPRESSIVE WAY WOULD THERE BE FOR A NEW MEMBER JOINING A CHURCH THAN TO STAND BEFORE THE CONGREGATION AND SAY, IN THE WORDS OF RUTH, "YOUR PEOPLE SHALL BE MY PEOPLE, AND YOUR GOD MY GOD"?

DEUTERONOMY 6:1-9 (RCL alt./BCP); 6:2-6 (RC)

Interpreting the Text

Most of Deuteronomy (4:44–30:20) is a speech in which Moses reminds the people of the events at Mt. Sinai (here called Horeb), reviews the stipulations of the Decalogue, and admonishes the people to observe these statutes and ordinances. Chapter 6 begins the commentary on the Decalogue with an authoritative *Shema Israel*—"Hear, O Israel" (vv. 3, 4). Indeed, the *Shema* in vv. 4-9 became the Creed of Judaism to be recited every morning and evening by Jewish males. The commandments are to be taught and observed from one generation to another. The chief commandment, from which all the rest follow, is devotion to the one true God. The issue is not really monotheism, but the single-minded love of Israel for the only One. The commandments are to be internalized so that they shape the will (the heart) and form a whole way of life (vv. 7-9). Even so, outward reminders are helpful. Verses 8-9 become the basis for the phylacteries (small boxes containing a miniature scroll of the *Shema*) worn on the forearm and forehead, and the *mazuzzah* (also a small capsule containing the *Shema*) fastened to the doorpost of the house, as is also done today.

Responding to the Text

There may be Christians who resist this introduction to the religion of the Law, the religion that it seemed Jesus and Paul rebelled against. They may object even more so to the outward ritual that the religion of Law encourages. There can be such a thing as "empty ritualism," but to apply this assessment to all ritual creates a problem since life itself is nothing but an endless series of rituals big and small. The issue is "meaningful ritual." Ritual is meaningful if it conveys meaning by doing it.

Deuteronomy functions like a catechism; it wants to teach the faith to the children. And by the act of teaching, the faith of the parents is also reinforced. How do children learn? They memorize and use little objects to remind them of what they have learned. There's no way around it, as every teacher knows. The memorization is odious, but the little boxes with their miniature scrolls compensate by the delight that they bring, so that one may truly grow up saying, "My delight is in the law of the Lord" (Ps. 1:2). In the Christian tradition, too, the texts of the catechism need to be taught and memorized and recited daily. Parents and sponsors promise at Baptism that they will teach their children the Ten Commandments, the Apostles' Creed, and the Lord's Prayer. In seventeenth and eighteenth century Anglican churches these texts were written out on tablets and placed on the wall of the sanctuary above the communion table. Lutheran children memorized these texts and their meanings from Luther's *Small Catechism*. They recall that the explanation of each of the Commandments begins, "We should so fear and love God . . ." because obedience to all the Commandments is contingent on obedience to the First. Hence, "We should fear, love, and trust in God above everything else."

Responsive Reading

PSALM 146 (RCL)

Interpreting the Text

This is a liturgical psalm that begins and ends with Halleluias. Pss. 146–150 have a place in the Jewish morning service. This psalm is appointed as a response to the First Reading from Ruth 1, probably because of v. 9: "The Lord watches over the strangers; the Lord upholds the orphan and the widow." The psalmist warns against placing trust in princes; instead the people should place their trust in the Lord.

Responding to the Text

The psalm extols God's favor toward the powerless who live at the peripheries of society. The theme of God lifting up "those who are bowed down" (v. 8) is connected with God's faithfulness to the covenant made with Israel. "Happy are those whose help is the God of Jacob, whose hope is in the Lord their God. . . . who keeps faith forever" (v. 5).

PSALM 119:1-16 (BCP); 119:1-8 (RCL alt./BCP alt.)

Interpreting the Text

This psalmody is appointed as a response to the First Reading from Deuteronomy 6. Psalm 119 is really a collection of psalms made up of twenty-two stanzas of eight lines each, in which each stanza uses, in order, the letters of the Hebrew alphabet to begin each of its eight lines. Thus, every line in vv. 1-8 begins with the letter *alef*, every line in vv. 9-16 with *bet*. These lines celebrate the Law as God's means of communication and as a guiding light for conduct.

Responding to the Text

Law might suggest something heavy and legalistic. But the psalmist uses the word *happy* (blessed) to describe those who observe the Law (vv. 1, 2) and speaks of "delight" (vv. 14, 16) as his response to God's decrees and statutes. It is undoubtedly difficult for Christians, after Paul (and Luther), to comprehend what is "delightful" about the Law. But there is also a reason why we should try to find out, since we still observe the Ten Commandments. It has to do with freedom. The people of Israel were free from wondering (and worrying) about how to be faithful to God in the various aspects of living since God had informed them in his Torah concerning what pleases him and how his will is to be done.

PSALM 18:2-4, 47, 51 (RC)

Interpreting the Text

The RC lectionary has chosen a different psalm as a response to the reading from Deuteronomy 6. Psalm 18 is a royal psalm of thanksgiving. The refrain (antiphon), taken from v. 1, "I love you, Lord, my strength," is a fitting response to the *Shema* and also an anticipation of the Great Commandment in the Gospel reading.

Responding to the Text

There is a great hymn based on this psalm, "Thee Will I Love, My Strength, My Tow'r" (*LBW* 502), by Johann Scheffler (1624–1677). Scheffler was born of a Polish Lutheran father in Breslau, Silesia (a region chiefly in the eastern Czech Republic and southwest Poland), studied medicine and the writings of the mystic Jakob Boehme, converted to Roman Catholicism, adopted the name Angelus Silesius, wrote poetry that influenced the pietistic writers of the next generation, including the Moravians, through whose use this hymn came to the attention of John Wesley, who translated it into English. It would be hard for one person to be more ecumenical! What others found attractive in Angelus Silesius was the ardent love of the Lord that he expressed in his devotional poetry, the same love that the psalmist expressed for the "great triumphs" (v. 50) God has given to his servants.

SECOND READING

HEBREWS 7:23-28 (BCP/RC)

(See the commentary on this reading for the twentieth Sunday after Pentecost, pp. 207–8).

HEBREWS 9:11-14 (RCL)

Interpreting the Text

The verses assigned in this reading are part of a literary unit that requires comparing them with vv. 1-10. Chapter 9 of "To the Hebrews" presents an accurate description of the Jewish tabernacle/temple which the priests alone could enter, and also an explicit picture of what the priests did in the sanctuary. A full description of the tabernacle is given in Exodus 25–27. Josephus also gives a full description of the Second Temple, which was arranged with the same layout. The author of Hebrews is critical of the whole cultic system. He describes the old cultus in order to contrast it with something superior: the high priestly ministry of Christ. In a detailed way, the author contrasts the earthly tent (v. 1) with the tent not made with hands (v. 11), the priests who had to enter the sanctuary continually (v. 6) with Christ who enters once (vv. 11-12), a ministry not performed without offering blood for himself as well as others (v. 7) with Christ's ministry performed through own blood (v. 12), the offering of gifts (v. 9) with Christ's offering of himself (v. 14), and the offering not able to purify consciences (v. 9) with that which cleanses our conscience (v. 14).

Responding to the Text

Preachers often use illustrations to make a point. Hebrews is one big illustration that shows how much better Jesus is than any other religious system. It uses the sanctuary and rituals of the old Israelite sacrificial cult in order to describe the high priestly ministry of Jesus. But Jesus fills that old system with new meaning. As good as it was, what Jesus has done blows it apart. The author's point is that if the old rituals had value, how much more valuable as a purifying influence on conscience is the example of Jesus whose life ("blood") was totally committed to doing the will of God? The author of Hebrews is leading up to the point that Jesus is the example of faith with his great image of Jesus as "the pioneer and perfecter of our faith" in 12:2.

HEBREWS IS ONE BIG ILLUSTRATION THAT SHOWS HOW MUCH BETTER JESUS IS THAN ANY OTHER RELIGIOUS SYSTEM.

It probably needs to be pointed out that the contrast here is not between Christianity and Judaism, but between the saving work of Jesus the Christ and the religious system of the old Israel. Both Judaism and Christianity are post-temple religions.

GOSPEL

MARK 12:28-34

Interpreting the Text

It would seem that this pericope is only loosely related to what precedes and what follows it. Luke, in fact, places this interchange between Jesus and a scribe earlier in his narrative; Matthew follows Mark in locating it in the confrontations between Jesus and the various religious parties within the Temple after Jesus' entrance into Jerusalem. Certainly one reason Mark had for placing the story in the context of Jesus' visit to the Temple was that the scribe agrees with Jesus that the Law concerning love of God and neighbor is "much more important than all the whole burnt offerings and sacrifices" (v. 33). In other words, it served Mark's anti-Temple polemic. Otherwise, the pericope seems out of place in this section of Mark since this courteous exchange between Jesus and a scribe is preceded by a series of entrapment questions from Pharisees, Herodians, and Sadducees, and is followed by Jesus' denunciation of the scribes.

Yet Mark's narrative is tightly developed, and we must wonder whether Jesus' affirmation that this scribe "is not far from the kingdom of God" (v. 34) is all that flattering. The scribe agrees with Jesus' interpretation of the Law, which certainly broke no new ground in understanding the faith of Israel. But agreeing is not enough. We are close to the moment of the cross, the moment of truth in which right answers must eventuate in right action. Only discipleship will bring this scribe all the way into the kingdom of God.

Responding to the Text

Scribes were highly trained teachers of the tradition who lived off the fees of students and the subsidies of patrons. Only the Temple scribes were paid directly out of the Temple treasury. This does not say whether the scribes were good or bad—only that they were professionals who studied deeply, were much given to dialogue, and were not afraid of being open to other opinions or of expressing their own. The preacher would do well to compare them with the theologians in the church rather than with ordinary believers in the pew who have questions about doctrine or practice. The professional theologian may also ask questions. The difference between the professional theologian and the ordinary lay believer is that the professional knows what questions to ask and what answers to look for. It's something of a game that operates according to certain rules of discourse and requires a certain level of understanding, although that does not cast judgment on the seriousness of the enterprise.

This particular theologian was even willing to defend the prophetic elevation of the Law above the ritual sacrifices, especially that aspect of the Law that concerns the love of neighbor. Jesus was not the first to equate the two tablets of the Commandments, but he stood in that tradition. There were those in Israel who also regarded the Temple as an institution that had not served the needs of all the people. Perhaps this was a scribe who stood closer to the Pharisees than to the Sadducees. By identifying with the prophetic tradition of denouncing those who do the rituals without honoring God in their lives by practicing justice, this scribe moved closer to Jesus. Any step we take toward Jesus puts us closer to the kingdom of God that Jesus represents in his person.

Yet is not something more required? If love of God and neighbor is "much more important than all the whole burnt offerings and sacrifices" (v. 33), then shouldn't one follow Jesus in the way Jesus went? The way of perfect obedience? It is perhaps at this point that the proclamation of Christ as the superior way in Hebrews can be brought to bear on the preaching of this Gospel reading.

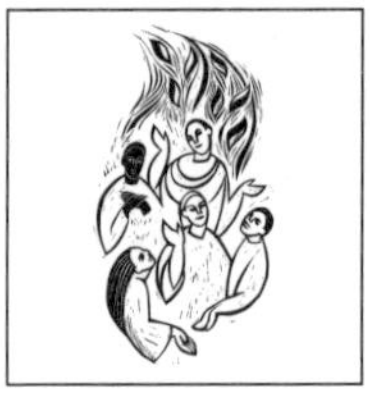

TWENTY-SECOND SUNDAY AFTER PENTECOST

NOVEMBER 12, 2000
THIRTY-SECOND SUNDAY IN ORDINARY TIME
PROPER 27

REVISED COMMON	EPISCOPAL (BCP)	ROMAN CATHOLIC
Ruth 3:1-5; 4:13-17 or 1 Kings 17:8-16	1 Kings 17:8-16	1 Kings 17:10-16
Ps. 127 or 146	Ps. 146 or 146:4-9	Ps. 146:7-10
Heb. 9:24-28	Heb. 9:24-28	Heb. 9:24-28
Mark 12:38-44	Mark 12:38-44	Mark 12:38-44 (12:41-44)

THE LAST THREE SUNDAYS of the church year traditionally focus on "last things" and have been called "kingdomtide." This eschatological emphasis pervades the whole month of November, beginning with All Saints' Day and continuing through the first Sunday of Advent. Eschatological themes are not prominent in today's readings, but they are present. The story of Ruth subtly raises the long-term question of how our personal redemption here and now relates to the eventual redemption of the human race. The other Old Testament reading, the story of the miraculous jar of meal and cruet of oil that do not fail during a time of drought and famine, testifies to God's faithful care of his people until the day of vindication comes. Psalm 146 celebrates God's execution of justice on behalf of the poor and the oppressed.

THE STORY OF RUTH SUBTLY RAISES THE LONG-TERM QUESTION OF HOW OUR PERSONAL REDEMPTION HERE AND NOW RELATES TO THE EVENTUAL REDEMPTION OF THE HUMAN RACE.

Poor widows are featured in both the First Reading and the Gospel. That widows would be poor is not surprising since in ancient Middle Eastern society economic well-being usually required a male head of the household to provide a living. Jesus contrasts the generous and genuine piety of the poor widow who puts her two copper coins into the Temple collection box with the stingy yet ostentatious show of the rich and powerful. This raises the question of stewardship, which always has an eschatological edge to it: What accounting shall we give of our management of God's gifts and our resources before the final judgment of God? In this light, Hebrews reminds us that we all need to throw ourselves on the mercy of Christ our high priest who offers in heaven the all-sufficient sacrifice to atone for our sins and who will come again to save those who eagerly await him. Our response to his ministry and self-offering, in the meantime, is to replicate it on earth in our own priestly service in the world.

First Reading
RUTH 3:1-5; 4:13-17 (RCL)

Interpreting the Text

This reading continues and concludes the story of Ruth. Ruth has settled into Bethlehem society with her mother-in-law Naomi. Naomi is concerned to find a husband for Ruth. The assigned verses leave out the most interesting part of the story: Ruth following Naomi's instruction on how to seduce Boaz. Going to Boaz's bed could just as likely get Ruth stoned to death as get her a husband. But Boaz recognizes that Ruth is motivated by *chesed*, loyalty to the family of Naomi. She did not seek a husband elsewhere but chose Boaz because he was the *go'el* (redeemer) to the two widows, Naomi and Ruth. Ruth and Boaz are married and in the final scene the women call the child born to this union "a restorer of life." In the last sentence we learn that this child, Obed, became the father of Jesse, the father of David. Ruth the Moabite is therefore the grandmother of Israel's greatest king and the ancestor of Jesus.

Responding to the Text

God does not have to be seduced, like Boaz was, into moving from general kindness to active redemption. But God does seem to like working with active human partners. This is not a matter of "God helps those who help themselves," as if God's involvement is irrelevant to the human enterprise or as if our efforts somehow manage to wring a blessing out of God. But God's concern for the powerless does not preclude their working on their own behalf, just as Naomi and Ruth worked for their own "redemption." And, as we see from the context of this story within the larger biblical story, God is at work even in ways in which God's plans are not at all apparent. God provided in Ruth a non-Jewish ancestor for Jesus who reached out to all people. Can we imagine God working through us to effect conditions that will pertain generations from now?

1 KINGS 17:8-16 (RCL alt./BCP); 17:10-16 (RC)

Interpreting the Text

This pericope stands in the context of Elijah's contest with King Ahab of Israel. Ahab married the Sidonite king's daughter, Jezebel, who induced Ahab to set up a sanctuary for the fertility god Baal. In retaliation, Elijah on his own authority predicted a drought, which the word of the Lord brought about. Elijah himself had to seek refuge from the drought, and this brought him to Sidonite territory, the very homeland of Jezebel, and the widow and her son who lived there, who were about to have their last meal. The great prophet comes in need to the needy widow and proclaims that the Lord will provide for them "until the day that the Lord sends rain on the earth" (v. 14).

Responding to the Text

One is left wondering why the widow was willing to respond to Elijah's request. Did she, in resignation, think that one final meal wouldn't make much difference? Did she feel the compunction of customary Middle Eastern hospitality? Was she willing to grasp at any faint hope of relief? Or was she willing to place her trust in a God who cares? She apparently knew something about Elijah's God, although she certainly was not a believer. And if she was willing to place her trust in the prophet's word that "the jar of meal will not be emptied and the jug of oil will not fail until the day that the Lord sends rain on the earth" (v. 14), what summoned the faith that was necessary? Was it the strong word of the prophet, "Do not be afraid" (v. 13)—not as a simple reassurance but as an oracle of salvation? Was this the "saving word" that the widow needed to hear in her context and that induced her to act in faith?

Responsive Reading
PSALM 127 (RCL)

Interpreting the Text

This psalm is appointed as a response to the First Reading from Ruth. As a hymn in proverbial style, the psalm teaches and acknowledges God's will being played out in human affairs. Only those human efforts that God makes his own can succeed. The subtitle "Of Solomon" and the image of building a house in v. 1 may refer to the fact that Solomon was one of the master builders in Israel's history. The reference in v. 3 to the much-desired birth of a son as a heritage or security for the parents relates most specifically to the story of Ruth and Boaz.

Responding to the Text

Human efforts to build structures and secure the future are useless unless God is involved in these enterprises. Our plans to create and procreate must be in conformity with the plans of the Creator. Therefore all human work must be undertaken with the proviso "if God so wills," which also has the effect of keeping us humble about our undertakings.

PSALM 146 (RCL alt./BCP); 146:4-9 (BCP alt.); 146:7-10 (RC)

Interpreting the Text

This psalm is appointed as a response to the First Reading from 1 Kings 17. (See the commentary on this text for the twenty-first Sunday after Pentecost, p. 235.)

Responding to the Text

The psalm invites us to trust God the Creator rather than human leaders (v. 3). We know that God is faithful to his covenant and executes justice for the powerless. Both the power and the love of God are proven in the very cases where human power and love fail, as in the story of God's provision for the widow of Zarephath.

SECOND READING
HEBREWS 9:24-28

Interpreting the Text

There are close parallels between vv. 11-14 and 24-28: the reference to the Temple not made with hands (vv. 11, 24); the once-for-all entrance of Christ into the holy place, into heaven (vv. 12, 24-26); the offering of himself, his appearance before God (vv. 14, 24); the blood of Christ cleansing our conscience, bearing the sins of many (vv. 14, 28); his sacrifice having accomplished eternal redemption, the removal of sins (vv. 12, 26). More than just a summary of the preceding verses, these verses sharpen the contrast between the old and the new covenants.

The author speaks of the earthly sanctuary as "a mere copy of the true one" (v. 24). The comparison of the earthly Temple with the heavenly sanctuary has misled some commentators into thinking that Hebrews is Platonic in its outlook. One wonders why they haven't considered that Plato himself might have been influenced in his typology by the standard Near Eastern view that the earthly temple is a replica of the heavenly throne-room of the deity? Because of the correspondence of the earthly and heavenly sanctuaries, if sacrifices took place in the earthly temple this action was also replicated in the heavenly temple.

While this might provide a framework for explaining the relationship between Christ's self-offering on the cross and his offering before the Father in heaven, the author of "To the Hebrews" does not deal with the historical Jesus but with the preexistent and glorified Son of God. The author has already made comparisons between the smoke of the sacrifices rising to heaven and the Son of God passing through the heavens, just as the high priest passed through the curtain into the holy of holies (4:14). There is no distinction made between Christ's crucifixion and his glorification. It is in his ascension that the Son of God carries his sacrifice to the Father. He has done this because the sacrifice is not for heaven, it is for the earth. It avails for those who are eagerly waiting for Christ to come again (v. 28).

Here is a point of view rooted in the futurist eschatology of apocalyptic literature. The author assumes that the future second coming of Christ will bring salvation to the believer. The believer's conscience is purified now by faith (9:14; 10:22), but salvation proper lies in the future. The author consistently understands faith as "the assurance of things hoped for, the conviction of things not seen" (11:1). He repeatedly warns against forfeiting what has been promised and urges perseverance—which may, in actuality, require our own acts of self-offering.

Responding to the Text

This is the classic text in Hebrews that proclaims Christ both as the eternal high priest who serves as the mediator between God and the people and as the sacrifice of atonement that never needs to be repeated. Yet in another classic text, 1 Peter 2:5, Christians are exhorted "to be a holy priesthood, to offer spiritual sacrifices acceptable to God through Jesus Christ." If Christ is the true high priest and if his sacrifice is eternally sufficient, in what sense are we priests and what further sacrifices are needed?

We need to see the close relationship between Christ and his church, which Hebrews describes in terms of siblings: "he had to become like his brothers and sisters in every respect" so that he could help us "who are being tested" (2:17, 18). We are Christ's brothers and sisters who experience suffering as he did. In Christ we are able to intercede even on behalf of those who test us and offer the sacrifices of our lives to God the Father. Liturgically, Christ the high priest is like the presiding priest over a priestly assembly that prays for a world that cannot pray for itself. Like Christ, in the liturgy we offer to God "our selves, our time, and our possessions" to support the church's ministries of medi-

IN CHRIST WE ARE ABLE TO INTERCEDE EVEN ON BEHALF OF THOSE WHO TEST US AND OFFER THE SACRIFICES OF OUR LIVES TO GOD THE FATHER.

ation and reconciliation. Intercession and offering are the ways in which believers exercise their priestly ministry and sacrificial service. Surrounded in our earthly sanctuaries by images of saints and angels, we have a sense that these true liturgical actions replicate here on earth the eternal priesthood and sacrifice of our brother Jesus in heaven, for our prayers and offerings are offered "through Jesus Christ our Lord."

Gospel

MARK 12:38-44; 12:41-44 (RC alt.)

Interpreting the Text

Jesus' courteous exchange with a scribe in last week's Gospel reading contrasts sharply with his denunciation of the scribal lifestyle and practices in today's Gospel reading. It is noteworthy that in 12:35-37 Jesus questions the scribes' identification of the Messiah with the Son of David; in vv. 38-40 he attacks their "royal" sense of power and prestige and their willingness to live off the offerings of poor widows under the pretense of piety.

An example presents itself as a poor widow drops her "widow's mite" into the Temple collection box. Her small act of devotion, performed in the midst of the rich pouring out their abundant gifts, is noticed by Jesus. He properly evaluates her contribution of two lepka, the smallest coins in circulation, because he knows that this is all she has. The standard of measurement for assessing gifts is not how much one gives to the work of God, but how much one has left for oneself. There is no romanticizing of small gifts here. Rather, Jesus observes that those who give "out of their abundance" still have an abundance left, whereas the widow "has put in everything she had, all she had to live on" (v. 44).

Responding to the Text

It is going to be difficult to avoid moralizing or even grandstanding on this text. It is easy to castigate ostentation, especially when it masks hypocrisy. Yet, as we read about the scribes dressing to indicate their official responsibility and acting according to the dictates of customary religious devotion, and as we imagine them receiving respectful greetings and preferred seating for public events, we realize that these practices are common to all religions and to all societies. Customs develop from the need for order. We often impose on our dignitaries a certain ostentation by expecting them to dress and behave in certain ways and deferring to them in public gatherings. In a sense, such dignitaries may even accommodate our human need for order by going along with these practices. Which was a more cultivated presidential image: Franklin Roosevelt's aristocratic bearing while riding in an open car in public, or Jimmy Carter's cardigan sweater when speaking to the public from the first family's living quarters in the White House? What matters with God is not style but substance. What Jesus penetrates is the core of our hubris. He does that to sensitize us to God's desire for genuineness in our relationship to him. What Jesus praised in the offering of the poor widow was, in fact, her genuine devotion to God.

"The Widow's Mite" is often used in stewardship sermons at this time of the year to chide us for our paltry pledges. In fact, stewardship has to do with a responsible management of what has been entrusted to us. If the poor widow had a small son at home to support, like the widow of Zarephath, she would not be a model of good stewardship for giving everything to the temple. How much we put in the collection plate is not the point of this story. But attaining social status at the expense of the poor might be. The condemnation of those who "devour widows' houses" but pray "for the sake of appearance" (v. 40) is directed at heedless hypocrites of any age who embark on grand schemes without regard for the consequences.

Those baptized into the priesthood of Christ, who identifies with his human brothers and sisters in their suffering as the agent of the God who looks after strangers and refugees and upholds widows and orphans, will naturally turn toward the oppressed. But doing so in a genuine way requires rethinking our values very carefully, because the ways we spend and invest our money have a lot to do with the economic conditions in the world.

We're not comfortable being asked to reflect on how we use our money. That's a harder stewardship sermon to preach than calling for proportional increases in our annual pledge. But being ill-at-ease makes for more intense listening. Maybe we listen to things for the first time. Maybe we begin to reflect, as the disciples of Jesus surely did when he praised the widow and condemned the scribes, on what it takes to follow Jesus in the kind of world in which we live.

TWENTY-THIRD SUNDAY AFTER PENTECOST

NOVEMBER 19, 2000
THIRTY-THIRD SUNDAY IN ORDINARY TIME
PROPER 28

REVISED COMMON	EPISCOPAL (BCP)	ROMAN CATHOLIC
1 Sam. 1:4-20 or Dan. 12:1-3	Dan. 12:1-4a (5-13)	Dan. 12:1-3
1 Sam. 2:1-10 or Ps. 16	Ps. 16	Ps. 16:5, 8-11 or 16:5-11
Heb. 10:11-14 (15-18) 19-25	Heb. 10:31-39	Heb. 10:11-14, 18
Mark 13:1-8	Mark 13:14-23	Mark 13:24-32

ON THIS PENULTIMATE SUNDAY in the church year, the readings are ominous and apocalyptic. The very idea that there will be an "end" may be threatening to people with good jobs, healthy families, sound retirement plans, economic security, and personal stability. For those who experience life as a roller coaster of ups and downs, the readings may actually be comforting. Hannah spends years feeling humiliated because of her inability to have a child; then "the Lord remembers her" and she bears a son. In Daniel, the people who go through a great tribulation and persevere shall be delivered, even resurrected to everlasting life. The author of Hebrews encourages his community to "hang in there," enduring in faith, hope, and love as they experience intimidation and persecution, and remembering their access to God's grace through Christ their high priest who is seated at the position of authority and power. In the Gospel reading, Jesus testifies that many people will be led astray by cataclysmic events and false messiahs, but those who remain faithful to the gospel of the kingdom of God will survive.

THE VERY IDEA THAT THERE WILL BE AN "END" MAY BE THREATENING TO PEOPLE WITH GOOD JOBS, HEALTHY FAMILIES, SOUND RETIREMENT PLANS, ECONOMIC SECURITY, AND PERSONAL STABILITY.

FIRST READING

1 SAMUEL 1:4-20 (RCL)

Interpreting the Text

The touching story of Hannah at the beginning of 1 Samuel is full of surprises. Contrary to social expectations, Hannah is highly regarded by her husband Elkanah for herself and not for her ability to bear children, because "the Lord had closed her womb" (v. 6). Yet it is clear that she wants more out of life than to be his favorite wife (v. 8), and therefore she cannot bear the cruel taunts of Peninnah, Elkanah's other wife. After years of enduring Peninnah's flaunting of her own fertility, Hannah is depressed even in the face of her husband's favor. Her sorrow and loss of appetite reach a point where she goes to the Lord in prayer, asking him to "remember me, and forget not your servant" (v. 11). If the Lord will give her a son, she promises to consecrate him to the Lord. The priest Eli sees her lips moving but no words being spoken and concludes that she is drunk. But after she explains her troubles, he sends her away with a blessing. That night Elkanah "knows" his wife and "the Lord remembered her" (v. 19). She bears a son whom she names Samuel.

At a deeper theological level, it may be, as Ann Hacket has suggested, that Hannah's hope is for more than social status; she seeks to claim her place as an heir of the covenant. Elkanah does not need more sons, but Hannah needs a son to be able to offer her first fruits to the Lord.[26] In the rest of the story, Hannah fulfills this vow and Samuel becomes the great transition figure in Israel's history between the time of the judges and the monarchy.

Responding to the Text

Hannah's prayer blends an authentic desire for personal fulfillment with a desire to claim a place within the covenant tradition of Israel. Like a number of other barren women in the Bible, Hannah is in need of a miracle. Yet the theological interpretation built into the text of the story indicates that Hannah's womb was "closed by the Lord." This alerts the reader that her barrenness served a purpose. This purpose is reinforced by the clear indication that Elkanah had no need for more sons. Hannah's pregnancy was finally to serve the Lord's purpose, not Elkanah's. The Lord needed the "fruit of her womb," Samuel. Samuel would lead God's people into the monarchy, first with the anointing of Saul and then with the anointing of David, who signified new hope for Israel and, by extension, new hope for the world with the reign of "great David's greater son," Jesus.

DANIEL 12:1-3 (RCL/RC); 12:1-4a (5-13) (BCP)

Interpreting the Text

Daniel is the only apocalyptic book in the Old Testament canon. It portrays a certain Daniel during the time of the Jewish exile in Babylon, but was probably written during the time of the persecution of the Jews by the Hellenistic king Antiochus IV Epiphanes, the Seleucid ruler of Syria whose desecration of the Jerusalem Temple in 167 B.C.E. (referred to in 12:11) precipitated the Maccabean revolt. Chapters 1-6 provide the Jews with heroic role models; chapters 7-12 holds out promise of deliverance in the new kingdom of God for those who persevere. This comes to culmination in chapter 12 when "Michael, the great prince, the protector of your people, shall arise" (help coming from heaven) and the dead shall be raised to "everlasting life" or "everlasting contempt" (v. 2). While Daniel is the last book in the order written to be included in the Old Testament canon, it has the first unambiguous statement of the idea of the resurrection of the dead that was to become a central tenet of Phariseeism. The precise meaning of "shame and everlasting contempt" (v. 2) is not clear, although in this context it probably does not mean the later concept of hell as a place of eternal punishment. The idea that "the wise," who "shall shine like the brightness of the sky" (v. 3), shall "understand" these things (v. 10) probably contributed to the placement of the book of Daniel among the Writings in the Jewish Bible, although it is one of the four major prophets in the Christian Bible.

Responding to the Text

Empires come and go. Tyrants strut their stuff on the world stage for a brief time and then they are toppled. The idea that people of faith can cling in hope to the assurance that God has a plan for the people—even to the point of raising them from the dead—gives them the courage to go through ordeals and testing. Heroic perseverance does not necessarily imply shunning all contact with the world. Indeed, Daniel was willing to serve as a wise counselor of gentile kings. What is rejected is an easygoing accommodation that flings all principles to the wind. The stories in the book of Daniel illustrate that even worldly rulers can come to respect the integrity of persons of faith.

RESPONSIVE READING

1 SAMUEL 2:1-10 (RCL)

Interpreting the Text

This canticle is appointed as a response to the First Reading from 1 Samuel 1. It also served Luke as the model for Mary's song, the Magnificat (Luke 1:46-55). Both songs express God's reordering of society in his kingdom to champion the interests of the poor and oppressed, as the kings of Israel were also to do. The personal reversal of fortunes is expressed in v. 5: "The barren has borne seven, but she who has many children is forlorn." But the song's theme is larger than Hannah's vindication: "The Lord kills and brings to life" (v. 6) and reverses the situation of the poor and the needy.

Responding to the Text

Like the Magnificat, Hannah's song sets out an agenda for rulers—beginning with David, who also demonstrates the reversal of fortune when Samuel anoints him as king since he is the youngest son of Jesse, but finally culminating in the reign of God inaugurated in Jesus' proclamation of the kingdom. This song, with its revolutionary program, is a source of deep but dangerous hope for the world. If God is the one who finally raises up the poor and needy, people have a right to expect no less from their earthly rulers.

PSALM 16 (BCP/RCL alt.); 16:5, 8-11 (RC); 16:5-11 (RC alt.)

Interpreting the Text

This psalm of supplication, perhaps prayed by the king, is appointed as a response to the First Reading from Daniel 12. Verse 3a, "the holy ones in the land [earth]," is a difficult translation, but it can be seen to relate to "those who sleep in the dust of the earth" (Dan. 12:2). Though there is no explicit mention of resurrection in the text, the psalmist trusts God not to abandon the faithful to Sheol, the place of the dead (v. 10). God shows "the path of life" (v. 11).

Responding to the Text

While the affirmation with which this psalm ends was not originally understood as referring to the resurrection of the dead, its hope has prophetic depths. The reach of this psalm extends beyond the reign of earthly kings to the reign of Christ who will lead believers of all nations on the path of eternal life (1 Cor. 15:20-29).

HEBREWS 10:11-14 (15-18) 19-25 (RCL); 10:31-39 (BCP); 10:11-14, 18 (RC)

Interpreting the Text

The RCL and RC readings continue the contrast between the Levitical priesthood and the priesthood of Christ, even to the issue of posture. The Levitical priest "stands" in his ministry; Christ "sat down at the right hand of God" (v. 12). Sitting down symbolizes work completed as well as authority "at the right hand of God." The author cites the royal Psalm 110:1, which suggests both God's favor (sitting at God's right hand) and vindication (until his enemies become a footstool for his feet). The work completed is the "single offering" by which Christ "has perfected for all time those who are sanctified" (v. 14), in contrast with offerings that must be made again and again—the daily sacrifices are referred to here rather than the annual atonement—yet "can never take away sins" (v. 11). "Perfecting the sanctified" does not denote moral perfection but initiating those who have been brought to God. To clinch the point about forgiveness, the author cites Jeremiah's prophecy of the new covenant (Jer. 31:31-34) that he had already cited in 8:8-12. Where forgiveness has been achieved, an offering for sin is no longer needed (v. 18). Indeed, it is the point of Hebrews that this offering cannot be repeated and therefore there cannot be a second forgiveness (4:4-6), which is a reason for all the exhortations scattered throughout this book. But this is probably not a message most worshipers want to hear, nor one that market-driven preachers would want to deliver.[27] The RC reading stops at this point, and these self-contained verses do deliver an upbeat message.

THERE IS A "NOT YET" IN THE TEXT OF HEBREWS: "*UNTIL* HIS ENEMIES WOULD BE MADE A FOOTSTOOL FOR HIS FEET." THE WORK IS DONE, THE VICTORY WON; YET THERE IS MOP-UP WORK THAT MUST BE DONE BECAUSE THE WORLD'S HEART AND MIND HAVE NOT YET BEEN COMPLETELY WON, AND EVIL STILL PROWLS AROUND SEEKING SOMEONE TO DEVOUR.

The RCL goes on to verses in which the author encourages the readers to apply this message to their own behavior. Since believers are now given access to the Holy of Holies by the blood of Christ, they should enter this formerly forbidden area. But like the priests of antiquity, they must observe the priestly rules for purification. Within the new covenant, this means boldly approaching God "in full assurance of faith" (v. 22), holding fast to "the confession of our hope" (v. 23), and provoking "one another to love and good deeds" (v. 24)—the same triad of virtues as in 1 Corinthians 13:13.

The BCP reading is also an exhortation, beginning with the text used in Jonathan Edwards' famous sermon, "It is a fearful thing to fall into the hands of the living God" (v. 31). The word "fearful," a word warning of punishments (and omitted in all the lectionaries), creates an inclusion for vv. 27-31 and sets the tone for vv. 32-39.Only after warning his readers of the terrible punishments that God would inflict on those who do not hold fast to the faith, the author reminds them of the good old days when their faith was strong and stable. They had endured a great deal of suffering (vv. 33-34). "Sometimes" they had been publicly "exposed" (i.e. exhibited) and embarrassed by being afflicted with insults and physical abuse. Other times they shared in the sullied reputation of those who had been so treated. They had visited those imprisoned for the faith and suffered with them and accepted with joy the "plundering" (confiscation) of their possessions. The author encourages them to endure and not "shrink back," but be "among those who have faith and so are saved" (v. 39). "Faith" is the introductory word to chapter 11, which praises the faith of the great saints of the past.

Responding to the Text

Depending on whether the lectionary uses vv. 11-14 or 31-39, there can be two different homiletical thrusts. In the earlier verses the contrast between a "standing priest" and a "sitting priest" is evocative. The standing priest is continually at the altar negotiating between God and humanity with repeated sacrifices and prayers. The ritual is never finished; it always begins again because the human situation has not been definitively resolved. The sitting priest has finished his work; the sacrifice has been made and the worship is complete. The reassuring word of forgiveness is pronounced and we go to our house justified. Yet there is a "not yet" in the text: "*until* his enemies would be made a footstool for his feet." The work is done, the victory won; yet there is mop-up work that must be done because the world's heart and mind have not yet been completely won, and evil still prowls around seeking someone to devour.

This leads to comments on the later verses in the chapter. The historical and pastoral context of this reading is a faith community facing intimidation and persecution from the outside and fear and fatigue on the inside. One source of assault is threatening; both simultaneously are a deadly combination that must be fought with the weapon of the Spirit the church has been given: prayer. Access to God is open, and the faithful who would endure must use it.

GOSPEL

MARK 13:1-8 (RCL); 13:14-23 (BCP); 13:24-32 (RC)

Interpreting the Text

Among the three lectionaries, almost the whole of Mark 13 is covered. Since chapter 13 is, in many ways, the heart of the Gospel of Mark, there may be some value in reading it in its entirety as the Gospel for this Sunday, and at the same time strike a blow for a truly "common lectionary."

Chapters 11-13 constitute Jesus' assault on the Temple, accomplished in three separate visits to the Temple. (One wonders if they parallel theologically the three Passion predictions in Mark.) Some of the material in chapter 13 is clearly apocalyptic (especially vv. 7, 8, 12, 14-22, 24-27). Willi Marxsen has postulated that this material may be based on an apocalyptic pamphlet circulating among the churches in Mark's day, although the chapter is entirely Mark's composition.[28] The chapter begins with the comments of Jesus' disciples about the large stones and buildings. The stones are indeed remarkable, as those who have seen the Temple foundation (the Western or "Wailing" Wall) for themselves can testify. Equally remarkable, therefore, is Jesus' prediction that "not one stone will be left here upon another" (v. 2). In fact, the foundation of Herod's Temple stands today, but the actual Temple building was reduced to rubble by the Romans in 68 C.E. The disciples' question, "When will this be?" is the pretext for the apocalyptic discourse that follows.

Apocalyptic literature usually addresses some political crisis. The crisis mentioned in Mark 13:14 is the "desolating sacrilege set up where it ought not to be (let the reader understand)." *The HarperCollins Study Bible* suggests that "*The desolating sacrilege* refers to pagan desecration of the temple in Dan. 9:27; 11:31; 12:11; 1 Macc. 1:54," but then says that what "the reader" is to "understand" is "unfathomable."[29] My view is that "the desolating sacrilege" is the standard of the Roman Legion that was erected in the Temple after Titus conquered the city. The reader is to "understand" that this is a sign for "those in Judea" (specifically the Jewish Christians) to "head for the hills" because of the great persecution and destruction that will follow when the Jewish defenders make a last stand in defense of the Temple. The evangelist thus has Jesus predicting the destruction of the Temple by the Romans and the revolt of the Zealots that ended at Masada. This may even have been the crisis that impelled the writing of the Gospel—namely, the need for Christians to distance themselves from the nationalist loyalties of the Jews in order to remain loyal to the mission of Jesus to proclaim God's kingdom for all people, as Jesus had demonstrated in his Galilean ministry.[30] Hence, most of the ministry of Jesus in the Gospel of Mark (followed by

Matthew and Luke) is located in "Galilee of the gentiles." Mark presumes a church of both Jews and gentiles and he writes to strengthen them in their belief that they are the true community founded by Jesus and therefore they have no more loyalty to the Temple.

In this time of great suffering "false Messiahs" (e.g. Zealots) were leading people astray (vv. 6, 22). There may even have been a concern that Christ had come again and the faithful have missed his parousia (vv. 24-27). Mark consoles his readers with an appeal to prophetic traditions (Isa. 13:10; 35:4; 50:2-3; Ezek. 32:7-8; Joel 2:10, 31; Amos 8:9; Dan. 7:13-14) that suggest the return of Christ, the Son of Man, is so awesome that the parousia could not possibly be missed. The readers should learn the lesson of the fig tree (v. 28) and watch for the signs. At the same time, they should know that "about that day or hour no one knows" except the Father (v. 32). Since only God knows when the end will come, they should stop calculating it from events that occur in history—including the destruction of the Temple.

Responding to the Text

If you're reading this, the end did not come at the stroke of midnight on January 1, 2000. But there was some disagreement about whether the new millennium began in the year 2000 or begins in the year 2001. So apocalypticists announcing the end may still be around worrying some folks with their message of doom. We have always had these predictors applying their allegorical arithmetic to current events, trying to calculate when the end will come. The "Markan Apocalypse" takes a stand against them.

Mark's message is this: Christ will come again. We do not need to worry that he has already come and that we have been left out. When he comes it will be obvious to all concerned. Nor do we need to calculate the exact time on the basis of signs and events and secret numbers. Since the exact time is known only by God, we're likely to get it wrong anyway.

But there are worse ways to be wrong than to miscalculate. Any teaching about the parousia that by panic or neglect pulls us away from the mission of Christ in the world is a false teaching. About that mission we do not need to depend on any secret information because a clear directive has been given. "Go into all the world and proclaim the gospel to the whole creation" (Mark 16:15). We may not have even made it all the way through our neighborhood yet. There is still mission work to be done.

ANY TEACHING ABOUT THE PAROUSIA THAT BY PANIC OR NEGLECT PULLS US AWAY FROM THE MISSION OF CHRIST IN THE WORLD IS A FALSE TEACHING.

CHRIST THE KING/LAST SUNDAY AFTER PENTECOST

November 26, 2000

Revised Common	Episcopal (BCP)	Roman Catholic
2 Sam. 23:1-7 or Dan. 7:9-10, 13-14	Dan. 7:9-14	Dan. 7:13-14
Ps. 132:1-12 (13-18) or 93	Ps. 93	Ps. 93:1-2, 5
Rev. 1:4b-8	Rev. 1:1-8	Rev. 1:5-8
John 18:33-37	John 18:33-37 or Mark 11:1-11	John 18:5-8

The Feast of Christ the King was instituted by Pope Pius XI in 1925 to counter the destructive forces of the modern world by proclaiming the kingship of Christ. It was moved to the last Sunday of the church year as a way of celebrating Christ as "the goal of human history, the focal point of the desires of history and civilization, the center of humankind, the joy of all hearts, and the fulfillment of all aspirations."[31]

The question posed by the readings today is: Who shall finally reign? We live in the vicissitudes of history and experience rulers coming and going. Even in the period after Pius XI instituted the Feast of Christ the King the world experienced the rise and fall of Fascism, Nazism, and Communism. None have finality. In North America, the kingdoms we build are found in our investments, and our loyalties are to our obsessive attention to our bodies and their comforts. Can we even contemplate the reign of consumerism falling at the feet of the selfless Son of God? If the title of "King" is too foreign or too male for Americans to grasp, how about "Conqueror"?

Our readings today direct us to God's gentle conquest through his Christ of all that stands against his reign of peace. They project a vision of a humane kingdom that shall supersede all the beastly ones, point to a faithful witness who testified to the truth before the politically powerful, and proclaim a violated one who shall come again to be vindicated.

FIRST READING

2 SAMUEL 23:1-7 (RCL)

Interpreting the Text

The words in this reading are described as the last words of King David. The Lord speaks an oracle through David, comparing the just ruler to "the light of morning," "the sun rising on a cloudless morning, gleaming from the rain on the grassy land" (v. 4). He then affirms his everlasting covenant with the house of David. "Ordered in all things and secure" (v. 5) means that the covenant has covered all points and is irrevocable. Verses 6-7 are somewhat obscure, but seem to draw on the metaphors of vv. 3-4 to say that when the just ruler shines on those who are disloyal, they are consumed in fire like uprooted thorn bushes.

Responding to the Text

It is significant that David's final testimony, apart from reaffirming the sure foundation of his dynasty within the covenant between Yahweh and Israel, reaffirms the king's duty to rule justly and in the fear of the Lord. The state is placed under the rule of God's law, which stands above the laws of any earthly ruler. Yet even David's descendants did not always see themselves as standing beneath a higher law; nor did they always fulfill their duty to protect and defend the weakest members of society. Inexorably this reading reminds us of Jesus' royal lineage and points us to his new kind of reign. It is interesting to note the difference between the enormous images of Christ the Pantocrator ("Ruler of all things") painted on the cupolas of Byzantine church buildings in a monumental style, and the smaller icons of Christ exposed to the faithful for veneration. Authorities inform us that ". . . on icons exposed to the veneration of the faithful, the type of the Christ-Pantocrator, while still keeping the same majesty, lacks all fearfulness. The grace expression of His face is full of sweetness; it is the compassionate Lord, come to take on Himself the sins of the world."[32]

DANIEL 7:9-10, 13-14 (RCL alt.); 7:9-14 (BCP); 7:13-14 (RC)

Interpreting the Text

Chapter 7 is a mixture of prose and poetry, originally written in Aramaic. The theme of the chapter—four kingdoms superseded by a fifth and more ideal kingdom—has a long history in the Near East before and after the time of the composition of Daniel. The persecution of the Jews by Antiochus Epiphanes (see the commentary on Dan. 12, twenty-third Sunday after Pentecost, p. 249) has negatively colored the assessment of these kingdoms (7:2-8), especially the fourth one. The verses in today's reading are a vision of an "Ancient One" on a throne (v. 9) and "one like a human being coming with the clouds of heaven" (v. 13). The NRSV rendering of "a human being" for "son of man" obscures whatever connection there may be between this image of the heavenly Man and *the* son of man in the book of Enoch and the Gospels. This man-like being comes with clouds (as does the Son of Man in Mark 13:26), but does not come to earth (as in Mark 13) but to God's throne. There he is invested with worldwide authority. Whereas the previous four beasts had rapaciously seized power, this man-like being receives his dominion from God. Moreover, whereas their authority was transient (that is, historical), his is permanent (that is, eternal). He represents the divinely ordained humane alternative to bestial history and may therefore be understood as a figure of God's people.

Responding to the Text

It is going to be very difficult to keep from jumping too quickly from the man-like being in Daniel 7 to the Son of Man in Mark 13 and to apply this apocalyptic image to Jesus. In fact, in the Gospel of Mark Jesus always speaks of the Son of Man in the third person, not in the first. This man-like being does not come down to earth but goes up to God from the earth. The figure is probably meant to be applied to Israel. It is a representative figure who symbolizes humanity in its acceptance of its God-given vocation, just as Israel did in its calling to be the people of God. The theological jump to seeing this figure as Christ-like requires regarding Jesus as Israel reduced to one representative person, the new Adam, the new humanity. If we see ourselves as being "in Christ," the idea embedded in Daniel is still vindicated. The human being is the masterpiece of God's creation. God's goal is to restore humankind to its rightful vocation, not to create a superman or a superhuman race. Well might we exclaim with the psalmist, "what are human beings that you are mindful of them, mortals that you care for them?" (Ps. 8:4).

Responsive Reading
PSALM 132:1-12 (13-18) (RCL)

Interpreting the Text

This psalmody is appointed as a response to the First Reading from 2 Samuel 23. It holds up to the Lord all that David has done to provide the Lord with a sanctuary: "Remember . . . how he swore to the Lord and vowed to the Mighty One of Jacob, 'I will not . . . sleep . . . until I find a place for the Lord'" (vv. 1-5). Verses 6-10 are related to a ceremony that dramatized David's discovery of the ark and his bringing it to the sanctuary. Verses 11-12 affirms the Lord's covenant with the house of David and vv. 13-18 celebrate the Lord's choice of Zion as "my resting place forever."

Responding to the Text

The hope of Israel rested not on any acts of piety or valor on the part of David or his descendant but on the Lord's oath to David and election of Zion. The good of the dynasty and the welfare of the holy city are intertwined. The relationship between Christ as the descendant of David and the church as the new Jerusalem is established on the same foundation: God's election.

PSALM 93 (RCL alt./BCP); 93:1-2, 5 (RC)

Interpreting the Text

This psalm celebrates God's kingship and his victory over the chaotic powers of anarchy, symbolized by the floods and the waves of the sea (vv. 3-4). The images of the floods probably come from Mesopotamia, whose rivers periodically but irregularly flooded (unlike the regularity of the Nile's floods). The Baal of the Canaanites also had to fight and defeat the sea god to restore order to creation, and was then acclaimed king of the gods. This Near Eastern mythology was applied to Yahweh. This psalm belongs to the category of "enthronement psalms" that may have been used in the fall festival in which Yahweh was proclaimed as king. In this festival the Lord's rule and his decrees (v. 5) were ritually reaffirmed.

Responding to the Text

This psalm is appropriate for the Feast of Christ the King on which we celebrate our expectation that the world will be brought to a new order in the kingdom of our God and of his Christ. God has created the world, preserves it against all efforts of the powers of chaos to undo it, and will finally bring it restored to himself through his Christ.

SECOND READING

REVELATION 1:4b-8 (RCL); 1:1-8 (BCP); 1:5-8 (RC)

Interpreting the Text

The RCL and the RC lectionary begin at vv. 4b and 5 respectively. Verses 1-4a introduce the revelation of Jesus Christ that John the Seer has received. Verse 3 introduces the first of seven beatitudes scattered throughout the book (14:13; 16:15; 19:9; 20:6; 22:7, 14). It is a double blessing: first, on the one who "reads aloud" these words in the Christian assembly; second, on "those who hear and keep" what is written. Verse 4 is the salutation of John at the beginning of his letter to the seven churches in Asia Minor. "Grace and peace" come from three sources: God, the seven spirits before God's throne (seven suggests a court full of servants—God's throne is surrounded by twenty-four courtiers in chapter 4), and Jesus Christ. Christ is described in three terms in v. 5: "the faithful witness" ("witness" = *martyria*), "the firstborn of the dead," and "the ruler of the kings of the earth." These three descriptive phrases seem to suggest Christ's death, resurrection, and ascension. Verses 5b-6a describe the church redeemed by Christ's blood and sanctified to be a kingdom of priests serving God. Verse 7 is a vision of Christ coming with the clouds, like the heavenly man in Daniel 7:13. At his coming again, he will be vindicated before those who were party to his crucifixion. Verse 8 proclaims God as the victor over time and history.

Responding to the Text

Though the reading begins and ends with God, Christ is its content. The temptation of preachers is to find something in a text that is applicable to humans or human society, so as to make the text seem "relevant" to the congregation. But this is the Feast of Christ the King. It is not our faithful witnessing but Christ's that the text extols. It is not our priestly service but Christ's coming in glory that the text proclaims. Is it possible to extol and proclaim Christ in a way that sums up his earthly mission and heavenly ministry as economically as v. 5 does? We have no witness to make other than to God's grace and power, made known in Jesus Christ. Let the sermon on this day be an example of faithful witnessing to Christ before the world rather than an exhortation to do so. Many Christians excuse themselves from witnessing on the grounds that they don't know enough. They may also have been browbeaten into believing that they have to have some kind of personal experience in order to witness. But witnessing to Christ is not a trip through "my psyche" or "my story." It is knowing the basics of the history of salvation, which are capsulized in the Apostles' Creed. It is living in such a way that the vision of Christ's saving death and glorious triumph alter my behavior in the marketplace, in my marriage, and in my home life, as well as my political commitments.

WE HAVE NO WITNESS TO MAKE OTHER THAN TO GOD'S GRACE AND POWER, MADE KNOWN IN JESUS CHRIST. LET THE SERMON ON THIS DAY BE AN EXAMPLE OF FAITHFUL WITNESSING TO CHRIST BEFORE THE WORLD RATHER THAN AN EXHORTATION TO DO SO.

GOSPEL

JOHN 18:33-37

Interpreting the Text

The Gospel reading is the dialogue between Jesus and Pontius Pilate. It continues the purpose of the Gospel in presenting Jesus as the revealer of God the Father and the Revealed One. Raymond Brown presents the Roman trial of Jesus as "a vehicle of Johannine theology."[33] The cryptic exchange pits Pilate's political power against Jesus' truth-claims. The situation suggests a reversal in which Jesus judges Pilate. Pilate asks, but really does not want to know who Jesus is. Jesus' reply, "You say that I am a king," has the sense of meaning, "those are your words, not mine." Jesus' sense of kingship is not one that Pilate can grasp without listening to his testimony to the truth. "Everyone who belongs to the truth listens to my voice" (v. 37). But this requires a leap of faith that Pilate is not willing to make. An implied question is evoked in the reader: Have I listened to the truth about Jesus?

Responding to the Text

Earthly politicians have to read a vote and assess their situation. Pontius Pilate was a politician who had to deal with the vote of the Jewish Sanhedrin to turn over Jesus to him as a messianic pretender and to assess the mood of the people. His job as governor was to represent Rome's authority and keep the peace. That was never easy in this volatile part of the Roman Empire. At times he used heavy-handed tactics. One report states that he was recalled to Rome for his mistaken slaughter of some Samaritans. Another report says that he retired to Vienne in Gaul. He just disappeared from history into the realm of legend. One legend has him become a secret Christian. He is listed as a saint in the Ethiopian Church. In this light it is interesting that the Gospel of John presents him in an almost sympathetic way as a man caught between a rock and a hard place.

When the Jewish Temple authorities demanded the death penalty for Jesus, Pilate had to question him. Pilate asks, "Are you the King of the Jews?" (v. 33). Jesus' answers throw him off balance as Jesus becomes Pilate's interrogator. Pilate's response, "I am not a Jew, am I?" (v. 35), seems to mask a deeper question, "Are you my king, too?" Rattled, Pilate asks Jesus what he had done. Jesus tells him that his way is not one of violence—which, translated into political terms, means, "I have no intention of trying to overthrow Roman authority." But Jesus' previous words, "My kingdom is not of this world," leads Pilate to press Jesus about his royal claims. Jesus reminds Pilate that the word "king" came out of Pilate's mouth and goes on to state his mission. By now Pilate is completely rattled and asks, "What is truth?" (v. 38). Was this a cynical reply, a lack of comprehension, or the beginning of some interest? In any event, Pilate does not wait for an answer and the question is left hanging in the air. Maybe the evangelist wanted his readers to reflect on what or who is truth. How do we assess the truth claims presented by Jesus of Nazareth? If he is more than a pretender, what claims does he lay on us?

In any event, Pilate is presented in this account as more than a mere representative of the Roman state. Raymond Brown, our great authority on the Gospel of John, suggests that Pilate represents another reaction to Jesus that is neither faith nor rejection—like Nicodemus. Pilate as presented here is not just typical of the politician's desire to maintain neutrality, but is typical of many well-meaning people who want to adopt the middle ground in a struggle that is total warfare. The wavering, lukewarm Christians of John's community in Asia Minor could probably see themselves mirrored in Pontius Pilate. How about us?

The Gospel reading today brings the kingship of Christ to us with uncomfortable questions. Where do we stand in terms of his royal claims? What do our actions and attitudes say about where we stand? If we're going to scramble to get "in" with the coming administration of Christ the King, we had better first come to terms with the fact that the One on the throne is the Lamb who was slain, and that self-giving love is his agenda throughout his dominions.

MARK 11:1-11 (BCP alt.)

Interpreting the Text

The story of Jesus' entry into Jerusalem reflects royal messianism, even though the entrance itself as described by Mark is somewhat less than "triumphal." Clear references to Zechariah 9:9 and 14:4 can be seen in the beginning of the passage. Psalm 118:25-26 is the source of the shout "Hosanna" and the words that follow. They were used in the *lulab* (branch) procession of the Feast of Tabernacles, which had become rife with messianic expectation. Hence the additional blessing of "the coming kingdom of our ancestor David" (v. 10).

Responding to the Text

Preaching on the story of Jesus' entry into Jerusalem on an occasion other than Palm Sunday provides another lens through which to view this story. Told at the beginning of Holy Week, the story is associated with the Feast of Passover and the Passion of Christ. But told on Christ the King Sunday (or on the first Sunday of Advent), the story can be associated with the Feast of Tabernacles and the royal coming of Christ. Jean Daniélou tells how this feast evolved from an agricultural festival (huts in the fields) to an historical one (tents in the wilderness) and how it acquired eschatological overtones in the period before first century C.E. (God coming to dwell with his people).[34]

In Mark's narrative, Jesus cannot inaugurate the reign of God without destroying the earthly Temple that has become subversive of God's true rule. His entrance into the city takes him directly to the Temple, which he surveys in v. 11 before regrouping in Bethany to prepare for his assault. What sacralized institutions and customs, preserved and defended by us, must be accosted before the reign of Christ can be inaugurated and God come to dwell among us?

Additional Resources

"All Saints Among the Churches." *Liturgy: Journal of the Liturgical Conference* 12/2 (1994).

Brown, Peter., *The Cult of the Saints: Its Rise and Function in Latin Christianity*. London: SCM Press, 1981; Chicago: University of Chicago Press, 1982.

"Christ Reigns." *Liturgy: Journal of the Liturgical Conference* 13/2 (1995).

Fuller, Reginald H., *Preaching the New Lectionary: The Word of God for the Church Today*. Collegeville, Minn.: The Liturgical Press, 1974. These commentaries on the Sunday and festival readings in the Roman Lectionary originally appeared in serial form in *Worship* magazine. They were collected into one volume which is, arguably, still the best single-author commentary on the entire three-year cycle of readings.

Pfatteicher, Philip, *Proclamation: The Lesser Festivals-2*. Philadelphia: Fortress Press, 1975. Commentaries on the Inter-Lutheran Commission on Worship lectionary that became the lectionary in the *Lutheran Book of Worship*.

Senn, Frank C., "Theological Exegesis: Mark 7-13." *Pro Ecclesia* 6 (1997) 351–58.

______, "Why Celebrate Reformation Day/Sunday?" *Homily Service* 31 (October 1998) 57–60.

"Souls, Saints and Services." *Liturgy: Journal of the Liturgical Conference* 14/3 (1998).

Notes

1. See George Wesley Buchanan, *To the Hebrews,* Anchor Bible 36 (Garden City, N.Y.: Doubleday, 1972).

2. See Mary Collins, *Worship: Renewal to Practice* (Washington, D.C.: The Pastoral Press, 1988), 123–32.

3. See Douglas John Hall, *Lighten Our Darkness: Toward an Indigenous Theology of the Cross* (Philadelphia: Westminster Press, 1976), 43–106.

4. See Frank C. Senn, *The Witness of the Worshiping Community: Liturgy and the Practice of Evangelism* (Mahwah and New York: Paulist Press, 1993), chapters 3–4 on the witness of Baptism and the Eucharist.

5. Artur Weiser, *The Psalms: A Commentary*, trans. Herbert Hartwell. Old Testament Library (Philadelphia: Westminster Press, 1962), 162.

6. Reginald H. Fuller, *Preaching the New Lectionary: The Word of God for the Church Today* (Collegeville, Minn.: Liturgical Press, 1974), 443.

7. Trans. in H. Bettenson, *The Later Christian Fathers* (Oxford and New York: Oxford University Press, 1970), 276, 277.

8. Ibid., 186.

9. *The City of God* 10, 5:6; trans. in Ibid., 244.

10. Werner H. Kelber, *Mark's Story of Jesus* (Philadelphia: Fortress Press, 1979), 56.

11. Robert P. Carroll, *The Book of Jeremiah*. Old Testament Library (Philadelphia: Westminster Press, 1986), 612.

12. John Bright, in *Interpretation* 20 (1966) 204.

13. For an interpretation of how important the means of grace had become to Luther already by 1518, see David S. Yeago, "The Catholic Luther," *The Catholicity of the Reformation*, ed. Carl E. Braaten and Robert W. Jenson (Grand Rapids: Eerdmans, 1996) 13–34.

14. See William L. Holladay, *The Psalms through Three Thousand Years: Prayerbook of a Cloud of Witnesses* (Minneapolis: Fortress Press, 1993), 29.

15. See the biography of Luther by Heiko Oberman, *Luther: Man between God and the Devil*, trans. Eileen Walliser-Schwarzbart (New York: Doubleday Image Books, 1992).

16. Rudolf Bultmann, *Theology of the New Testament*, Vol. I–II, trans. Kendrick Grobel (New York: Charles Scribner's Sons, 1951, 1955), I, 270ff.

17. Krister Stendahl, *Paul among Jews and Gentiles* (Philadelphia: Fortress Press, 1976), especially 23ff.

18. See Eric W. Gritsch and Robert W. Jenson, *Lutheranism: The Theological Movement and Its Confessional Writings* (Philadelphia: Fortress Press, 1976), 2ff.

19. Joint Declaration on the Doctrine of Justification 3.15.

20. *Luther's Works*, Vol. 31, ed. Harold Grimm (Philadelphia: Fortress Press, 1957), 346.

21. For a starter see Gerard S. Sloyan, "In the End-Time is the Beginning," *Preaching on Death: An Ecumenical Resource* (Silver Spring, Md.: The Liturgical Conference, 1997), 31–35.

22. For an excellent comparison of the ethical teachings of Jesus with the ethics of the Graeco-Roman world, see Frederick W. Danker, *Jesus and the New Age: A Commentary on St. Luke's Gospel* (Philadelphia: Fortress Press, 1988), especially 138–51 for commentary on this pericope.

23. William J. Bennett, *The Book of Virtues: A Treasury of Great Moral Stories* (New York: Simon & Schuster, 1993), 11.

24. Fyodor Dostoevsky, *The Brothers Karamazov*, trans. Andrew R. MacAndrew (New York: Bantam Books, 1970), 344–54.

25. See *Butler's Lives of the Saints*. Ed., rev., and supplemented by Herbert Thurston and Donald Attwater, 4 vols. (New York: Kenedy, 1956); also Philip H. Pfatteicher, *Festivals and Commemorations: Handbook to the Calendar in the Lutheran Book of Worship* (Minneapolis: Augsburg, 1980).

26. See "1 and 2 Samuel," in *The Women's Bible Commentary*, ed. Carol A. Newsome and Sharon H. Ringe (Louisville: Westminster/John Knox Press, 1992), 89–90.

27. It would be worth pondering the data amassed in Marsha G. Witten, *All Is Forgiven: The Secular Message in American Protestantism* (Princeton, N.J.: Princeton University Press, 1993).

28. Willi Marxsen, *Mark the Evangelist*, trans. J. Boyce et al. (Nashville: Abingdon Press, 1969), 162.

29. *The HarperCollins Study Bible: New Revised Standard Version*, ed. Wayne A. Meeks (New York: HarperCollins Publishers, 1993), 1944.

30. See James M. Robinson, *The Problem of History in Mark*. Studies in Biblical Theology 21 (Naperville, Ill.: Alec R. Allenson, 1957), 60ff.

31. *The Pastoral Constitution on the Church in the Modern World,* 45. See Adolf Adam, *The Liturgical Year*, trans. Matthew J. O'Connell (New York: Pueblo Publishing Company, 1981), 177–80.

32. Leonid Ouspensky and Vladimir Lossky, *The Meaning of Icons* (Crestwood, N.Y.: St. Vladimir's Seminary Press, 1989), 73.

33. Raymond E. Brown, *The Gospel According to John XIII–XXI*, Anchor Bible 29A (Garden City, N.Y.: Doubleday, 1970), 862ff.

34. Jean Daniélou, *The Bible and the Liturgy* (Notre Dame, Ind.: University of Notre Dame Press, 1956), 333ff.